Y0-BZZ-249

Theological Ethics and Global Dynamics

Theological Ethics and Global Dynamics

In the Time of Many Worlds

William Schweiker

350 Main Street, Malden, MA 02148-5020, USA
108 Cowley Road, Oxford OX4 1JF, UK
550 Swanston Street, Carlton, Victoria 3053, Australia

First published 2004 by Blackwell Publishing Ltd

Library of Congress Cataloging-in-Publication Data

Schweiker, William.
Theological ethics and global dynamics : in the time of many worlds / William Schweiker.
p. cm.
Includes bibliographical references and index.
ISBN 1-4051-1344-8 (alk. paper)—ISBN 1-4051-1345-6 (pbk. : alk. paper)
1. Christian ethics. 2. Globalization—Moral and ethical aspects. I. Title.

BJ1275.S39 2004
241—dc22

2003021332

A catalogue record for this title is available from the British Library.

Set in 10 on 12.5 pt Caslon
by SNP Best-set Typesetter Ltd., Hong Kong
Printed and bound in the United Kingdom
by TJ International Ltd, Padstow, Cornwall

For further information on
Blackwell Publishing, visit our website:
http://www.blackwellpublishing.com

This book is dedicated to my teachers and my students. I have been blessed by having insightful and demanding teachers throughout my life. Each of them was willing to take a risk on my capacities and then to labor to further my thought. I mention just a few: Loren C. Gruber, during my BA studies at Simpson College; Jill Raitt, Robert Gregg, Harmon Smith, Thomas Langford, and Fred Herzog who taught at Duke Divinity School where I took the M.Div degree. Most important, this book is dedicated to James M. Gustafson, David Tracy, and Langdon Gilkey, who in different ways profoundly shaped my thought while I undertook doctoral studies at the University of Chicago. In fact, I am bold enough to fancy that this book continues insights I first learned from them. I can only hope that each of them sees some evidence of influence in my ongoing work.

I also thank my students, too many (happily) individually to name. It has been one of the true gifts of my life to work with exceedingly intelligent students. These men and women seek to ponder and to respond with integrity to the hopes and possibilities of life. I have learned more from you than you could possibly learn from me.

So, to my teachers and students:

May your thoughts ever deepen and your lives always flourish

Contents

Acknowledgments

Several of the chapters in this book have been published in other volumes or were originally given as lectures at international conferences. I wish to acknowledge gratitude for permission to publish these sources in this new, revised form and also to express my thanks to everyone who has made my work possible. I especially want to thank the institutions that have supported my work at the various stages of writing: the University of Chicago Divinity School, the Center for Theological Inquiry in Princeton, and the Wissenschaftlich-Theologisches Seminar of the University of Heidelberg.

I have also benefited from conversations with friends and colleagues. I thank Maria Antonaccio, Hans Dieter Betz, Don S. Browning, Kelton Cobb, Kristine Culp, Wendy Doniger, Jean Bethke Elshtain, Franklin I. Gamwell, Clark W. Gilpin, David E. Klemm, Robin Lovin, Patrick D. Miller, Richard B. Miller, Terence J. Martin, Piet Naude, Douglas Ottati, Andreas Schüler, Günter Thomas, Michael Welker, and Charles Wilson. These friends and colleagues have enriched my thought and life. I also want to thank my assistants Aimee Burant, Michael Johnson, Kevin Jung and Jonathan Rothchild for their excellent help with the text. Ms. Sandy Crane aided with the final production of the manuscript.

Chapter 1 was published as "A Preface to Ethics" in the *Journal of Religious Ethics* 32: 1 (2003): 13–37.

Chapter 2 was published in a different form as "Verantwortungsethik in einer Pluralistischen Welt: Schöpfung und die Integrität des Lebens" in *Evangelische Theologie* 59: 5 (1999): 320–35.

Chapter 3 was written for the Project on Property, Possession and the Theology of Culture funded by the Lilly Endowment, Inc. It was published in a different form in *Having: Property and Possession in Religious and Social Life*, edited by William Schweiker and Charles Mathewes (Grand Rapids, MI: Eerdmans, 2004).

Chapter 4 was published in a different form as "Time as a Moral Space: Moral Cosmologies, Creation and Last Judgment" in *The End of the World and the Ends of God: Science and Theology on Eschatology*, edited by John Polkinghorne and Michael Welker (Harrisburg, PA: Trinity Press International, 2000).

Chapter 7 was originally published in a different form as "Images of Scripture and Contemporary Theological Ethics" in *Character and Scripture: Moral Formation, Community, and Biblical Interpretation*, edited by William P. Brown (Grand Rapids, MI: Eerdmans, 2002).

Chapter 8 was originally given for the series "9/11 Causes and Consequences: Beyond the Clash of Civilizations" held at the University of Chicago, November 2001. That lecture then appeared in *Sightings* in a three part series in October 2001.

Chapter 10 appeared in a different form as "Theological Ethics and the Question of Humanism" in the *Journal of Religion* 83: 4 (2003): 539–61.

Introduction

We live in a time of twilight. The sun sets too often on a pitiless and weeping world. Or is this half-light the dawn when a new global reality emerges into day? The travail of the twentieth century – the horrors of mass death and terrors of tyranny – is now matched by a sense that we live amid a global whirl and confusion in which meaning and orientation are difficult to attain. Many people feel their hopes and dreams fade in the dusk of an age. The anxieties of our time drive them to seek comfort in the past. And yet others, blinking in dawn's gray light, struggle to step forth and embrace the future. Mindful that half-light conceals, these people nevertheless bend their wills to fashion a world worthy of high aspirations. In truth, twilight can be dusk and dawn.[1]

The purpose of this book is to make sense of the current situation and to discover truths needed to guide life realistically in our time. People around this planet must orient their existence by the commitment to respect and enhance the integrity of life. This is the challenge and the great possibility of our age. Sadly, most forms of ethics hardly seem adequate to the present task. There is a profound symbolic and conceptual poverty in much current thought. The inadequacy and poverty of ethics, I contend, is due in some measure to the modern banishment of religious sources from moral thinking, coupled with the assumption by many religious thinkers that valid ethical arguments are confined to their community. Beyond that banishment of religious resources, I seek in the course of this book to deploy in a comparative way the insights of the Christian tradition for the purposes of outlining an adequate ethics. I hope to show how this approach to moral thinking provides a richer way than other options in moral philosophy to understand and respond rightly to the current twilight situation. Yet this book is written not just for Christians or people with religious sensibilities. It is written for anyone concerned to think profoundly about the demands of responsible existence. Religious sources are not just thinly veiled pious wishes. They can provoke and fund thought about how best to live within a complex vision of reality. Of course, the religions, all the religions, continue to fuel hatred and ignorance. They too are part of the global whirl and confusion facing us. One must defuse the potential viciousness of these resources and also overcome their systematic distortions. The way to overcome the inadequacy and poverty of ethics, as far as I can see, is to use religious and other resources in a genuinely critical and constructive way, thereby to enrich moral thinking and transform those resources. This is just what I do in the following chapters.

Many themes link together the chapters of this book. I develop the idea of the integrity of life in order to articulate the central moral good needed to orient existence in our age. Throughout the chapters there is also an ongoing comparative analysis of various symbolic and mythic forms, especially ones about creation and moral order. I also explore the deep connection between emotions and the cultural forms that saturate human experience in an age of global media. At a deeper level, I address the problem of religious and cultural violence that rages in every society and among nations. So, many themes link the chapters into a multidimensional theological–ethical analysis and response to global dynamics.

That being said, two basic themes structure the argument of the book. One basic theme centers on an account of the global situation and the challenge it places before us. I name this the "time of many worlds." The other basic theme is about a particular perspective in ethics called theological humanism. In order to provide some guidance through the thicket of what follows, it is wise at the outset to put these themes in high relief. After explaining them, a few words are offered about the method and structure of the book.

The Time of Many Worlds

Every work in ethics must provide some account of what is going on. Mindful of the sense of twilight, I write about the present age as the "time of many worlds." The idea of a "world" signals the fact that human beings always inhabit some space of meaning and value structured by cultural and social dynamics. Currently, diverse peoples and cultures, diverse "worlds," are merging into an interdependent global reality. As one scholar has noted, the era "is creating a stronger sense of shared destiny among diverse peoples of the world, even while it is also generating a more stressful sense of ethnic, religious, and cultural difference."[2] The stress of "worlds" colliding can take horrific expression in war and in terrorist attacks like the one on the World Trade Center in New York City in 2001 that killed thousands of innocent people from many cultures and religions. The stress of shared destiny can also take positive form, say in the human rights movement and growing ecological awareness around the planet. Interactions among peoples are forging, for good or ill, the future of planetary life. No one remains untouched by this emerging reality. From tiny villages in sub-Saharan Africa to high-tech businesses on Wall Street and in Tokyo, a defining feature of this age is the collision and confusion of cultural forms. How people meet this situation will shape forever life on this planet.

However, there is a paradox captured by the idea of the "time of many worlds." For long stretches of Western history, time was imagined like a stream, a process. Christians can quickly recall the great hymn of Isaac Watts:

> O God, our help in ages past,
> Our hope for years to come,
> Our shelter from the stormy blast,
> And our eternal home . . .
> Time, like an ever-rolling stream,
> Bears all its sons away;
> They fly forgotten, as a dream
> Dies at the opening day.[3]

Human beings contend with the limits that time places on life. Our lives are swept in and out of existence. The marking of time by natural processes (e.g., the rate of decay in particles, the movement of planets, the aging of our bodies) forms a background of regularity to human experiences of time. That is why the idea of time as a stream or process intuitively makes sense. And yet something subtle is now happening in human consciousness. What provides a basic order and limit to existence nowadays is no longer just the relentless press of time that bears all life away. Time is given meaning through human descriptions of temporal processes.[4] Increasingly, people can communicate in a shared, universally present "real time" despite the fluctuations in personal life and natural processes. While it may seem odd, human time is being accelerated and homogenized around the planet. Humanity is now becoming omnipresent to itself amid its diversity. The fusion of experience and technological speed is changing existence forever. The moral order of life is increasingly an all-too-human reality.

Oddly enough, we must speak at one and the same moment about the interaction and even conflict of diverse "worlds," diverse cultures and moral spaces, but within a shared global time. The uniformity of "real" time is the space of human differences. Put somewhat abstractly, the present situation is the conjunction of an accelerating homogeneous present amid reflexively interacting "cultures." The fact of human diversity amid unified time is signified by speaking of the "time of many worlds" as the emerging global moral order. Within this idea are to be found others that span the chapters of the book, namely, ideas about value, moral spaces and cosmologies, the "compression of the world" that too often leads to violence, and, of course, the reality of moral diversity and the reflexive interactions among "worlds." It will take many chapters to explain the full meaning of the "time of many worlds." But the real question is how best to consider the age from an ethical perspective. How do we find orientation in the twilight of dying and emerging worlds?

To be human is to be constantly engaged in the task of world-making, culture creation. This is because we are profoundly social creatures and also beings that must, come what may, make sense of our lives. Outside of the bonds of culture, existence would be meaningless and wretched. We are unavoidably creatures who seek to "humanize" reality. However, there is a downside to the work of culture creation, especially in the time of many worlds. More and more, human power intervenes to change and direct the dynamics of life on this planet. As Régis Debray notes, people increasingly live within "transistorized, fiber-optically cabled, air-conditioned, video-surveilled surroundings." Night and day are awash in human light. Does this give us a sense of twilight? Some wonder if there is something toxic about the extension of the human kingdom. Debray rightly observes that "humans still crave, in order to breathe, nonhuman spaces."[5] There seems little outside the human realm in which spirit can live and move. There is a loss of a sense of human transcendence. That is the challenge of the time of many worlds. We can call it the challenge of "overhumanization."

The modern age in the West, if nothing else, involved the relentless pursuit of knowledge in order to extend our power so that we might possess and control nature and make it serve human purposes. Overhumanization designates the triumph of will and with it the conviction that all that is of worth, what should direct actions, relations, and social projects, is the extension of the human power to shape and create realities. The inscribing of forms of life within cultural projects, symbolic forms, and power is meant to further human flourishing. This project brought great rewards: advances in knowledge, the lessening of disease and want, and the formation of freer and more open democratic societies. Yet it has also led, ironically, to the demeaning and the profaning of human existence and all of life through wars, ecological endangerment, and cultural banality.

We can now state more boldly the central moral question of our time, the time of many worlds. Is the present age best characterized by the domination of an overhumanized, even anti-human, age that extends the most brutal dynamics of the modern world (mass death; concentration camps; totalitarian systems; rampant consumerism; overly managed social systems; environmental destruction) into an inescapable global reality? Conversely, is there the possibility of forging an awareness of human dignity not apart from or against nature but within the integrity of life? The fate of the earth and other forms of life are bound to the future people envision and choose to enact. And this means that whenever human responsibility is demeaned, all forms of life are put at the mercy of forces released from moral evaluation. This is why so many people sense the twilight of our age, dusk and dawn. It is difficult to discern in the half-light clear markers that provide guidance for the use of human power.

In order to provide some orientation and guidance for life, this book develops a theory of value and specifies a norm for moral action and choice within an ethics of responsibility. The theory of value is multidimensional and centers on the idea of the integrity of life before God.[6] As argued throughout the book, the "integrity of life" is the proper relation among natural, social, and reflexive goods. Further, a life dedicated and lived in responsibility to and for the integrity of life is marked by yet another form of goodness, moral integrity or, same thing said, the rectitude of conscience. I also develop this account of the source and scope of value in order to articulate within moral thinking the complex symbolic discourse of creation and new creation. Yet, in addition to a theory of value, any adequate ethics must provide some norm or directive for choices about human actions and relations. I formulate the imperative of responsibility in this way: *in all actions and relations respect and enhance the integrity of life.* Responsible actions and relations are ones that respect and enhance the right interaction of complex goods and also manifest and contribute to moral goodness, moral integrity.

As we will see in the course of the book, the imperative of responsibility needs to provide orientation for responses to overhumanization, a way to protect the fragile goodness of life. Yet the imperative must lend guidance for decisions about how to respond to others, especially in circumstances of conflict that scar the current global situation. In order to clarify the imperative in that global context, I unfold its determinate meaning in terms of the double love command and the Golden Rule. These two religious specifications of the imperative, we will see, are intended as answers to the problem of human conflict and situations of struggle and suffering.

Once we grasp that the norm of choice and action, the imperative of responsibility, and its distinctive specifications aim to guide responsible existence for the integrity of life, then we have some needed orientation in the time of many worlds. And what is more, a basic directive about how to live is shown to be part of a vision of reality as God's good creation. This allows one to meet the twilight of value and to curtail the relentless drive of overhumanization, while also celebrating human beings as moral creatures, responsible beings. In other words, an adequate theological ethics for this age must focus on the marks of human distinctiveness and the forces that impede or advance responsibility for the future. We can neither demean human power nor uncritically celebrate its relentless extension.

In order to face the ambiguity of power, one must have not only a theory of value and some directive for choice and action. An ethics also needs to be clear about the vantage point from which life is understood, evaluated, and also lived. This brings us to the other basic theme of this book, the perspective of theological humanism. There is a paradox in this idea as well. In order to combat overhumanization, we need, surprisingly, a deeper grasp of the dignity, moral vocation, and vulnerability of human beings. And we need to see human existence from a theological or religious point of view.

Theological Humanism

We are in the midst of a global struggle about the worth and dignity of humanity. For most of Western history there have been those who held a moral outlook that was deeply humanistic and naturalistic.[7] "Nature" and the "human" were understood to exist within a domain of value or worth wider and deeper than physical processes or human self-interest. That wider reality was understood religiously in terms of God's being and action or metaphysically through ideas about the moral order of reality. Human beings were believed to have distinctive worth and human well-being was defined in terms of what respects and enhances natural capacities. Within current Western societies the affirmation of human distinctiveness intrinsic to this moral heritage has become separated from a more encompassing realm of value and purposes, religious or metaphysical, so that human power is now given free reign to conquer and control life. That is the project of overhumanization.

In the chapters of this book I will argue that the triumph of overhumanization and with it the decay of a vibrant humanistic and non-reductionistic naturalistic moral outlook poses a deep threat within Western cultures. The core of the threat is the widespread loss of the sense of worth that backs and grounds finite existence. Religiously construed, the sense of creation as gift has been eclipsed and with it an awareness of the moral depth of reality and the reach of human transcendence. Metaphysically considered being is now considered value neutral. The background assumption of high modern cultures is that we dwell in a morally empty universe, the nightfall of value. With that nightfall the triumph of human power is the supposed source of all value.[8] High modernity aims to dignify human existence and yet, ironically, dislodges human worth from any source other than the mechanisms of social power. Human beings are pictured as having to create meaning and value in a vacant universe, and, correlatively, human dignity is thereby seen as a threat to the worth of other forms of life or it is believed to be a shining light surrounded by endless night. This is, again, why one must reclaim and revise naturalistic and humanistic impulses within ethics.

Yet, it is fair to ask here, why use the contentious language of *humanism*, much less *theological* humanism, to speak about this agenda in ethics? For one thing, adopting a "humanistic" stance means that one grants the finite and limited character of all thinking. This position admits the risky, partial, broken, foolish, and violent facts of human existence and how those "facts" touch everything a theologian and moral philosopher says. No one escapes finitude in order to attain "God's" perspective on existence. Some thinkers bemoan this limit; others seek to deny it by offering a Theory of Everything. A "humanist" accepts the limit. And this is because a humanist of whatever kind believes that despite the folly, partiality, and brokenness of existence, it is possible to discover basic truths about how to respect and enhance life. One affirms a simple, but profoundly important, claim about human beings, namely, that we are incomplete creatures who must constantly labor to fashion lives worth living. The moral life is thus not about constraining our humanity but, in fact, freely and fully living with a profound love of life.

Importantly, a host of twentieth-century thinkers leveled penetrating criticisms of classical and modern ideas about "Man." They believed that the only way to counter the drive of overhumanization was to challenge "humanism" and to adopt an anti-humanist stance. This is a significant strand of thought that will be addressed in various ways throughout this book. Yet the attack on "humanism" has too often left us without standards by which to orient human powers. As Kate Soper has nicely put it, "We must be wary, in fact, lest by focusing on the philosophical 'end of man' we encourage a passivity that may hasten the actual demise of humanity."[9] Conversely, there also developed over the last centuries modern secular humanism. These thinkers and movements were strident in the criticism of all religious outlooks, calling them "other-worldly" and deceptive. They sought to curtail human transcendence in the name of human betterment. This meant a celebration of human freedom and power. The demand, as they saw it, was to fashion an utterly mundane ethics of human achievement. This agenda has too often unwittingly aided the project of overhumanization. The ethics could not envision a trans-human good. I speak of theological *humanism*, then, to signal the importance of human responsibility within the fragile landscape of existence. *Theological* humanism specifies that the source of goodness is wider than human projects and powers and so the nightfall of value. This is to make the audacious claim that the living God sustains and empowers struggles to discover how rightly to live.

I advance, then, a form of religious, non-reductionistic humanism. Here, too, honesty is required. The religions are ambiguous forces on this planet. They foster communities of care, but also violence and hatred among the peoples of the earth. The religions enrich our lives with music, art, literature, and guidance that deepen and answer spiritual longings. They are also forces of repression, ignorance, and deception. The religions speak of redemption and human wholeness, but they often fail to provide real answers to real problems. For all of these reasons, one must insist on a critical engagement as well as constructive use of religious resources. By adopting "theological humanism," one counters the dulling impulses of so-called "secular humanism." One likewise moves beyond the loss of standards in too much "anti-humanism." The theological humanist embraces a realistic and yet vibrant love of life. And because of this commitment, she or he holds that resources for moral thinking, even our dearest religious ones, must be interpreted and evaluated by whether or not they aid in respecting and enhancing the integrity of life. The insight is that moral thinking ought to be free to use in a non-dogmatic way whatever resources, religious and non-religious, are available to ponder and orient human life.

The theological and yet humanistic cast of this book not only moves beyond debates about secular humanism and anti-humanist positions. It also entails a certain perspective on morality. There is a legacy of thinkers who predicate "moral rectitude" of the orientation of a person's heart. A great problem of human life is the character of loves and dispositions so that we can respond rightly to others, see others not as enemies but in relation to God, and behold the divine not only as tyrant or destroyer but also as the source of goodness.[10] This book stands in that tradition. It outlines an ethics of transformation or regeneration that begins with conscience and reaches out through structural social change to how we can and must live in relation to other forms of life on our planet.

However, the argument of this book is also a radical revision in that long-standing idea about the basic problem facing human beings. A "good person" can intend well within narrow confines, the confines of "my" community, or goodness can be imagined located only in this world or some other world to come, say "heaven." My point throughout is that responsible existence is the capacity to move among "worlds"; it is the ability to navigate moral spaces that reflexively structure social existence in time. That was one point, after all, of speaking about the time of many worlds. The hallmark of moral rectitude is the capacity to move responsibly between worlds in such a way as to respect and enhance the integrity of life. That is an unqualified virtue in the present age. And saying this is admittedly a particular vision of the mode of our moral being, even if it has continuity with a legacy of thought. But how are we to speak about responsible agents who can and must navigate colliding and conflicting worlds? How are we to think about a sense of integrity and even the awareness of the disintegration of self, community, and society in the time of many worlds?

Conscience is one way to talk about what is most basic, most definitive, about human beings as moral creatures. It is one of the richest ideas in Western moral discourse. Given the complexity of the idea and the range of theories of conscience, it is obviously neither possible nor desirable to explore its many facets in this book.[11] But the focus of my interest is with "conscience" as a way to explore the mode of moral being. To use rhetorical terms, it is a synecdoche. A part is used to speak about the whole of human existence. It suggests, in the very etymology of the word, that we know (*scientia*) ourselves with (*con*) others and a demand of what is good and right upon us. Human beings on my reckoning are creatures with the strange and wonderful capacity radically to interpret existence in relation to others and the felt claim to respect and enhance the integrity of life. We can observe and question our self-perceptions, the pictures we form of our selves, others, and our worlds, and test them by the demands of responsibility.

John Wesley, the founder of Methodism, stated the matter well:

> God has made us thinking beings, capable of perceiving what is present, and of reflecting or looking back on what is past. In particular, we are capable of perceiving whatsoever passes in our own hearts or lives; of knowing whatsoever we feel or do; and that either while it passes, or when it is past. This we mean when we say man is a conscious being: he hath a consciousness, or inward perception, both of things present and past, relating to himself, of his own tempers and outward behavior.

Wesley goes on to note that "conscience" presumes "consciousness" but adds to it. Conscience's "main business," Wesley insists, "is to excuse or accuse, to approve or disapprove, to acquit or condemn."[12] Mindful of contemporary psychology and the impact of cultural forces on consciousness, one can no longer believe that the self is as transparent to itself as Wesley and other classical thinkers seem to assume. Still, conscience is a way to speak about the most fundamental way we live as moral creatures. It designates the moral integrity of existence manifest in and through acts of evaluation, criticism, and responsibility with and for others. The so-called "fallen conscience" is thereby a fit symbol for the frightful disintegration of self and constitutive relations with and for others. It indicates the realm of "sin" as a structure of lived reality and the kinds of moral madness we will explore throughout this book.

I try to show how the idea of conscience enables us to articulate the shape of the moral life in an age when people must move between diverse "worlds." Conscience so construed is a practice of moral examination that necessarily draws on the linguistic and conceptual resources of a community's values and norms. The labor of our moral being is obviously bound to and shaped by the communities in which we exist. And this means that traditions and communities must likewise be tested for systematic distortions. More generally, conscience as a kind of radical interpretation names the way we can draw on and yet submit to evaluation the working of the personal and social imaginary. To be sure, "natural moral knowledge," the *sensus divinitatis* as John Calvin would later call it, is not all that is needed to live rightly.[13] Conscience itself must be tested; our moral being must be evaluated, judged, and even transformed. Yet this is just to say that conscience, as I will develop the idea, provides the means to analyze and articulate the depth, reach, but also danger of our lives as creatures defined by actions and relations.

So, the argument of this book is that we now live in the time of many worlds. This age is endangered by the threat of overhumanization in such a way that a deep commitment to the integrity of life is required. There is also the demand to adopt a humane and yet ardently theological perspective on existence in order to escape anti-humanism, a dulling secular humanism, and religious fanaticism. The time of many worlds is not simply a description of the global social situation. It also touches our lives as individual agents. In a world awash in the flow of media images and so the triumph of the social imaginary, how ought we to think about our lives as creatures committed to the integrity of life? In order to do so, we need "conscience" as a way to articulate the character and labor of moral being.

Style and Structure

With basic themes in hand, it will be helpful to conclude this introduction with some words about the method and structure of the book. The method of this book is hardly a linear path of argument. Much like the time of many worlds itself, thinking must now move through complex and interacting dimensions of reality. The chapters take different routes into the same territory of thought. The reader will quickly see connecting links between chapters and even parts of the book, like, for instance, the connection between emotions and the cultural forms that shape and distort human existence. There is also throughout the book an extended exegesis of the biblical creation narrative in comparison to other symbolic and mythic forms of thought about the moral order of life. This is meant to help overcome the banishment of religious resources from ethics and also to show the significance of those resources for anyone interested in the moral challenges of this age.

Presently there is considerable debate among thinkers who engage the symbols, narratives, and sacred texts of communities and traditions. The debate is about the best method for the interpretation of those resources, especially when they are religious resources. In many respects, these differences in method hinge on how a thinker interrelates, if at all, historical inquiry aimed at understanding the strangeness or otherness of inherited texts, symbols, and discourses with the purpose of showing their contemporary meaning and truth. In the course of this book, various positions found in the current debate are examined.

Two forms of hermeneutics clearly seem inadequate for work in ethics. Precritical kinds of reasoning seek to move from a straightforward literal reading of a text, say the Bible, to current life without any reflection on the historical and cultural context of the text or the situation of the interpreter. Similarly, so-called historical-critical methods too often locate the meaning of the text in its historical setting with the implication that past resources have little to say to current thought. Historical distance trumps contemporary meaning. Most contemporary theologians and religious thinkers avoid these options and seek some version of what is called post-critical hermeneutics. These positions are *critical* in that they submit sources to dense historical readings through the use of philosophical, literary, political, psychological, and even gender forms of analysis. Yet they are *post*-critical in that analysis is part of the act of interpretation, not its end or point. The point of interpretation for any post-critical theory is to show the contemporary meaning and truth of the work. It is to open the text or symbol or event for renewed engagement within the dynamics of current life.

Yet here too there are differences. For some thinkers, the hermeneutical task is to trace the connections internal to scripture (or any text) as constitutive of experience and moral identity. In my judgment these intertextual or narrative approaches risk forgetting, like precritical readings, the historical distance between reader and text. They make the assumption that one can simply think within the linguistic world of the Bible or a community's belief system. Conversely, there are thinkers who seek to correlate the text and current experience. Correlational approaches seem problematic as well. They must assume that somehow a text "expresses" a meaning in symbolic form that can be correlated to common human existential experiences open to non-symbolic analysis. It is not at all clear that there are such experiences, especially in the time of many worlds, or that any human experience is unchanged by its expression through symbolic and linguistic forms. Finally, there are deconstructionist or poststructuralist theories. These positions seek to isolate instabilities within a text that fuel the proliferation of meaning in every act of interpretation. While helpful in overturning entrenched understandings, it is difficult to see how this approach can provide much aid for moral thinking. The purpose of these positions is to isolate the point where the question of the validity of one interpretation over another is rendered mute and what remains is just the proliferation of meanings. But the generation of meaning without judgments of validity provides little real orientation for actions and relations.

The approach developed in this book is also post-critical. It is an explicative, or, as I have called it elsewhere, "mimetic" hermeneutic.[14] The interpretation of texts or myths aims to articulate the density of lived practical experience so that a new understanding of the moral space of life is possible. While "correlationists" are right that there are shared human needs, challenges, and even goods, how life is actually understood is linked to the distinctive resources we have to articulate its meaning. And yet in order for any specified meaning to be morally valid, it must be recognized as explicative of the density of actual existence while also providing direction for life. In this way, the act of interpretation does not just dwell in the world of the text, but, rather, confirms or enacts anew a text or symbol or event in actual life even as practical existence validates or negates that proposal for life. This means, along with poststructuralist positions, that at times we will read a text against itself and thereby isolate points of instability in a narrative or symbol. The point of that "reading" is not to trace the generation of meanings, but, rather, to provide a better grasp of the lived structure of experience. Texts, symbols, and concepts must be understood in terms of their descriptive power – their semantic and phenomenological structure – and also their historical and social indebtedness. Without such an analysis, we too easily fall prey to abstractions that blind us to the real dynamics of human life. The interpretation of texts, concepts, and experiences undertaken in this book uncovers forces that shape life even as it explicates features of moral existence.

Put more technically, the method of thinking found in this book of theological ethics, or Christian moral philosophy, is a kind of hermeneutical phenomenology. I seek to articulate and analyze the lived structure of reality as this "appears" within symbolic, textual, and narrative forms that are often historically and culturally distant to us. One assumes thereby that we have access to the complexity of our existence indirectly through the labor of interpretation even as life itself is not ultimately irrational or chaotic. And, further, I undertake this hermeneutical and phenomenological labor as a way, ultimately, to specify a moral ontology, that is, to offer an account of the structures of the moral space of life and also the most basic mode of moral being as conscience. Summarily stated, theological ethics is a way of analyzing and articulating the lived structure of reality in order to provide orientation and guidance for life.[15] Its distinctive character is that reality and human life are understood from a theological perspective, existing before God. Its ethical purpose is to aid human beings as agents in thinking about and responsibly conducting their lives. The style of the book signals the coherence between the form of theological ethical thinking and what we are trying to think about, that is, how to live in the time of many worlds. And it is structured in such a way as to develop fully the ideas presented in this introduction.

The book is organized in three parts and each part moves through a similar progression of thought. Part I is an examination of the current world situation and ideas about creation and new creation. Within Part I there is a movement from an initial description of the situation (chapter 1) through a more detailed account of the challenge of pluralism to ethical reflection (chapter 2) to, finally, an inquiry into greed (chapter 3) insofar as the time of many worlds is driven by economic as well as cultural and political forces. In a word, Part I explores the interaction of "worlds" in contemporary existence as a space of meanings.

Part II of the book shifts to the theme of time. It begins in chapter 4 with a comparative analysis of the moral meaning of Christian beliefs about time. This is followed in chapter 5 by a more detailed consideration of how beliefs about time relate to a pressing ethical issue, specifically the problem of how to respond to the enemy. This parallels the reality of pluralism explored in chapter 3, but now with explicit attention to problems of human conflict. Part II concludes in chapter 6 with an inquiry into political forgiveness and its necessity if human history is to endure in the time of many worlds. The picture of the time of many worlds that spans Parts I and II is presented in a comparative and interpretive way while also addressing global problems.

Part III moves to the social imaginary and conscience. It brings to reflection issues already present in the previous parts of the book, insofar as they too engage the imaginary from a distinctive ethical perspective. Part III starts with a general discussion of the connection between types of moral theory, claims about the use of scripture in religious and philosophical ethics, and what this means for conscience (chapter 7). This is followed, in chapter 8, by engaging in comparative analysis of religious frameworks in order to isolate the possibility of religious fanaticism. Here too the question of pluralism reappears in ways parallel to chapters 2 and 5. Yet the focus in chapter 8 is on religious pluralism and the reality of conflict. Chapter 9 examines the idea of moral madness. This failure of conscience shows the ways in which deeply held religious and moral beliefs can lead to destruction. The question of how to counter the vicious potential of religious beliefs is thereby drawn into the work of conscience and ethical reflection.

The book ends with a return to theological humanism. It does so with the full awareness of the complexity of our current situation, the deep moral challenges now facing us, and mindful of the global collision of moral worlds. Beyond the grip of overhumanization, theological humanism articulates a space of transcendence where spirit can live and move.

The Tumult of Thinking

This book is the product of years of reflection on the tumultuous, often violent, reality of our lives amid the current global situation. The question is how to orient life in the twilight. What is required, I believe, is a moral revolution within religious and cultural forces motivating belief and action around the world. People of good will and serious conviction must repent the sad legacies of their traditions, learn from the moral insights of others, and set about the task of living by the most humane and gracious teachings of their faith. The aim of the following pages is to aid this tumult of thinking that now confronts everyone in the time of many worlds.

NOTES

1 The image of "twilight" resonates with diverse strands of philosophical and theological thought. In the nineteenth century, Nietzsche wrote about the twilight of the gods and also the dawn. In the twentieth century, thinkers like Paul Tillich explored boundary situations demarcating present and past. In a similar vein, Langdon Gilkey examined the "whirlwind" of contemporary life, whereas David Tracy has written on a "blessed rage for order" amid cultural plurality and ambiguity. James M. Gustafson has in various ways explored "treasures in earthen vessels," the historical and social nature of Christian convictions. Erazim Kohák wrote about the dusk, embers, and the stars to explore the moral sense of nature. The image of twilight is used here in a distinctive way to speak about the felt meaning and ambiguity of a specific temporal space of life, the time of many worlds. Later in this book we explore different responses to living in a complex temporal present at once dying and yet struggling for birth. Chapter 2 engages a similar image in the poetry of Yeats, whereas chapter 5 explores eschatological ideas in early Christian thought.

2 Richard A. Falk, *Human Rights Horizon: The Pursuit of Justice in a Globalizing World* (New York: Routledge, 2000), p. 2. For a discussion of the problem of evil in Christian thought with respect to social and political matters, see Charles T. Mathewes, *Evil and the Augustinian Tradition* (Cambridge: Cambridge University Press, 2001).

3 Isaac Watts, "O God, Our Help In Ages Past" in *The Methodist Hymn-Book* (London: Methodist Conference Office, 1972), no. 878.

4 See Niklas Luhmann, *Theories of Distinction: Redescribing the Descriptions of Modernity*, edited with introduction by William Rasch (Stanford, CA: Stanford University Press, 2002).

5 Régis Debray, *Transmitting Culture*, translated by Eric Rauth (New York: Columbia University Press, 2000), p. 63.

6 I am aware that the idea of the "integrity of life" is politically contested. Conservative thinkers use similar language to curtail any intervention in natural processes, say, abortion, while liberals often use it to speak about ecological holism. I hope the reader will see the distinctiveness of my account of this moral norm and how I seek to avoid polarized positions. For a discussion of the idea of "integrity," see William Schweiker, *Responsibility and Christian Ethics* (Cambridge: Cambridge University Press, 1995). For a related, if somewhat different, account, see Darlene

Fozard Weaver, *Self-Love and Christian Ethics* (Cambridge: Cambridge University Press, 2002).

7 See Daniel C. Maguire, *The Moral Core of Judaism and Christianity: Reclaiming the Revolution* (Minneapolis, MN: Fortress Press, 1993) and Michael J. Perry, *The Idea of Human Rights: Four Inquiries* (Oxford: Oxford University Press, 1998).

8 On this see William Schweiker, *Power, Value and Conviction: Theological Ethics in the Postmodern Age* (Cleveland, OH: Pilgrim Press, 1998) and Hans Joas, *The Genesis of Values* (Chicago, IL: University of Chicago Press, 2000).

9 Kate Soper, *Humanism and Anti-Humanism* (LaSalle, IL: Open Court, 1986), p. 153. Also see Timothy G. McCarthy, *Christianity and Humanism: From Their Biblical Foundations into the Third Millennium* (Chicago, IL: Loyola Press, 1996).

10 For a classic statement of this point, see H. Richard Niebuhr, *The Responsible Self: An Essay in Christian Moral Philosophy*, introduction by James M. Gustafson with foreword by William Schweiker. Library of Theological Ethics (Louisville, KY: Westminster/John Knox Press, 1999). For other attempts to rethink this tradition, see Iris Murdoch, *Metaphysics as a Guide to Morals* (New York: Allen Lane/Penguin Press, 1992) and also Maria Antonaccio, *Picturing the Human: The Moral Thought of Iris Murdoch* (Oxford: Oxford University Press, 2000).

11 Generally speaking, the language of conscience has been used in two ways. It has been used to designate a specific faculty or habit of moral reason, and it has been used to speak about the distinctive character of our entire existence as moral creatures. There are problems in speaking about conscience in either way, let alone how, if at all, to explain the relations among these different senses of the idea. Why use the idea of conscience to speak about the whole of our moral being rather than some other term or set of terms? If conscience is about moral reasoning, why not just talk about practical reason or casuistry? In the course of the book I try to answer these worries. Likewise, I understand the existential meaning of "conscience" to extend insights announced by St. Paul in his letters to the Romans and the subtle connection he makes between conscience, the law of God, and creation.

12 John Wesley, "The Witness of Our Own Spirit" in *Sermons on Several Occasions* First Series (London: Epworth Press, 1944), p. 124. I understand my own account of conscience and the practice of radical interpretation to be in continuity with Wesley's and thus a contemporary, hermeneutical account of a basic claim in Methodist theology. For a fuller account, see Schweiker, *Responsibility and Christian Ethics*, esp. ch. 7.

13 Calvin argues, in Book 1.3.1 of the *Institutes of the Christian Religion* (1559), that "the human mind, even by natural instinct, possess some sense of a Deity . . . some sense of the Divinity is inscribed on every heart." Later (Book 2.8.1), he clarifies matters: "conscience does not permit us to sleep in perpetual insensibility, but is an internal witness and monitor of the duties we owe God, shows the difference between good and evil, and so accuses us when we deviate from our duty. But man, involved as he is in a cloud of errors, scarcely obtains from this law of nature the smallest idea of what worship is accepted by God, but is certainly at an immense distance from right understanding of it." Calvin's point is that relying on our moral sense to indicate what is right worship leads too easily, not to God,

but to works righteousness and thus false pride that denies the need for Christ's redeeming action.

14 See William Schweiker, *Mimetic Reflections: A Study in Hermeneutics, Theology and Ethics* (New York: Fordham University Press, 1990).

15 James M. Gustafson has helpfully defined theology as a way of construing the world. I amend that definition in order to emphasize specific tasks of theological inquiry (analysis and articulation), its experiential and existential focus (the lived structures of reality), as well as the practical intent of thinking (to orient and guide life). On this see James M. Gustafson, *Ethics from a Theocentric Perspective*, 2 vols. (Chicago, IL: University of Chicago Press, 1981, 1984).

PART I

Creation and World-Making

CHAPTER 1

Global Dynamics and the Integrity of Life

Aristophanes' World

"Whirl is King, having driven out Zeus."[1] This line from the Greek dramatist Aristophanes seems strangely current. Recall the myth behind the poet's verse. Zeus escaped the fate of his siblings, all of whom were swallowed by their father the Titan Chronos, whose name means "time." In his maturity, Zeus tricks Chronos into freeing his siblings – "time" heaves forth his children from his belly – and these same children wage war against the father and the Titans. Victorious, Zeus is enthroned on Olympus as the sky god, the high governor of the world. Order triumphs over chaos. The world is born in violence and warfare. But now, Whirl – the primal titanic force of reality – has returned with the power of the repressed. Whirl has vanquished the order of the world.

No matter what the story meant to the Greeks, this ancient myth resonates deeply in our age.[2] "Globality," an intensive awareness of the world as a whole, was lately born from the bloody political, ethnic, economic, and colonial conflicts of the twentieth century. We know all too well that modern, Western politics has given us not only democracy, but also gas chambers. Science and technology have discovered new medicines for old diseases, but bequeathed an ecological crisis. The spread of global capitalism is not just about fantastic economic productivity, but also grotesque, deadly poverty for untold numbers of people. Little wonder, then, that many theorists of globalization focus on these shifts from "modernity" to "globality" within political relations, economic systems, and the spread of technology.

Sadly, too often theorists fail to take seriously the profound impact of the world's religions on globalization, or they fasten on the extreme expressions of religion, say worldwide fundamentalism. This is odd. Buddhism, Islam, Christianity, Judaism, and other traditions are the oldest and yet still most powerful operative forms of global civilization on this planet. These religions cross through nations, languages, cultures, economies, and races, reworking (for good or ill) those human processes and also being changed by them. The religions have been "globalizers" for a very long time indeed. Furthermore, theorists who do consider the cultural dimension of globalization, and thus give at least passing reference to the religions, usually define culture in decidedly non-moral terms. This too is odd. "Culture," as John Tomlinson has noted, can be defined as "the order of life in which human beings construct meaning through practices of symbolic representation."[3] Yet any "meaningful" way of life entails beliefs about how one should live and also norms of human actions and relations. Whatever else we say about human beings we are, come what may, valuing creatures. Whoever defines what is valued, what kinds of life a culture esteems, has a unique social power.[4] Within any exploration of culture, even global cultural flows, moral matters are present.

In this light, we can unfold *cultural* dynamics of globalization mindful of religious and moral matters as well as an ancient cosmogonic myth, a story about the origin of the world.[5] The myth is used for heuristic and diagnostic purposes, but one could show in detail how close it is to basic conceptions of social existence found among a host of Western theorists. Thinkers no less than Thomas Hobbes, at the dawn of the modern world, and as recent as political realists during the Cold War era, saw the sociocultural world created by conflict and the struggle for power. Marxist social analysis, built on class conflict, no less (oddly enough) than neoclassical theories about the nature of markets, insists that struggle is at the root of social life. The story of Zeus and Chronos nicely captures an idea basic to much modern Western social theory. And insofar as globalization can be seen, in the apt terms of Arjun Appadurai, as "modernity at large," then attending to this "myth," a product of the moral imagination, might aid us in understanding and responding to global dynamics and cultural flows.[6]

At issue in this chapter is, then, the working of the moral imagination within culture creation, world-making. "Central to the moral imagination," writes Jonathan Glover, "is seeing what is humanly important. When it is stimulated, there is a breakthrough of the human responses, otherwise deadened by such things as distance, tribalism or ideology."[7] Later, we will try to reclaim different stories than the myth of the Titans in order to enliven our moral imaginations. The intent in making this kind of argument needs to be grasped, however. This argument is not an appeal to confessional resources aimed at showing Christian uniqueness against the violence of the "world." That kind of argument, quite popular among conservative, postliberal North American theologians, fails to grasp the complexity of the social situation we inhabit.[8] It assumes that a community's "identity" can be shaped in ways free from the pressure of global dynamics. But the idea that any community, any tradition, can remain pure from reflexive interactions with other cultures and communities is not tenable in the time of many worlds. Even to reject or to deny those reflexive relations is to be implicated in global processes. Roland Robertson has astutely commented: "the idea of tradition is a modern phenomenon – a form of *countermodernity* that became a feature of modernity itself."[9] So one makes the hermeneutical move to engage the moral meaning of various "myths" of origin and moral order not out of the desire to remain within the comfortable walls of one's own "tradition." Any perception of the world is informed by some tradition and this fact allows us openly and critically to explore the religions. The moral challenges posed by this age mean that an ethicist *must* engage the religions and their reflexive relation to global cultural flows.[10]

One further introductory comment is in order. Besides the experiential resonance of Aristophanes' words, the line is a banner for our inquiry in this chapter for another reason. In 1929, Walter Lippman, an eminent newspaper columnist, wrote a famous book titled *A Preface to Morals*.[11] Lippman took this very same line from Aristophanes as the focus of his work. He argued, in brief, that the modern world is one in which the erosion of traditional social order has led to a loss of religious belief and social cohesion. Whirl has returned. Lippman set out to praise the genius of modernity and the possibilities of life in an age of unbelief. Our world is no longer Lippman's modernity. The time of many worlds is one in which the fate of all forms of life – from molecular structures to rain forests – is intimately bound up with the expansion and use of human power and cultural forms. What is threatened is the integrity of life.[12] Can the religions respond to this new situation, advance human flourishing, and protect the earth?

To meet this challenge to the integrity of life, the remainder of this chapter sketches a new preface to the ethics developed in the rest of the book. The first step is to clarify the meaning of globalization as one element of the time of many worlds.

Global Dynamics and World-Making

The term "global dynamics" signals the simple but important fact that we are concerned with sociocultural and economic processes and structures and not something called "Globalization" with a capital "G." Alfred North Whitehead had a nice term for the penchant of academics to use words beginning with capital letters, words like "Modernity" or the "Enlightenment" or "Globalization." He called this the fallacy of misplaced concreteness.[13] We have to avoid mistaking an abstract idea, like globalization, for an actual concrete thing. And we should avoid other forms of reductionism as well, say, believing that one form of analysis – economic, political, cultural, theological, or ethical – alone says it all. Like many phenomena, so too with globalization: miss the complexity and you have missed the thing. "Globalization" in this chapter is a complex reality uncovered through descriptions of interlocking social and cultural dynamics and structures.

One can be more precise. Globalization is "the rapidly developing and ever-densening network of interconnections and interdependence that characterizes modern social life."[14] Robertson rightly insists that globalization denotes a "compression of the world." The world seems smaller, and, increasingly, we imagine it as one world. In this respect, "globality" is "an enlargement of modernity, from society to the world. It is modernity on a global scale."[15] The compression of the world can be characterized, first, by the increasing socio-cultural density of life brought on by the migration of peoples and economic developments. It is no longer the case – although some groups around the world would like it such – that societies are in any simple sense homogeneous entities. The mass movement of peoples in our time has made multiculturalism a fact in most places. When social density becomes reflexive, that is, when we begin to understand ourselves in and through our relations to those who are really different or other than ourselves, then we have what can be termed "proximity." "Proximity" does not mean simply that people who were at a distance are now close at hand, either by the media or migration. "Proximity" is a moral challenge: how to live with others amid powerful forces shaping one's own society and identity.[16] It is as if other people's worlds and minds enter into our own and we enter their minds and worlds.

A clear example of social density and proximity enlivened by economic forces is globalized cities. Saskia Sassen, in her volume *Globalization and its Discontents*, notes that the "city has indeed emerged as a site for new claims: by global capital which uses the city as an 'organizational commodity,' but also by disadvantaged sectors of the urban population, which in large cities are frequently as internationalized a presence as is capital."[17] Anyone who watched recordings of the 2000 New Year's celebrations had to be struck by the way the event focused on events in cities: Paris, London, Moscow, New York. Large cities are one crucial site or location of globalization as a heterogeneous and yet coherent economic and cultural process. International cities are a "place" in which people's identities, sense of self, others, and the wider world, as well as values and desires, are locally situated but altered by global dynamics.[18] For example, a nightclub in Jerusalem features music that fuses traditional sounds and rhythms with rock and jazz. This can lead, as sociologists note, to social anomie and conflict, seen, for instance, in the debate raging in Israel over who is a Jew. The compression of the world found in massive cities is thus a boon for the formation of new self-understandings, especially for dislocated peoples. Yet "proximity" – a traditional Israeli confronted with global music – is the problem of how to relate to those who are "other" and yet enter into our lives. This is especially pointed when those "others" are implicated in histories of suffering. The compression of the world confronts us with the problem of how to live amid others, even enemies. Globality is a space of reasons marked by violence as much as creativity and discovery.

The world is compressed because of social density. But, second, the very same compression of the world means that human consciousness is expanding to see the world as a whole. There is a long history to this expansion of consciousness. In the West, ancient Greek historians tried writing "world histories" even as early Christian thinkers and Roman Stoic philosophers spoke about the "ecumene" or the whole civilized "world." The idea of "world-making," that is, a conception of human coherence beyond local identities, is an old idea. The temptation to understand the movement of "globalization" as somehow solely the product of Western imperialism or capitalism seems to miss the historical complexity of the reality we are trying to understand. And yet we should not deny the novelty of our situation. Pictures of the earth as a blue-green orb floating in a silent dance about the sun have only been available to the human imagination during the so-called space age. The spread of global capital has also bound people in a complex web of interdependence. It is not simply that we now have access via TV, radio, the Internet, and the market to information about other parts of the world, although that is important. Much more, the "compression of the world" means a new moment within the imaginative project of world-making. People are increasingly living in a mediated and yet simultaneous present. World-making, like proximity, is a reflexive process: to understand the world as one is to relativize all places in it, or, as often is the case, to claim that one's own culture, religion, and nation is the *axis mundi*, the center of the world. But with so many cultures and societies, can there really be just one center to the world?

From a cultural perspective, globalization is a complex, interrelated dynamic: compression and so the proximity of peoples as well as the expansion of consciousness and world-making. The paradox is that at the very time when people can imagine the world as one, the reality of social density confronts one with the problem of proximity, with otherness. How we see the world and others, and even the perceptions of us by others, bends back to shape our actions, relations, and identities. There is a host of ways to respond to those who are other, different, than ourselves. Sometimes, say in the face of massive destruction by terrorists as with the World Trade Center, revulsion over the event is morally right and required.[19] But one also knows that there are some ways of life, some belief systems, which we would like to enter but really cannot do so.[20] Global reflexivity comes with massive moral challenges in responding to others.

Let us be clearer about the meaning of reflexivity. It can be found in economic as well as cultural forms. Ponder the link between imagination and worldwide consumption. Through the circulation of commercials, people's consumption patterns are being shaped and transformed by what is other, what is different. The image of Michael Jordan endows Nike shoes with increased market value wherever that "image" can penetrate a culture. Even the Dalai Lama was used by Apple to sell computers! Appadurai has noted that "consumption is now the social practice through which persons are drawn into the work of fantasy."[21] The ways in which communities and individuals fashion meaningful lives out of the welter of images and ideas that mediate global reflexivity can be a way to resist economic powers. This is also the means to participate in those structures and processes. Consider another example of reflexivity that is distinctly religious and cultural: a Hindu temple recently built in Atlanta, Georgia. The difficulty arises from what Thomas Thangaraj has called Hindu "bio-piety."[22] Piety demands that the Hindu community in Atlanta attempt to reduplicate a specific "space" in India, but now obviously within a radically different physical–social–cultural context. Building the temple is an expansion of consciousness wherein members of the community see their lives differently in the global scene. Yet it also refashions piety. Caste and arranged marriages are breaking down in these "American" Hindu communities. There is a loss of traditional identity.

Many theorists think about global dynamics primarily in economic terms or through international relations. One reads, for instance, about the "McDonaldization" of the world wherein cultural differences are crushed under the weight of economic standardization, rationalization, and consumerist sameness.[23] Similarly, the development of international tribunals, accords, NGOs, and political organizations ranging from NATO to the EU, the UN to the World Court, signal forums for the meeting and interaction of nations aimed at cooperation and the minimization of conflict. Whether justice is served by these developments remains a question. Other thinkers rightly point out that behind the supposed "sameness" of international law and spreading market capitalism are actually profound forces of difference. This dialectic of sameness and difference, homogenization and heterogenization, global and local, seems to be a lasting mark of the reflexive dynamic of "globalization" in the time of many worlds.

It would be very odd indeed to deny the fact that we must explore the economic forces and international relations driving and impeding globalization. These are undoubtedly operative in the present "concrete structuration of the world as a whole."[24] We will return to economic matters later in the book (see, for instance, chapter 3). And yet, as it has already been shown, globalization in whatever form (economic; political) is a cultural dynamic. Nike shoes, as a commodity, are the same material objects everywhere, but they have a different cultural significance and meaning on a New York City basketball court than in a shanty-town in South Africa. And this is partly why they have different market value in diverse cultural contexts. Even the meaning and working of democracy are more culturally dependent than some political theorists previously believed. And further, there is, no doubt, a complex interaction among these factors, namely, desired commodities (Nike shoes) used within social practices (athletics) amid political aspirations (democracy) and economic interaction (international trade). Whether one considers the formation of new identities by dislocated peoples in postcolonial social and economic situations or the worldview of information technology, the symbiosis of social structure and cultural labor shapes how we think and live. "Culture" – which is not a unified thing (remember Whitehead's warning) – is the human work of rendering life meaningful through practices of symbolic representation. Cultural forms have impact on social life insofar as *representations* always entail *valuations* and *motivations* that, taken together, create a space of reasons for human conduct.[25] Cultural labor in all its forms is one of the forces forging globality; it is part of the dynamic behind the sameness and differences found in the reflexivity and the compression of the world.

We now have before us some dynamics of globalization: (1) the movement of money and people epitomized in gigantic cities, a movement that breaks down homogeneous social realities and poses the problem of "proximity"; (2) the expansion of consciousness via media and market so that we increasingly picture the world as one and in a unified "time" but in doing so relativize our lives; and (3) the dynamic of reflexivity in economic, political, and cultural dynamics that changes identities through what is other, manifest precisely in the expansion of consciousness and the compression of the world. In some respects none of this is new. People have always been on the move for a variety of reasons; there has always been an economy of money and images; divergent peoples and traditions have long interacted, often violently. And yet global dynamics uniquely mark this age. One dare not be naive about these developments. We ought to expect that social density – the problem of proximity – and the expansion of consciousness will lead to systemic conflict and psychic dislocation, especially around scarce natural resources and legacies of hatred and suffering. Disintegration and conflict reign within the dynamics of globalization as much as powers of integration and increasing interdependence. Whirl and Zeus contend with each other.

The global dynamics now isolated, i.e., proximity, expansion of consciousness, and reflexivity that works in and through social systems (economy, media, politics), are deeply bound to cultural matters, that is, representation, valuation, and also motivation. As a space of reasons, globality is actually a representational space, an emergent cultural and imaginary reality. We see ourselves and others and the world in specific ways that shape a sense of self, other, and world. Global dynamics are driven by and also challenge deep cultural valuations, a fact manifest in widespread ethnic and religious conflict. Cultural forces, along with economic and political ones, are clearly motivating peoples to enter the global scene. These global social and cultural "dynamics" must be grasped as forming a moral space if we are to understand the force of the religions in the worldwide scene. Thus we turn to a second and more controversial step in this new preface to ethics.

Globality as a Moral Space

A moral space is any context in which persons or communities must orient their lives with respect to some ideas about what are higher and lower, better and worse, ways of conducting life.[26] In this "space" we are concerned with *reasons for actions* rather than causes of events; one wants to *explicate* human conduct, not *explain* natural phenomena. So defined, every culture – and globality itself – is a moral space; it is a space of normative reasons. This insight into moral spaces requires that we conceive of agents (individual or social) having capacities or powers to act knowingly, to give reasons and guide actions, with respect to some orienting ideas about what is good. If there were no agents (say, persons or larger social entities like corporations or nations) or they were subjected to unbending determinism, or these agents lacked powers of action and decision making, or there were in fact no orienting ideas about what is better and worse held by agents who did have the power to act knowingly, then the very notion of a moral space would make no sense. But while it might be philosophically tempting to argue that there are no agents, in our actual practical existence there can be little doubt about their reality. The current dynamics of globalization in fact rest upon and radicalize the emergence and influence in the West of the unitary nation-state from the late fifteenth century onward as well as developing concepts of the individual and even "humanity" during the same period.

One can bemoan this development, of course. One can see the modern idea of the individual and nations as alienating and destructive. Thinkers have tried to redress fundamental flaws in the modern, Western conception of the individual by focusing on the reality of interdependent, internal relations.[27] Yet the fact remains that from these modern agents – individuals and nations – globalization in its current form has emerged. Equally clear is the fact that these agents act in a space with respect to reasons about what counts as good, say, national self-interest or maximizing utility or moral values like human rights and economic justice.[28] Come what may, the global scene is one in which agents of various sorts (corporations, ethnic groups, nations, individuals) act and orient themselves in ways that further or destroy life. To understand this scene requires exploring reasons used to explicate behavior. Insofar as the dynamics of globalization are intrinsically bound to representational, evaluative, and so motivational forces working on and in these agents, then globality is a moral space, a space of perception, motives, and choice.

In this light, recall a previous example. The massive international cities that dot the face of the earth are "spaces" in which persons must orient their lives. Sassen has shown that through the Internet and labor by persons in their homes, the "household" has become a key analytic category in global economic processes. The household as a site of global economic activity linked by the media to others is a place of global reflexivity. We see "new forms of cross-border solidarity, experiences of membership and identity formation that represent new subjectivities, including feminist subjectivities."[29] The city, the household, and even cyberspace are contexts in which persons orient their lives with respect to some idea of what is good. They are moral spaces.

There is one more facet of globality we must isolate. This "facet" shows why the time of many worlds must be seen as a moral space, that is, a space of normative reasons about actions and relations. Nothing so much characterizes the age of globality as the fantastic, even terrifying, expansion of the human capacity to respond to, shape, and even create reality, that is, the explosive growth of human power. Globality is about the titanic power of human beings, a power that increasingly is beyond our capacities or desire to control and orient. From genetic technology to space exploration, from ongoing massive deforestation around the world to atomic power in all its ambiguity, from hideous economic inequality to high-tech warfare, we live within a space of human power. Cultural processes increasingly intervene and restructure natural processes. The genetics revolution and the ecological crisis have pressed this fact upon us. Are we able to sense the moral challenge which the vulnerability of planetary life puts to human power? Do we have the ears to hear the "cry of mute things," as Hans Jonas so beautifully put it?[30] Whirl and Zeus are symbolic of this all too human power. The fantastic growth of human power was simply missed by Lippman in his "preface to morals."

At this juncture we can grasp the deeper reason for insisting that globality is a space of reasons. The massive growth and uneven distribution of human power means that various agencies – individuals no less than corporations, nations no less than international NGOs – are shaping life and also the very conditions necessary for future life. Given the radical increase of human power in the so-called First World, we need to think about how the future is presently imagined and how it ought to be imagined. It is as if human power is about to swallow Chronos, planetary time. Part of the rhetoric of global technology, it seems, is that one can imagine a radical discontinuity between the past and the present and the future. Many fantasize about a day in which disease, age, fertility, and hunger will be under human control and thus discontinuous with previous biological constraints. Ideas about cyborgs or genetic engineering and "fabricated man" to improve our species represent a future that orients action in the current space of life. Some theorists, blindly enthusiastic about these ideas, speak of the "reinvention of nature."[31] These forces and ideas are emblematic of what was called "overhumanization" in the introduction to this book. The difficulty in addressing this new reality is that traditional forms of Western ethics assumed a limited reach of human power. The determination of the distant future was always thought beyond the touch of human action. How then are we to think ethically about the new reach of human power?[32]

Importantly, it is at this point that the religions have resources for ethics too long banished in modern moral philosophy. The idea that human power can exceed its usual spatial and temporal limits is not foreign to the religions. Images of heavenly realms and beings, transformed and perfected souls, heaven and hell, journeys to other worlds, and other images of the future have informed the moral outlooks of peoples. The religions are wildly complex imaginary and ritual forces that shape life and courses of action by picturing time and eternity beyond the usual limits on human power and thereby transform human consciousness.[33] But when the fate of future life is in our hands, how much novelty should we imagine in representations of the world, selves, and others? In a moment we will have to return to this question and with it the place of myth within ethics.

The expansion of human power and with it dreams of reinventing nature or securing a world order means that what is valued most profoundly in "modernity at large" is the never-ending maximization of human power. Things gain value (they matter and are good in themselves) with respect to the extent they derive from or actually increase human power, the ability to respond, shape, and create reality. Of course, this has always been the case. As creatures that seemingly cannot escape the realities of death, want, and frustration, any means to stave-off death, answer want, and secure fulfillment is grasped intuitively as valuable, as mattering. Here, too, the religions are illustrative. From magical rites to beliefs about immorality, from ascetic practices to hope in divine help and fulfillment, the religions are in part about access to power or powers that will enable human beings to face inescapable realities of existence. But the assumption that human power alone is at the root of all moral value is a dangerous one in an age when future life is at our mercy.

The increase of human power is profoundly uneven, held mainly by the so-called First World nations. The inequality of power threatens global stability and just might swallow the future in unending violence between the "haves" and the "have-nots." The very same power bears on the compression of the world and the moral challenges it entails. It is easy to see how this is the case. The increasing social density of life fosters the problem of proximity. How are very different people to live together, especially when their lives and histories are marred by legacies of mutual violence and hatred? The Balkans, the Middle East, Northern Ireland and racial conflict in the United States all manifest the ways in which the remembrance of injustice continues to permeate human time. With the increase of communicative power working through global media, hatred is becoming globalized as well as access to weapons – including nuclear, chemical and biological weapons – that continue the suffering. At issue is not simply justice or respect for the other, but forgiveness as the power to enact mercy, thereby reconstituting human community after ruinous violence. Proximity as the reflexive presence of enemies in one's own life means that the logic of retributive justice must be curtailed by mercy. But to love mercy as the context for any viable idea of justice is to limit human power, limit the power of retaliation. Can we so limit power or will the fires of hatred merely increase until they engulf the world?

The question of the proper limit on human power exposes the most pointed moral meaning of the myth about Chronos and Zeus. Human technological power can swallow the future, destroy the conditions needed for future life, even as memories of suffering and violence, how the violent past is inscribed in the present, threaten to engulf us in unending hatred and retribution. We need to learn to hear the cry of mute things and also to love mercy as well as justice. But immediately upon saying this, the ethicist typically confronts a blank stare. The profound differences in moral outlooks and convictions makes everyone skeptical about whether a global ethics is really possible. Can one really imagine that any set of moral values, Christian no less than Islamic, Eastern no less than Western, Indigenous no less than transcultural, will suffice for everyone? And yet without some such shared moral convictions, it is not at all clear how we might escape the destruction of future life or the fires of hate and violence. The world of globality seems born in violence and warfare, and, sad to say, it might well die as it was born. Our new preface to ethics appears, ironically enough, to force us into a rather tragic judgment, namely, that we are at the mercy of powers and processes beyond control, swept along by titanic forces of our making but which might swallow lives and dreams.

Myth and Global Ethics?

We have been pursuing a rather complex and disturbing journey in thinking about globalization and the integrity of life in the time of many worlds. The present age confronts us with challenges and possibilities that global dynamics cannot answer. Globality cannot help us escape legacies of violence, since social density and global reflexivity accentuate memories of suffering and hatred even as they open new possibilities for understanding and forgiveness. Surely in the wake of the attacks on the World Trade Center this has become abundantly clear. Global dynamics will not limit human power, simply because they are the children of that power no less than the nation-state or ideas about humanity. The very same power that produces immense wealth and relieves much misery also creates suffering and unjust poverty. Globalization shapes the future even as it drags a violent past along with it. The "myth" about the origin of the world in violence and warfare – the Olympians against the Titans – seems to mean in its most profound reach that the world is caught, dreadfully trapped, in a never-ending cycle of destruction and wrath.

Of course, it is true that this myth has never been the sole operative belief system of Western, let alone Eastern, peoples. This is so even though cosmogonic myths about the birth of worlds through destruction are exceedingly widespread. The very idea of "modernity," and globalization as "modernity at large," feeds on the idea of a new time, *Neuzeit* as the Germans call "modernity," of human freedom born from the religious and cultural violence of the past.[34] But the fact that Aristophanes' myth is not our myth is utterly beside the point. Sometimes we understand ourselves best through others' eyes; sometimes we must use others' stories reflexively in order to know our own situation. The point is that we need to think about how to imagine the world if we are to meet the challenges of the day. The ethicist can and must draw from and yet refashion inherited myths under the demand of moral necessity.[35]

It is time to pull together this argument and to show the contribution of Christian convictions to a global ethics. Among thinkers concerned with the challenge of global ethics, two different approaches can be noted that are closely related to the present argument. Some, like Hans Küng and the "Declaration Toward a Global Ethic" by the Parliament of the World's Religions (1993), try to isolate common values, standards, and attitudes found among the religions.[36] Critics have rightly noted that the Declaration looks suspiciously like a version of the Ten Commandments and thus expresses Western, Jewish, and Christian values. Yet it is interesting that all of the religions endorse some idea of truth-telling, prohibitions of murder, sexual morality, and similar values and norms. By signing the Declaration, the representatives of various traditions affirmed those standards, but also, and this is important, relativized their own traditions in light of human commonalities. Here is found at the level of moral norms and value the dialectic of the local and global that characterizes globalization as an element of the time of many worlds.

This is true of another major option in developing a global ethics, namely, the turn to human rights.[37] Of course, it is often argued that the very idea of "rights" is incurably Western. In religions and cultures with a different conception of what it means to be a self or a human being, does the idea of "rights" inhering "naturally" in an individual as a free decision maker have any plausibility? Many thinkers doubt it. Jeremy Bentham insisted that the idea of natural rights was "rhetorical nonsense, nonsense on stilts."[38] Yet it is important to note that virtually no nation, culture, or tradition wants to proclaim before the world that it is against human rights. And this once again makes the point about global reflexivity, proximity, and the expansion of the consciousness: the dynamics of globalization are changing (for good or ill) local moral values and beliefs about humanity. In the face of poverty, legacies of hate, and the environmental crisis, peoples around the world understand themselves in a shared moral space and are finding commonalities while insisting on human rights.

There is much to endorse in these strategies for developing a global ethics. Yet the force of our inquiry is to suggest that what is at issue most basically is how we "picture" or imagine the moral space of life. It is not enough to isolate common standards, values, and attitudes, even those about human rights, if we leave in place a construal of the world that foils moral aspirations. The contribution the religions can make to global ethics is not only about common norms and attitudes as well as beliefs about human dignity. The contribution is also in terms of what has been most suspect in religion during the modern age, namely, the moral significance of myth. Modernity, at least in the West, has been in large measure about demythologization in the face of the triumph of scientific knowledge. Religious beliefs and the stories, or myths, which encompass them have been seen as projections, fantasies, or simple lies. The very idea of "myth" carries a negative meaning. This is one reason why, incidentally, many non-Western cultures find globalization threatening. Globality seems a wholesale demythologizing, a relentless cleansing of cultures of all inherited beliefs and sacred stories.

Ancient myths like that of Chronos and Zeus can be a goad to moral understanding. The point, first recognized by Plato, is that there is neither "mythless" morality nor any "myth" that fails to inspire and require ethical interpretation. The kind of hermeneutical moral inquiry practiced throughout this book engages the dialectic of myth and morals in the labor of construing and orienting life. What is needed is an ethical reinterpretation of stories about the world and others so that we might escape or at least curtail the globalization of hate and the annihilation of the future. Of course, ethical inquiry comes at a cost; it does not leave inherited religious beliefs and practices in place. We can now take the final and most controversial step in this inquiry by practicing just that form of moral reflection with respect to Christian faith. The wager is that there are parallel insights in other traditions that could be explored and engaged by further comparative study.[39] The argument offered now will be expanded in other chapters of the book, both in terms of the theory of value and in terms of the norm of choice it entails.

The Enemy and Creation

The most basic challenge facing global ethics, as we have seen, is how to understand and value the created order (the cry of mute things) and also the other, even the other as enemy, in a way that can guide moral action beyond the celebration of human power that now threatens the integrity of life.[40] Beliefs about the origin of the world in warfare and violence simply do not help us. These beliefs too easily warrant just the kind of world we find: "modernity at large," where overhumanization has been too often violent and destructive of others and the natural world. Claims made by some Christian theologians that the world is wrapped in sin and destined to divine destruction are also morally dangerous. Naive convictions among critics of the West about ecological wholeness strangely blind to human distinctiveness and suffering are below the complexity of the world in which we actually live. Thankfully, Jews, Christians, Muslims, and others have different mythic and conceptual resources. These mythic resources can be explored precisely along the lines of inquiry outlined in this "preface" to ethics. We can explore the "moral meaning" of religious myths. When we do so, we find resources (not answers) for considering the connection between power and value important for the time of many worlds, as well as claims about the worth of finite life and even how to respond to the enemy.

The Genesis story in the Christian and Jewish Bibles is a creation myth that can be read along a number of lines. Two are important for the present inquiry. They show the ways in which "creation" is a construal of the interaction of natural processes and cultural dynamics. First, this story depicts through the "days" of creation human beings set amid a complex reality of different times, forms of life, rhythms, and patterns of nature. There is the time of light and dark, day and night, but also the span of mortal life distinct from the time of God's action. The divine blessing is poured out on creatures, human beings, and even the Sabbath. Michael Welker writes that creation is "the differentiated structural pattern of reciprocity of natural and cultural forms of life and events, oriented and ordered toward the human capacity to experience."[41] Creation is the interaction of nature and sociocultural processes (e.g., night and day no less than naming creatures) with their own distinctive dynamics. Chronos, that is time, in the rhythm of day and night, does not swallow all else; it too is a creature of God.

Second, this complex reality is called "good" by the divine. "And God saw that it was good." Worth is written into the nature of things recognized by God wherein God's act of recognition is creative. The goodness of finite being is not simply an expression of divine power. God blesses creation and then rests in its completion. The creation story is about world construction in which blessing, not warfare, is the key to understanding reality. This insight culminates in the narrative of Noah and the Flood (cf. Genesis 6–9). After destroying the world because of human evil, God the warrior hangs his bow in the heavens and makes a covenant ever to sustain life. Throughout the biblical texts in their canonical form is an ongoing tension between God as righteous but wrathful judge and God as the sustainer and redeemer of life.

What is surprising, and little noted, is that deep within the Christian and the Jewish mindsets is a connection between creation as good, and thus worthy of our care, and the problem of the enemy. The ethicist responding to the time of many worlds must use this connection in reclaiming beliefs about creation and also ideas about forgiveness. Hans-Dieter Betz notes:

> The human being as rebel and enemy is what God has to deal with. The command of Torah in Leviticus 19:18 says: "Love your neighbor as yourself." Now, how do you love your neighbor? Look at creation: this is the way God loves the neighbor. God provides the bounty of life even to the enemy, to the rebellious and ungrateful humans . . . The Sermon on the Mount says, provocatively, that he wastes all these goods like rain and sunshine on the undeserving folks. Why doesn't he take any retributive action against evildoers?[42]

Within the Bible there is a moral interpretation, a midrash, of the creation story in the light of the problem of the enemy. Love of neighbor, even the enemy, is given content by the thematic of a good and yet complex creation; creation is drawn into the depths of the moral life through its interpretation by the love command. Creation overcomes chaos not through Zeus-like coercion or conflict, but through an ordering that brings forth life. God can no longer be seen as responding to enemies by destruction and violence (the "Flood"), but in the bounty of creation aimed at conversion and reconciliation. This deep linking of creation and care for the other continues in the stories of Jesus healing the sick and feeding the hungry.[43] The feeding stories manifest a logic of abundance and reconfigure communities so that all might partake of God's reign. Healings transform social boundaries beyond traditional social markers; they include the stranger, the outcast. Jesus challenges the line between clean and profane. Creation and God's rule is a moral space that is imagined as abundant and merciful. From this insight flows other convictions about the connection between God's creative and sustaining activity. The challenge is to live rightly within this space committed to creation, justice, and also mercy. It is this insight that will be continued and yet deepened in the remainder of this book.

Rather than engaging at this point in further biblical analysis, what is the point? Will the problems of globalization be answered if we simply read the Bible? Hardly! The challenge before us is the mighty task of overcoming the ways in which proximity can devolve into continuing violence and global technological power endanger the viability of planetary life. We need ways of understanding and picturing reality, ways to engage in the imaginative, cultural task of meaning-making, that link forgiveness with respect for the worth of finite, natural life. There are resources for engaging in this work buried within religious texts, narratives, and symbols.[44]

Those very same resources are operative within the cultural memory of civilizations shaped by these religious traditions.[45] This is why Aristophanes' line about Chronos and Zeus is in some primal way foreign to most Western peoples. At a profound level, it is hard for anyone touched by the symbolic power of Judaism and Christianity and Islam – and that is, after all, very many people – to see reality arising from murder and warfare and also to believe that the "enemy" is a virtual principle of a moral order (creation). But the fact that Zeus and Whirl now resonate in our experience shows us a possible shift in moral worldviews. In fact, the time of many worlds may just be an experiment in the plausibility of this Zeus-like outlook for actual life. But one is not without resources in making a response. The ethicist has an inexhaustible wealth of symbols, metaphors, and narratives that have in fact shaped the moral consciousness and sensibilities of a civilization. The task is to articulate, to bring from the oblivion of forgetfulness, resources for orienting life.

One can make the point in the language of responsibility ethics and thereby move between symbolic and conceptual matters. The symbolic contribution of biblical thought to an ethics of responsibility requires that one wed claims usually torn asunder: one claim is a regard – even love – for the enemy that reestablishes justice on the other side of retribution, thereby breaking cycles of violence (cf. chapter 6); a second claim is the primal affirmation of the goodness of creation that warrants responsibility for future life, the cry of mute things (cf. chapter 2). The affirmation of creation backs *respect* for life, regard for the enemy, as the extreme form of the other in one's midst, and grounds the struggle to *enhance* life beyond the logic of retribution. These two convictions permeate the symbolic and ritual resources of Christian faith and can be formulated as an imperative for the responsible direction of human power: *in all actions and relations respect and enhance the integrity of life before God.* Later in this book the imperative of responsibility will be specified in Christian and Jewish terms, namely as the double love command (chapter 5) and the Golden Rule (chapter 9) to address problems of conflict. Yet these norms are themselves warranted by the goods of creation.

The task of an ethics for the time of many worlds working with these distinctly Christian sources is to show how the imperative of responsibility expresses what has already shaped a view of the world and life, but which, when formulated as an imperative, resonates with deep moral sensibilities and can provide guidance for meeting the moral challenges of globalization. An ethics can do so at two levels. First, the ethics specifies the central moral value, the supreme good, as the integrity of life and so a good creation. As we know from the introduction to this book, the integrity of life curtails the maximization of power as necessarily the central human aspiration. Second, the ethics functions as a directive for action within the distinct, but related, social subsystems in a society or even globality: economics, politics, law, media, etc. A global ethics must show, in other words, how an understanding of the integrity of life and the imperative of responsibility can inform character and conduct amid the complex and reflexive dynamics of global processes. The basic insight is that the conjunction of creation and the enemy in biblical, symbolic discourse serves as one resource for meeting the moral challenge of today, namely, the threat to future life and the problem of proximity.

We conclude this chapter not by recalling a classic myth or the moral resources of biblical texts, but with a real life story. It captures most of what has been said about the moral challenge of globalization. And it shows us the way in which religious sources can and must shape lives. While deeply personal, similar stories have been lived out in untold ways by morally sensitive persons.[46]

In the Eyes of the Enemy

Near the end of World War II the allied forces attacked Okinawa, the largest of the Ryukyu Islands off the southern tip of Japan. Okinawa was one of the most brutal battles of the Pacific campaign, a foretaste of any actual invasion of Japan. The invasion of Japan was never undertaken; atomic bombs ended the war. And even to this day, the presence of the United States military in Okinawa is disputed and troubled. A legacy of suffering endures. Yet amid these past and present global realities, life is lived out in the concrete, in flesh and blood.

Several days into the actual landing on Okinawa and after the initial flush of brutality and blood, a young Marine captain, son of devout Methodists back in Iowa, took his platoon on routine rounds.[47] They came to a cave and entered it in search of the enemy. Near the back of the cave on the floor lay a Japanese soldier who was dying. The American soldiers wanted to finish the job. As the captain later told the story, the men were determined to cut out the Japanese soldier's teeth for the gold fillings and take anything else of value. The captain was morally outraged. He ordered his men to leave the cave while he remained behind. He stooped down and cradled the dying man in his arms. They looked into each other's eyes. The Japanese man, knowing that he had been spared violation, torture, and further agony, smiled and uttered a few words. In that moment, the American soldier felt the claim and depth of shared humanity. The enemy he held, who died in his arms, had entered him and yet remained other. In the eyes of an enemy whom he had been compelled to protect out of religious conviction came a glimpse of shared humanity, a common dignity and destiny.

The task of ethics in the time of many worlds, an age too easily trapped in legacies of hatred and too ready to forsake future life, is in good measure to make sense of stories like this one. For in these acts of goodness, the world is born not of violence and warfare but remade from within the bounty of life.

NOTES

1 This chapter was originally given as "A Preface to Ethics: Global Dynamics and the Integrity of Life" for the Religious Studies Forum, Bucknell University, February 2000.

2 One could, of course, draw on psychological categories, especially Freudian ones, to examine this myth of the struggle between children and father! Part of the point of this chapter is to engage in the complex dialectical relation between sociocultural patterns of thought and the interpretation of religious discourse. Given this, psychological categories, while important, are not exclusively deployed in what follows. Yet it should be noted that throughout this inquiry the titanic myth is overturned by a different vision of creation rich in psychological import.

3 John Tomlinson, *Globalization and Culture* (Chicago, IL: University of Chicago Press, 1999), p. 18.

4 This is the profound and enduring insight of Friedrich Nietzsche. See his *On the Genealogy of Morals*, translated by Walter Kaufman and R. J. Hollingdale (New York: Vintage Books, 1989).

5 Problems of definition beset "myth" no less than "culture" and "globalization." Without entering those debates, I have been informed by work in the history of religions and also hermeneutical theory. On this see Wendy Doniger O'Flaherty, *Other Peoples' Myths: The Cave of Echoes* (Chicago, IL: University of Chicago Press, 1995) and Paul Ricoeur, *Hermeneutics and the Human Sciences*, edited and translated by John B. Thompson (Cambridge: Cambridge University Press, 1981).

6 See Arjun Appadurai, *Modernity at Large: Global Dimensions of Globalization* (Minneapolis, MN: University of Minnesota Press, 1996).

7 Jonathan Glover, *Humanity: A Moral History of the Twentieth Century* (New Haven, CT: Yale University Press, 2000), pp. 408–9.

8 For the originating statement of this perspective, see George Lindbeck, *The Nature of Doctrine: Religion and Theology in a Post-Liberal Age* (Philadelphia, PA: Westminster Press, 1984).

9 Roland Robertson, "Globalization and the Future of 'Traditional Religion'" in *God and Globalization* vol. 1: *Religion and the Power of Common Life*, edited by Max L. Stackhouse with Peter J. Paris (Harrisburg, PA: Trinity Press International, 2000), p. 58.

10 Put otherwise, I am, in this chapter, submitting to the demands specified by Immanuel Kant and most modern philosophy, as well as amending them. Recall that in recognizing and insisting on the limits of human reason, Kant, in the *Critique of Pure Reason* and elsewhere, nevertheless granted that we *may* engage in speculation about matters that continually preoccupy the human heart, like the origin and end of things or even death and immortality. Added to this, I am suggesting that the problem of globality means that we *must* ponder these things and draw on the symbolic resources of traditions to do so. All of this remains within the context of moral reflection, however. Thus for the sake of this discussion, I am making a fully public argument about the contributions of the religions to ethics. In another context, say my own religious community, other arguments would be germane. But the concern now is with what H. Richard Niebuhr called "Christian moral philosophy." See his *The Responsible Self: An Essay in Christian Moral Philosophy*, introduction by James M. Gustafson and foreword by William Schweiker. Library of Theological Ethics (Louisville, KY: Westminster/John Knox Press, 1999).

11 Walter Lippman, *A Preface to Morals* (New York: Time, 1964).

12 A fuller account of the idea of the "integrity of life" is found in chapter 2 and also the introduction to this book.

13 Alfred North Whitehead, *Science and the Modern World* (New York: Macmillan, 1948).

14 Tomlinson, *Globalization and Culture*, p. 2.

15 Roland Robertson, *Globalization: Social Theory and Global Culture* (London: Sage, 1992), p. 142. Also see Anthony Giddens, *Modernity and Self-Identity: Self and Society in the Late Modern Age* (Stanford, CA: Stanford University Press, 1991) and U. Beck, A. Giddens, and S. Lash, *Reflexive Modernization* (Cambridge: Polity Press, 1994).

16 Some theorists, like Tomlinson, speak of "complex connectivity" rather than social density and understand "proximity" in geographical terms. This is to miss the moral challenge of social density. See Tomlinson, *Globalization and Culture*, esp. chs. 1 and 5. In speaking of "proximity" I mean to signal the moral challenge nestled in connectivity itself. For a thinker who does explore "proximity" as the challenge of the "other," and yet without attention to matters of globalization, see Emmanuel Lévinas, *Otherwise than Being or Beyond Essence*, translated by Alphonso Lingis (Boston, MA: Martinus Nijhoff, 1981).

17 Saskia Sassen, *Globalization and Its Discontents: Essays on the New Mobility of People and Money* (New York: New Press, 1998), p. xx.

18 David Harvey, *The Condition of Postmodernity: An Enquiry into the Origins of Cultural Change* (Oxford: Blackwell, 1990).

19 The point, obviously, is not to demonize other people, cultures, and religions. The point is that toleration has its justified limits and that it is important to make moral judgments about actions and events. On the complex connection between toleration and judgments about the intolerable, see chapter 6 below.

20 For a sensitive discussion of this issue see Lee Yearley, "New Religious Virtues and the Study of Religion" (Tempe: Arizona State University Press, 1994).

21 Appadurai, *Modernity at Large*, p. 82.

22 M. Thomas Thangaraj, "Hinduism and Globalization: A Christian Theological Perspective" in *God and Globalization* vol. 3: *Christ, The World Faiths and the Civilizational Dominions*, edited by Max L. Stackhouse, et. al. (Harrisburg, PA: Trinity Press International, 2001).

23 See B. Barber, *Jihad vs. McWorld* (New York: Time Books, 1995) and G. Ritzer *The McDonaldization of Society: An Investigation into the Changing Character of Contemporary Social Life* (Thousand Oaks, CA: Pine Forge Press, 1993).

24 Robertson, *Globalization*, p. 53.

25 For an instructive account of debates about culture, see Kathryn Tanner, *Theories of Culture: A New Agenda for Theology* (Minneapolis, MN: Fortress Press, 1997). For a brief, if somewhat controversial, account, see also Tomoko Masuzawa's "Culture" in *Critical Terms for Religious Studies*, edited by Mark C. Taylor (Chicago, IL: University of Chicago Press, 1998), pp. 70–93. The old idea of economic substructure and ideological/cultural superstructure – which was, in any case, never adequate – must surely be overcome in thinking about global dynamics. The importance of these factors (representation, valuation, motivation) was always noted by the giants of classical sociology. Karl Marx, for instance, tried to understand the development of capitalism with respect to class struggle as a representational space underwritten by ideologies that together move worker and capitalist in the toil of economic life. The same could be shown of Max Weber's analysis of the rise of modern capitalism.

26 I borrow the term "moral space" from Charles Taylor, but develop it in a distinctive way. See Charles Taylor, *Sources of the Self: The Making of Modern Identity* (Cambridge, MA: Harvard University Press, 1990). Also see William Schweiker, *Power, Value and Conviction: Theological Ethics in the Postmodern Age* (Cleveland, OH: Pilgrim Press, 1998).

27 See Douglas Sturm, "Identity and Otherness: Summons to a New Axial Age (Perspective on the Earth Charter Movement)" (Lewisburg, PA: Forum on Religion and Ecology, Department of Religion, Bucknell University, October 1999). One should note that theorists as different as Alexis de Tocqueville, J. S. Mill, Karl Marx and Friedrich Nietzsche, as well as others, already in the nineteenth century challenged certain ideas of the "individual" in relation to the rise and spread of modern democracy.

28 I want to leave aside debates about whether claims about national interest á *la Realpolitik* or utility and rational choice made by neoclassical economists require a more deterministic account of social and individual agents. Without arguing the point, the force of my position is that any attempt to understand global dynamics, and with this its main "actors," from a unitary perspective – say economics or politics – is inadequate. That is why I have insisted on not only social scientific but also cultural analysis in trying to understand globalization.

29 Sassen, *Globalization and Its Discontents*, pp. 84–5.

30 Hans Jonas, *Morality and Mortality: A Search for the Good after Auschwitz* (Evanston, IL: Northwestern University Press, 1996).

31 See Donna J. Haraway, *Simians, Cyborgs, and Women: The Reinvention of Nature* (New York: Routledge, 1991). For a critique of such positions, see Paul Ramsey,

Fabricated Man: The Ethics of Genetic Control (New Haven, CT: Yale University Press, 1970).

32 See William Schweiker, *Responsibility and Christian Ethics* (Cambridge: Cambridge University Press, 1995) and also Hans Jonas, *The Imperative of Responsibility: In Search of an Ethics for the Technological Age* translated by Hans Jonas and David Herr (Chicago, IL: University of Chicago Press, 1984).

33 What is meant by "religion" is hotly debated. Yet any account of religion would want to include some dimension of experience, say the experience of transcendence, as well as symbolic, ritual, and ethical elements. As Theo Sundermeier has noted, "Religion ist die gemeinschaftliche Antwort des Menschen auf Transzendenzerfahrung, die sich in Ritus und Ethik Gestalt gibt." See his *Was ist Religion? Religionswissenschaft in theologischen Kontext. Ein Studienbuck* (Gütersloh: Chr. Kaiser/Gütersloh Verlaghaus, 1999), p. 27.

34 See Stephen Toulmin, *Cosmopolis: The Hidden Agenda of Modernity* (New York: Free Press, 1990).

35 Honesty is needed. Some beliefs simply are not up to the task of our age; some worldviews, some myths, are below the level of the complexity of the world in which we in fact live. Put differently, the reality of globality is relativizing even the religions; it is forcing us to ask about what contribution they can make to a realistic response to the threats to the integrity of life on our planet.

36 See *A Global Ethic: The Declaration of the Parliament of the World's Religions*, edited by Hans Küng and Karl-Josef Kuschel (New York: Continuum, 1995).

37 See John Kelsay and Sumner B. Twiss, *Religion and Human Rights* (New York: The Project on Religion and Human Rights, 1994).

38 Jeremy Bentham, "Anarchial Fallacies" in his *Works* vol. 2 (Edinburgh: William Tait, 1843), p. 523.

39 For instance, one might explore how Hindu ideas about Karma imply both a journey of salvation, and thus answers problems of hatred and suffering, and connect persons to the rest of reality and even the future. Similar explorations could be undertaken with respect to craving and suffering and the Buddhist response to these in universal compassion. Comparative inquiry along those or other lines is not possible in this chapter.

40 Recall a previous note. I am making the move to distinctly religious concerns within the ambit of ethical reflection. It is important that this move arises in the light of the problem of suffering and violence. As Kant knew, the problem of evil rightly provokes reflection beyond the limits prescribed by philosophical method. This also relates to the note above about a mimetic or explicative hermeneutics. I have made some of the argument of the following pages in other writings. See William Schweiker, "Verantwortungsethik in einer pluralistischen Welt: Schöpfung und die Integrität des Lebens" in *Evangelische Theologie* 59: 5 (1999): 320–34, or chapter 2 below.

41 Michael Welker, "Creation: Big Bang or the Work of Seven Days?" in *Theology Today* 52: 2 (1995): 183–4.

42 Hans-Dieter Betz and William Schweiker, "Concerning Mountains and Morals: A Conversation about the Sermon on the Mount" in *Criterion* 36: 2 (1997): 23. Also see his *The Sermon on the Mount* (Philadelphia, PA: Fortress Press, 1997).

Of course, we ought not to assume that God is all "sweetness and light" in the biblical texts. Quite the contrary: God is also depicted as destroyer and slayer. The argument is that there are the means within the text for the moral critique of such accounts of the divine. Ironically, it may well be important in some domains of moral and political existence to insist that God's ways are not our ways, that God is the slayer of human purposes.

43 On this see John Dominic Crossan, *Jesus: A Revolutionary Biography* (San Francisco, CA: HarperSanFrancisco, 1994).

44 Not surprisingly, theologians have been drawn into long discussions about the relation between creation, redemption, and providence. Without entering the details of these dogmatic issues, the force of my remarks is to link much closer than usual claims about God's creative action with beliefs about redemption and providence. My interpretation might not be as novel as it seems, although the full ethical implications of this move have not been traced by others. Consider other analogous arguments. Karl Barth, in his *Church Dogmatics*, insists that divine election, God's decision to be God for us, is the primal reality and this sets creation in the context of redemption. Thomas Aquinas, in the *Summa Theologiae*, argues that the "logos" is the paradigm in the divine mind for the creation of the world, but this is the logos that is incarnate in the redeemer. More recently, Jürgen Moltmann argues for a connection between eschatology and creation and thus ideas of new creation. See his *The Coming of God: Christian Eschatology*, translated by Margaret Kohl (Minneapolis, MN: Fortress Press, 1996). My point is that the old division between an "ethics of creation" and an "ethics of redemption" must be rethought in the global context by Christian thinkers and that there is some precedence for doing so.

45 While some skepticism is in order about the power of religions actually to shape the moral beliefs, attitudes, and actions of persons, we should always remain open to the evidence. In this light, the recent work of Robin Gill on the ways in which religious membership does in fact help foster moral outlook and action is extremely important. See his *Churchgoing and Christian Ethics* (Cambridge: Cambridge University Press, 1999).

46 I am of course mindful of the many ambiguities that surround any moral encounter amid the terrors of war. Granting that fact, this story, I believe, manifests some basic features characteristic of when, in the midst of those terrors, responsibility and moral sensitivity remain undefeated. For an insightful account of this point, and one that includes other stories like that to follow, see Jonathan Glover, *Humanity: A Moral History of the Twentieth Century* (New Haven, CT: Yale University Press, 2000).

47 That captain was my father. I have long pondered over his story and what it has taught me about the power of human care. In love and gratitude I owe so much to Dad, now lost to me.

CHAPTER 2

Pluralism in Creation

A Feature of Our Age

In 1921, W. B. Yeats, in his poem "The Second Coming," wrote difficult yet beautiful lines that announce a kind of modern apocalypse.

> Turning and turning in the widening gyre
> The falcon cannot hear the falconer;
> Things fall apart; the center cannot hold;
> Mere anarchy is loosed upon the world . . .[1]

These words seem to express the spirit of our age. We live in a time of twilight, when persons' lives are fragmented and strained by multiple roles: parent, professional, lover, citizen. The clamor of private freedom, runaway consumption, and ethnic conflict and war around the world threaten us with anarchy or a breakdown of social ties. There are also endless debates about how democratic societies can negotiate moral diversity as well as multiculturalism.[2] The same could be said of the current global situation. Ethnic groups, religious traditions, ancient cultural divides are reasserting themselves. The chorus of voices will not go away and, indeed, ought not to go away. How to think about the moral life in our age?

In the face of this question, the temptation is to let Yeats have the final word. The temptation is to think of our time as caught between an anarchy of values and the longing for a new revelation. This is a skeptical and pessimistic response. It renders us powerless in the face of complex social forces; it condemns us to long silently for another age. Given that attitude, it is not surprising that much current moral, philosophical, and theological reflection focuses on the anarchy, either by celebrating postmodern "play" or trying to curtail its anarchic violence. Another response to this twilight is now demanded of us.

The previous chapter began to fashion a response to the current situation, what was called the time of many worlds. Chapter 1 outlined a "new preface to ethics" that tried to grasp the most general features of our age and also respond to questions about the value of creation and the integrity of life. This chapter addresses another feature of the age, namely, matters of moral pluralism and the fantastic expansion of human power that characterize the contemporary compression of the world. I want to show, surprisingly, that the Christian symbols of "creation/new creation" and the idea of the integrity of life help us combat the moral skepticism too often associated with the time of many worlds. These symbols provide a way to affirm a robust sense of pluralism while also establishing strong limits on conflict and its power to engulf our lives and communities.[3]

As we saw in chapter 1, facing the problem of proximity and the reality of scarce resources in a hungry world too easily and too often leads to unending cycles of violence. To respond to the time of many worlds requires in part careful consideration of how rightly and best to break those cycles of hatred and conflict. By drawing together creation and new creation a bold revision is made in Christian moral convictions. Creation as a distinctly theological idea includes, but is more than, "nature." Creation so defined extends the realm of responsibility to all people. Additionally, the transformation and renewal of conscience – the primary mode of our being as moral creatures – is precisely how best to live within the reality of God's gracious creative activity. It is to live in the new creation. Finally, the claim is that a new ethics of responsibility is the best way to articulate the moral meaning of these religious convictions. The inquiry can thereby begin with a statement of the agenda for responsibility ethics.

The Agenda for Ethics

"Responsibility" is a relatively recent term in ethics. The word entered Western moral discourse only a few hundred years ago. It signified a novel way of thinking about our lives. H. Richard Niebuhr argued that responsibility ethics fastens not on ends and consequences, as in so-called teleological ethics, nor insists on a universal, categorical obligation as definitive of morals, as deontological forms of moral theory do. An ethics of responsibility offers an alternative to these mainstays of moral theory. Niebuhr insisted that human beings are primarily responders to others, participants in complex patterns of communicative interaction. But there are other accounts of "responsibility." Karl Barth spoke of responsibility. He understood the moral life in terms of a free, responsive obedience to the command of God in each situation of choice. Max Weber argued that an ethics of responsibility was about accountability for actions and consequences in situations where adherence to absolute norms is not possible. Other thinkers, like Georg Picht and Heinz Eduard Tödt, explored responsibility and time. Tödt insisted on the importance of conscience and claimed that responsibility was originally an eschatological word in Christian thought. As Hans Jonas has astutely noted, responsibility is about power. Advances in technology as well as the forms of violence that mark this century make responsibility basic in ethics. Wolfgang Huber, in Germany, as well as Charles Curran and James M. Gustafson in the US, have all worked in responsibility ethics. Johannes Fischer has developed ideas about responsibility within a theological ethics focused on the Christian ethos and its claims about reality. Hans Küng has been a staunch advocate of a global ethics of responsibility. Recently, proponents of discourse ethics, like Jürgen Habermas, Karl-Otto Apel, and Seyla Benhabib, have argued for an account of responsibility in terms of communicative action and rationality. There are, of course, vast differences among these thinkers. We cannot possibly explore those differences in this chapter.[4] Yet in each case, a conception of our lives as responsible agents is basic to the normative stance of an ethics.

The thinkers just mentioned address the breakdown in the West of long-standing beliefs about what it means to be a human being, and also, given moral diversity, the loss of a consensus about moral norms. Responsibility ethics has been a way to conceive of our lives as moral beings, as responders to, with, and for others. The ethics for the integrity of life offered in this book agrees with the basic point of these positions: persons exist in complex, communicative patterns of interaction; moral norms must specify ways to respond to the complexity of life. However, a new problem has surfaced in ethics. This problem arises when pluralism is seen to reside internal to a culture and the interactions among cultures are expanded. With the compression of the world through the rise of global systems, we begin to ask about a shared human time of moral diversity. How, then, are we to conceive of a pluralistic world as a moral space of life, and, additionally, how do conceptions of the world shape moral consciousness? Is Yeats right? Is the space of our lives a gap between anarchy and longing? Should we see the world in this way?

There is a good deal at stake in this question about the connection between worldviews and moral consciousness. As agents, we always orient our lives with respect to some idea of goodness, some scale of better or worse. Human beings necessarily hold strong evaluations in order to guide their lives.[5] And those ideas of worth or moral goodness are embedded in and expressed through our beliefs about the world. The new challenge of pluralism to ethics is precisely about the connection between morality and reality. In rather old terminology, the problem facing ethics in the time of many worlds is to clarify the link between metaphysics and ethics.[6] In order to save us the embarrassment of using the term "metaphysics," we can talk about ethics providing a "moral ontology," that is, a conception of reality and directives for how to live rightly in that world.[7] The pluralistic character of reality, I argue, is best explicated by the biblical symbol of creation. The idea of the "integrity of life" is a concept of moral goodness apt for a pluralistic age. This chapter aims to show that the "integrity of life" articulates at the level of axiology, or theory of value, the moral meaning of creation. Responsibility, therefore, is the practical task of living in creation committed to the good as the integrity of life.[8] Later in this book we will explore norms of right choice, especially the double love command and the Golden Rule, consistent with the integrity of life as the core good of responsible existence. At this juncture our concern is less with the connection between the good (the domain of value) and the right (a principle of choice) and more with the challenge pluralism puts to any conception of the reality of value.[9] In later chapters, especially chapters 5, 6, and 9, we will have more to say about the norm of choice, the imperative of responsibility and its specification in Christian discourse.

In terms of ethical theory, pluralism challenges moral realism. Most approaches to pluralism insist that we must disconnect moral beliefs from claims about the nature of reality. That is, a host of thinkers and lots of people believe that norms for how we ought to live must be determined without reference to claims about reality, social or natural. A moral realist, conversely, is someone who thinks that there is in fact some connection between morality and reality. In a strong sense, we can get it right and wrong morally, because "morality" is not simply a matter of social convention or personal preferences. Realists come in many stripes: divine command ethics, rationalists, and naturalists. Most religions and certainly the Christian faith, we should note, have always been strongly realist. Believers hold that goodness is rooted in the nature of things, the sacred, God's will. The position offered in this book is called hermeneutical realism. The domain of goods to which we must rightly respond in order to live morally inheres in the complex relations among things, relations that either foster or destroy life. In ways that will be noted later, this position stands in some continuity with traditional Christian natural law ethics.[10]

However, the approach offered here to moral realism is not old-style natural law. We cannot simply read out of nature norms for living. All perceptions of value, every grasp of norms for actions and relations, are factored through complex acts of imagination, understanding, and interpretation. The work of the moral imagination is constant. The interpretive act, moreover, draws on the ambiguous, open-ended resources of traditions, linguistic forms, symbols, and images in order to discover the meaning and direction of life. This is why we will have something to say later about the symbol of creation in contrast to Yeats's vision of our age. The symbol of creation is a construal of the world, and it requires critique and interpretation within ethics. Yet the confusing thing confronting us nowadays is not that we must revise our traditions. The confusing thing is that we must decide which resources, which images, symbols, traditions, ought to shape our own understanding of life. That is the reason to speak of hermeneutical realism and, as a moral and religious orientation, theological humanism.

What was just noted might appear painfully abstract. People tend to think that ethics is about social norms and policies, a set of do's and don't's. For instance, one might see the "ethical" as just the logic of giving and receiving respect in the domain of social life. Someone else thinks morality is about codes of sexual conduct or personal honesty. We like to think that ethics talks about one domain of our lives, the domain of burdensome duties, but not all of life. But this book assumes a wider, and, in fact, more classical, conception of ethics and the moral life. The most basic moral question is this: how should we live? Any answer to that question – any ethics – entails beliefs about human existence and about the world in which we can, must, and may live. Now, whatever else we want to say about it, the word "pluralism" seems to capture something true about the current situation, the time of many *worlds*. Let us turn to the challenge of pluralism as the next step in presenting an ethics of responsibility for the integrity of life.

Three Aspects of Pluralism

The ethical challenge of pluralism is simple yet radical. As Mary Midgley has noted, morality is "our large-scale cognitive and practical attitudes – our whole policies for thinking and living, our ways of relating to those around us."[11] Pluralism seems to imply that there can be no commonly held "policies for thinking and living." It threatens to shatter the very idea that we inhabit a more or less coherent moral space. But if that is the case, how does one avoid social conflict and breakdown? Is mere anarchy loosed on the world? Yet it is also the case that genuine pluralism can combat social and political tyranny through the interaction of diverse social forces. What is needed, then, is an operative and not destructive pluralism. On the way to that insight, one must begin by clarifying what is meant by pluralism.

The first and most obvious aspect of pluralism is cognitive and axiological *diversity*. People think about and value life in different ways. Some seek wealth and others want martyrdom; some believe in human rights while others insist on ecological holism. Moral diversity is a central fact of the time of many worlds. Roland Robertson has put it well: "Globalization is, it should be clearly recognized, a multidimensional process. In other words, it is simultaneously cultural, economic, and political. Moreover, we should not conceive of this process as necessarily leading to global integration in the strong sense of the word."[12] Pluralism and globalization are deeply linked. The time of many worlds is just that: it is a time in which different moral worlds, different cultures, are interacting, colliding, fusing into an unknown future. It is not at all clear that the future will be one of greater coherence among peoples, or greater conflict, or both.

The diversity of cultures and values is not the only meaning of pluralism. Pluralism also denotes, second, a social situation that easily disconnects policies of thinking and living from claims about the nature of things. While they are mentioned above, we need to be clearer about these arguments. Consider some exemplary positions. Because of cognitive and axiological diversity, Jürgen Habermas, in his discourse ethics, and John Rawls, in his political theory, insist that no general conception of reality or the moral good, no comprehensive ideal as Rawls calls it, is possible or needed in pluralistic societies. As the argument goes, all we need are politically or communicatively warranted norms of justice.[13] Morality need not go deeper than socially warranted convention. In a related way, proponents of global ethics like Hans Küng draw on the resources of religious traditions. Yet they insist that moral codes of the religions can be disconnected from the beliefs found in the religions about the sacred and reality. Again, comprehensive beliefs are unimportant for meeting the moral challenge of pluralism. This means that a pluralistic society must ground moral norms in something other than comprehensive ideals. And it further implies that pluralism itself is not a conception, no matter how implicit, of the reality in which we live. Is this true?

We have isolated two aspects of pluralism: diversity in ways of thinking and valuing, and, given that, the belief that morality must be disconnected from any comprehensive beliefs about life and the world. There is a third aspect to pluralism. Pluralism also describes any social or natural reality in which different forces interact through mutual, reflexive adjustment rather than simple hierarchical ordering. As social theorists from Max Weber to Niklas Luhmann have shown, complex societies are functionally differentiated and each subsystem (law, economy, media, etc.) works by its own logic, values, and discourse.[14] In this respect, "pluralism" is an ethical challenge because it is the shape of the social contexts, the public realms, in which persons must orient their lives.[15] Images of sports heroes speed around the world, feed the market system, and also are used by persons to fashion their personal identities and their cultures. The images of religious leaders or sport heroes facilitates the interaction of functionally differentiated systems – the market, media, sports, religion – even as this brings about shifts in knowing and valuing. Pluralistic realities so understood necessarily shape the moral imagination, deadening or enlivening it.

We can now state more pointedly the ethical problem of pluralism. Contemporary people around the world mostly live in highly differentiated societies wherein social subsystems (market, law, etc.) entail diverse ways of knowing and valuing. The interaction of social subsystems brings about shifts in those frameworks of knowing and valuing and shapes the moral imagination: the economy, for example, must adjust to legal practice; educational systems (sad to say) are increasingly permeated by the logic and value of the economic market. These shifts in knowing and valuing reach from the level of individual consciousness to the relations among communities and nations. The worldwide media means nothing less than the images flowing from spreading market systems penetrating into the consciousness of people around the world and informing their moral imaginations. The media enlivens or deadens what is seen as humanly important.

Given the shifts in thinking and valuing, it seems impossible to offer any comprehensive beliefs about human existence. Moral codes are disconnected from beliefs about reality. Not surprisingly, a great anxiety of our time is rooted in the fact that increasingly persons sense that they are not in control of forces shaping their own consciousness or the social systems that define their roles and lives. It is difficult to gain reflexive distance on the images, pictures, and stories that flow through consciousness and shape perceptions of self, others, and the world. But at the same time, we are the producers of images, the ones who picture, imagine, the world. To borrow from the introduction to this book, the current world is, paradoxically, overhumanized (nature and consciousness are increasingly enfolded into all-too-human ways of picturing and valuing the world) even as we sense it as dehumanizing and profaning. It is a situation in which the "distinction between life and art, reality and appearance becomes impossible . . . Life becomes the proto-type of the world of appearances and these the proto-types of life."[16] This is why Yeats's poem resonates so deeply within our cultures and our hearts.

Creation as a Pluralistic Reality

Notice what has been argued thus far in this chapter. Pluralism is best understood as defining any social and cultural reality that fosters shifts in thinking and valuing in and through the interaction of different subsystems. Awareness of diversity seems to make it difficult to speak of any shared policies of living other than the flow of information in social systems. In terms of ethical theory, what is at stake is the connection between reality and morality, that is, some construal of the space of life and our ways of living. And the challenge, as suggested, is felt in personal life in terms powerfully set forth by Yeats. There is a sense that anarchy is loosed on the earth and that people long for some new revelation. Is Yeats's vision the only possible picture of our moral situation?

We need to be absolutely clear about what is being asked. In order adequately to respond to Yeats's vision, one must shift levels of inquiry. The discussion above of the aspects of pluralism was an *analysis* of our situation. What Yeats offers is not analysis, but, rather, an imaginative *depiction* of the domain of human life and how we presently exist in it. The poet seeks to *articulate*, rather than *analyze*, the texture of experience. He engages the moral imagination. His picture is necessarily symbolic in form, since he wants to capture the lived density of reality. Yeats's poem has widespread resonance expressing how many people in fact see their lives. If one is ever to counter moral skepticism what is needed is not a different analysis of pluralism. We need a different *depiction* of the shape of lived reality. This depiction will be admittedly evaluative; it will be an imaginative framework of thinking that is shaped by ways of appraising or valuing life. In other words, any alternative to Yeats will be nothing less than an imaginatively construed moral ontology. The ontology must, first, provide some way to understand the interconnection of divergent social and natural processes and the forms of valuing and knowing. And, second, this alternate depiction of life needs to warrant a policy of living different than waiting for whatever slouches towards Bethlehem to be born.

Proposing such a construal of the world is a massive task. This book can only outline the basic elements of such an argument. In order to do so we can examine the resources of the Christian tradition as a treasure trove of images, symbols, myths, and narratives for construing reality. The purpose, initially, is simply to see what work these religious resources can do in ethics. Against theorists like Rawls and some global ethicists who banish religious resources from ethics, our hope is to show the importance of beliefs about reality to the moral life. Given this, we turn again to the symbol of creation and new creation and their moral meanings.[17]

Traditionally, the idea of "creation" in Christian theology has been expressed in terms of the "dependence" of all things on God. This "dependence" could be understood metaphysically (God is the cause of all that is, as Thomas Aquinas put it) or psychologically (the Christian has a sense of the dependence of life on God, in the thought of Friedrich Schleiermacher) or intersubjectively (creation configures God's being God for us in Jesus Christ, as Karl Barth insisted). But in all cases, everything that exists supposedly remains in existence because of God's immediate creative and sustaining activity (*creatio continuum*). The idea of dependence was to show the relation and yet transcendence of God to the world. And, further, the idea of dependence was linked to a political image of power: God as the sovereign Lord. Recently, theologians have turned away from the concept of dependency and ideas about political power in order to explore creation within the narrative resources of Christian thought. Feminist theologians, for instance, have insisted on the doctrine of the trinity in order to articulate a relational understanding of the being of God, an understanding that undercuts hierarchical ideas of power built on dependence.[18]

With hermeneutical sensitivity, one must insist on a literary interpretation of the biblical creation narrative in order to escape the conceptual problems that surround the metaphysically and politically loaded idea of dependence. One can isolate two distinct arguments about this narrative: one is about creation and the pluralistic shape of reality; the other, embedded in later strata of tradition, is about how God's response to the world is a model for human moral existence. The strategy of reading in this and other chapters is to explore these arguments in and through each other; it is to read creation texts and claims about forgiveness and redemption together. Undertaking an explicative reading will (1) present a symbolic depiction of the moral space of life, and yet (2) revise this symbol under the pressure of moral reflection. Further, a concept – the integrity of life – must replace dependence in understanding the moral meaning of creation.

First of all, creation within the biblical narrative is an account of reality not in terms of dependence but *abundance* and *fecundity*. God's relation to the "world" is not as a simple cause, a principle of origin, or a metaphysical support. As God "creates," that which is created (heaven/earth; animals; human beings) begins immediately to participate in the ongoing event of world-making. In Genesis narrative, human beings are given the power to name the world, that is, to dwell linguistically, and thus culturally, in reality. They are set amid a complex differentiation of times, forms of life, rhythms and patterns of nature. The divine blessing is poured out on creatures, human beings, and the Sabbath. The blessing is the capacity to participate in bringing forth life in all of its complexity and diversity. "Creation produces a complex unity between diverse structural patterns of life and events."[19] In other words, creation is the interaction of natural and social/cultural processes along with their logics. The symbol provides a *depiction* of reality that can be *analyzed* as pluralistic in character.

How does this account of reality relate to a policy of thinking and valuing, to moral existence? This brings us to the second argument about the creation narrative that centers on God's response to the world. As argued in the previous chapter, there is a deep connection in the biblical texts between love of neighbor and creation. Acts of righteousness and justice are "creation events" precisely because they enable people to participate anew in world-making. God loves the neighbor, even God's enemies, by providing the bounty of existence. In the Sermon on the Mount, Jesus teaches a radical and seemingly harsh thing: God lets the rain, the waters of life, fall on the just and the unjust

(Matthew 5–7). Does this mean that God does not care about the difference between justice and injustice? God's way of dealing with the wrongdoer, with God's enemies, is not through retribution in which the enemy is made a means to the end of securing justice. The divine's extravagant care for the world and persons, seen in creation itself, is to lead to conversion of the enemy.[20] Of course, this is hardly what God's "enemy" wants. In its extreme form, the "enemy" champions words John Milton put in the mouth of Satan. "Evil, be thou my good." The conversion of evil through goodness, drawing good from evil, is also a judgment. The evil heart, the heart bent on demeaning and destroying the integrity of life, ceases to orient life, is rendered powerless, and is converted to what was previously despised, that the integrity of life should be respected and flourish. Conversion is demanding; it is a fundamental transformation of existence. None of us, if we are honest, easily bear such a fundamental judgment and change. The redemption of evil by merciful goodness is bound in Christian faith to the connection between creation and new creation won through Christ. Within scripture and even the teachings of Jesus, a principle meant to end the cycle of retribution is injected back into the event of creation itself. In Christ, that principle becomes a person.

Throughout scripture the bountiful creativity of God can be read as a non-retributive and non-coercive *overcoming* of the "enemies" of God. Justice is done. That which is destructive of life will not long endure. Creation overcomes chaos not through coercion or conflict as seen in myths like the Greek tale of Chronos and Zeus examined in chapter 1. Creation works through an ordering that brings forth life; it is a multi-causal event of world-making. Adam and Eve are set within a garden meant to evoke gratitude and joyful obedience. Slaves are created into the people of Israel through the Exodus. YHWH gives the Law and the Land, thereby fulfilling the promise of abundant heirs made with Abraham and Sarah. Jesus heals the sick and feeds the hungry. The feeding stories manifest a logic of abundance and reconfigure communities so that all might partake of the reign of God. The feedings revise the boundaries of social life beyond traditional demarcations and conflicts between the clean and the profane. The death and resurrection of Christ are followed by the outpouring of the Spirit that overcomes within the Church the split of Jew and Gentile. Preaching and Eucharist are, in the life of the community of faith, the linguistic and ritual enactments of the bounty of the divine bearing toward the world. In this way, the story of grace, new creation, articulates the core meaning of creation. Creation is abundant and merciful even if the natural world is marked by want and suffering.

Taking these arguments about the biblical narrative together, we can say that "creation/new creation" imaginatively depicts the moral space of life and sets forth a policy of living. The logic of these symbols seeks to ground ways of thinking and valuing in a claim about the divine activity as abundant and non-retributive. The moral life is and ought to be an imitation of the divine action. Yet this account of the idea of creation is admittedly a profound revision of traditional theism. The core moral demand of reciprocity, the backbone of justice expressed in the claim to love others as you would have them love you, provides a conceptual transformation of how we understand God's bearing towards the world. The problem of retribution internal to the biblical picture of God (see the flood; acts of divine repentance; the Cross of Christ) is overcome throughout the intertextual connection between the Sermon on the Mount and Genesis.[21] Put more pointedly, Jesus Christ in his teaching, actions, death, and resurrection is the very being of God radically interpreted beyond the logic of retribution. In Christ, one confesses, the reality of God is made known and present in the world, enabling and requiring a life imitative of the divine way. Conduct and social structures that foster possessiveness, violence, and animosity – say, in class conflict, absolute poverty that demeans and destroys persons, and even civil war – are, religiously speaking, the realm of sin. Yet when life is used to further human dignity, foster the common good, and overcome conflict it is a genuine good rooted in God's non-coercive dealing with hostile powers.[22] This outlook fosters a deep affirmation of the goodness of life even in the face of conflict as well as a commitment to restorative justice (cf. chapter 6).

We have reached some genuine insights. The first insight is that creation is an apt symbol for understanding ethically the pluralistic shape of lived reality untarnished by "sin." It enlivens the moral imagination to grasp what is humanly important. The creation narrative explicates life as a realm of goods in and through the interworking of multiple forces and realities (heaven/earth; light/dark; etc.). Genuine pluralism is not anarchy loosed on the earth. It is a complex, interacting reality affirmed as good but also marked by the ever present possibility of conflict and violence. Next, by reading the love command within creation, the principle of reciprocity is seen to specify the moral meaning of God's creative abundance in the face of conflict and so the reality and realm of sin. This is not to reduce the text to a single moral principle. Joseph Sittler has rightly written that the "desire to extrude principles from the Christ-life may be a form of man's hidden longing to cool into palpable ingots of duty the living stuff of love and so dismiss . . . the Holy One with whom we have to do."[23] To seek justice is not to live by some generalized principle. It is, rather, to live in accord with creation amid the structures of sin but under the power of new creation. This is a realistic conception of justice necessary to counter forces of destruction and conflict that too often and too readily infest all human communities. But, third, this is also an utter transformation of justice and our usual ideas of creation. When creation is conceived on the model of reciprocity within the integrity of life and not metaphysical dependence, when God's abundant dealing with the enemy through the goods of life grounds the principle of justice, then justice and creation are transvalued. Justice is no longer only the claim to one's due and the duty to render fairly to others. Justice is not simply fairness, as John Rawls contends. It is, rather, the merciful establishment of right relations among persons and social and natural processes. It is a creation event. Our ideas about creation are also transformed in the light of moral demands. Creation is not simply a claim about the pluralistic shape of reality, although it is that. It is also a way of living out restorative justice and redemption. Morality and reality are connected in the moral imagination, deepening one's perception of what is important.

A depiction of reality as creation, a comprehensive belief, warrants an attitude towards life that is markedly different than Yeats's poem and too much postmodern skepticism. It is an attitude that affirms life and can curtail cycles of retribution. This attitude is required in order to live in a world of diversity. Yet our interpretation of this symbol is incomplete. We have insisted that the idea of reciprocity – do unto others as you would have them do unto you – specifies God's abundant, merciful dealing with enemies. This is a claim about the connection of thinking and valuing within policies of living. Creation is also pluralistic in character. Here is a statement about the depth of value, the status of goodness. The question now is how to link these points about a norm for right action and a claim about the source of goodness into a coherent position, into an ethics. In ways analogous to traditional natural law ethics, we are concerned with an order of right moral reasoning (the principle of reciprocity) and the order of nature indicative of the good (the fecundity of creation). In order to complete the argument, we must return to an ethics for the integrity of life.

Ethics for the Integrity of Life

We now make the third and final shift in thinking. The argument of this chapter has moved between an *analysis* of pluralism and competing *articulations* of the moral space of life, namely, Yeats's and the biblical symbol of creation. We have done so in order to clarify and to meet the challenge of pluralism to ethics. By understanding the symbol of creation at the intersection of Genesis and the Sermon on the Mount, it was shown to provide (1) a policy of living and thinking that (2) affirms a robust pluralism, and (3) connects morality to a picture of reality. In this way, to borrow Paul Ricoeur's famous idea, the symbol gives rise to thought.[24] Specifically, the symbol of creation so interpreted provokes reflection aimed at responding to aspects of pluralism. The task at this point of the inquiry is to draw together *analysis* and *articulation* within the work of a *prescriptive* ethics.

Actually, the dimensions of God's abundance in creation and in Christ can be drawn together once we see that they relate to different elements of normative ethical thinking. These elements are, first, some norm for right choice and conduct, and, second, a theory of value, the good that we ought to seek in all actions and relations. God's dealing with "enemies" through the outpouring of the necessities of life specifies a norm for right choice and conduct. This is why, as noted, it is articulated by Jesus in the Sermon on the Mount in terms of love of neighbor. The so-called Golden Rule is nothing less than the creation event interpreted as a norm for conduct and choice. Acting on this rule is in part how human beings imitate God; it is how, on the other side of retribution, Christians imitate Christ and so live in the new creation. We can make this point stronger by including the active, merciful dimension of creation as norm. Let me put this as an *initial* formulation of an imperative of responsibility: *in all actions and relations respect and enhance life.* The directive to *respect* life captures the idea of reciprocity; the demand to *enhance* life signals the abundance of creation. Acting on this norm fulfills justice. It limits retribution while also protecting the innocent. The full implications of this imperative formulation of creation will be traced throughout other chapters of this book.

What then of a theory of value? As we have seen, "creation aims from the very beginning at the differentiated communion of God with human beings in particular and with creatures in general, and thus at knowledge of God and of creation."[25] In order to capture the moral meaning of creation, we need the idea of the integrity of life. This concept designates two things, as suggested in the introduction to this book. First, integrity means the *integration* of complex goods into some coherent, complex whole. Value inheres in the interactions among various dimensions of life: natural existence (say, health), social interaction and processes, and also reflective goods, goods of culture and meaning. Integrity is life characterized by richness and yet also coherence or wholeness. The integrity of life indicates that intrinsic worth is found in the right relation of complex goods.[26] This is the meaning of the statement in Genesis that God saw it and it was "good." Second, the integration of human life, our existence as moral agents, is always through commitment to something that brings wholeness of life. That is why we speak of a person of integrity as someone who acts on principle, who actually lives out her or his convictions. The distinctly moral good is a life whose wholeness is found through dedication to respecting and enhancing the integrity of life. Integrity is thus also a critical principle to judge those forces operative in pluralistic societies working to shape our view of others and the world. Dedication to living responsibly is nothing less than retaining the freedom and dignity of one's life and consciousness.

We can now join the elements of our reflections on God's abundant creativity. The integrity of life is a pluralistic conception of the good. It suggests that what we mean by "goodness" is precisely the integration of complex realities symbolically depicted in biblical texts as creation. The responsible life is service to that good. It is a life shaped by commitment to the integrity of life. Given this, the precise formulation of the imperative of responsibility is possible: *in all actions and relations respect and enhance the integrity of life before God.* This is an imperative for responsible living because it articulates a norm for responding to complex domains of reality. What one is required to endorse as the norm of actions and relations is the worth of complex, integrated realities, the interaction among natural, social, and reflexive goods. The imperative of responsibility links the basic claims about creation that have emerged from our hermeneutical inquiry. Later in the book this will be explored through the double love command (chapter 5) and also the so-called Golden Rule (chapter 9) as religious specifications of the imperative of responsibility.

However, immediately on seeing this point about the diversity of goods we reach a stark and troubling realization. It returns us at a deeper level to the problem of comprehensive ideals and pluralistic societies. Life is never orderly and harmonious. The clamor of voices and social disputes rages in our world. Retributive violence too easily engulfs whole societies and maybe the planet. Life competes with life for the goods of this earth. Time spent with friends detracts from family. Work brings fulfillment but at emotional and physical cost. Insofar as our lives are situated in roles within a highly differentiated society – father, citizen, student, consumer all at once – then the competition of life with life invades existence. More profoundly, we daily confront the reality of sin, the wanton demeaning and destroying of the integrity of life.

By affirming the integrity of life, one is also and simultaneously acknowledging the fact of moral tragedy. Given limitations of finite life, the pluralistic structure of social existence, and genuine evil, not all things that ought to be respected and enhanced can be respected or enhanced. Is Yeats, ironically enough, right in the end? If one endorses the goodness of creation, does the moral center no longer hold and a tragic anarchy break into our lives? One suspects that we have, at long last, reached the deepest worry of the time of many worlds. If one sees the diversity of our world as a genuine human good, if one affirms pluralism, then tragic events seem everywhere. How then to love life? What is at issue in a picture of reality is actually a response to moral tragedy.

One response of our day is found in Yeats's poem. This picture of life is a comprehensive ideal. It tells us to endure the conflicts of life, a twilight of idols, hoping for some new revelation, some new savior.[27] Drawing on religious sources, we have tried to outline a different response and policy for living. In fact, biblical texts were read through each other in order thereby to link creation and redemption in a comprehensive view of life. Redemption has already transformed creation, even as we await and struggle for fulfillment as new creation in others and our own existence.[28] This is, possibly, an odd response. The point is that we ought to live responsibly, we ought to respect and enhance the integrity of life, not because it will free us from tragedy, but, quite simply, because it is good and right to live as creatures of God. In other words, there is no prudential justification for the moral life, no self-interested reason for a dedication and commitment to the integrity of life. All that remains is the intrinsic claim of this vision of life and the risk it entails, a risk that even the divine bears. The deepest challenge of pluralism, as I have noted, is that by shaping our ways of thinking and valuing it can blind us to the intrinsic claim of the integrity of life to be respected and enhanced. Pluralism can blind us to the reality of God among us.

Yet we are not left empty handed. The imperative to respect and enhance the integrity of life before God resonates deeply in people's lives. The good is not without its witness. Through the complex interactions of family, community, education, tradition, loves, and natural endowment we do in fact sense that we ought not to demean and destroy the integrity of life. This sense of responsibility is nothing less than an awareness of God's good creation, whether it is named as such or not. It is the claim of conscience. Given this sense of responsibility, we are called and empowered to imitate the divine bearing toward the world. The basic question of the moral life, therefore, is whether or not people will live out that sensibility of life's real worth. The task in the time of many worlds is to find resources that enable persons and communities to meet life resolutely and responsibly. Imagining the world creatively fosters a perception of the depth of goodness beyond the anxieties of the age.

NOTES

1 W. B. Yeats, "The Second Coming" in *The Oxford Anthology of English Literature* vol. 2 (New York: Oxford University Press, 1973), p. 1700. In a note on this poem, Yeats insisted that "our scientific, democratic, fact-accumulating, heterogeneous civilization belongs to the outward gyre and prepares not the continuance of itself" (ibid, p. 1699). In this note, Yeats gives poetic expression to many of the forces we have noted in the time of many worlds and the problem of overhumanization.

2 See Michael Walzer, *On Toleration* (New Haven, CT: Yale University Press, 1998). See also George Kateb, "Notes on Pluralism" in *Social Research* 61: 3 (1994): 511–37.

3 On this also see Donald W. Shriver, Jr., *An Ethic for Enemies: Forgiveness in Politics* (Oxford. Oxford University Press, 1995) and Jean Bethke Elshtain, *New Wine and Old Bottles: International Relations and Ethical Discourse* (Notre Dame, IN: University of Notre Dame Press, 1998).

4 H. Richard Niebuhr, *The Responsible Self: An Essay in Christian Moral Philosophy*, introduction by James M. Gustafson with foreword by William Schweiker (Louisville, KT: Westminster/John Knox Press, 1999). See Heinz Eduard Tödt, *Perspektiven theologischer Ethik* (Munich: Chr. Kaiser, 1988); Georg Picht, *Wahrheit, Vernunft, Verantwortung: philosophische Studien* (Stuttgart: Ernst Klett, 1969); Hans Jonas, *The Imperative of Responsibility: In Search of an Ethics for the Technological Age* (Chicago, IL: University of Chicago Press, 1984); Wolfgang Huber, "Toward an Ethics of Responsibility" in *The Journal of Religion* 73: 4 (1993): 573–91 and his *Konflikt und Konsens: Studien zur Ethik der Verantwortung* (Munich: Chr. Kaiser, 1990); Johannes Fischer, *Theological Ethik: Grundwissen und Orientierung* (Stuttgart: W. Kohlhammer, 2002). Also see Hans Küng, *Global Responsibility: In Search of a New Global Ethic*, translated by John Bowden (New York: Crossroads, 1991) and Karl-Otto Apel, *Diskurs und Verantwortung: Das Problem des übergangs zur postkonventionellen Moral* (Frankfurt: Suhrkamp, 1990).

5 Charles Taylor, *Sources of the Self: The Making of the Modern Identity* (Cambridge, MA: Harvard University Press, 1989).

6 A number of thinkers are making this point. See William Schweiker, *Responsibility and Christian Ethics* (Cambridge: Cambridge University Press, 1995) and *Power, Value, and Conviction: Theological Ethics in the Postmodern Age* (Cleveland, OH: Pilgrim Press, 1998). Also see Franklin I. Gamwell, *The Divine Good: Modern Moral Theory and the Necessity of God* (San Francisco: HarperCollins, 1990); James M. Gustafson, *Ethics from a Theocentric Perspective* 2 vols. (Chicago, IL: University of Chicago Press, 1981, 1984); Erazim Kohák, *The Embers and the Stars: An Inquiry into the Moral Sense of Nature* (Chicago, IL: University of Chicago Press, 1984); Iris Murdoch, *Metaphysics as a Guide to Morals* (London: Penguin Press/Allen Lane, 1992); and Maria Antonaccio, *Picturing the Human: The Moral Thought of Iris Murdoch* (Oxford: Oxford University Press, 2000).

7 See William Schweiker, "Power and the Agency of God" in *Theology Today* 52: 2 (1995): 204–24. As we will see, the three cognitive acts of analysis, articulation, and prescription basic to moral ontological reflection set forth in that essay structure the present chapter as well.

8 I am aware that the World Council of Churches as well as several theologians have spoken of the "integrity of creation" as the basic moral value. While I am in agreement with much of the intent of that discourse, I find it manifesting a category mistake. On my account, "creation" is a distinctive linguistic expression, a symbol, for the lived texture of reality; integrity is a moral concept for the good. I have thus related, yet distinguished, creation and integrity. The WWC, it seems to me, is not careful enough to explore the distinctions and relations between symbol (creation) and concept (integrity) and how these ought to be properly related in theological ethical reflection.

9 Debates about the relation between claims about goodness and norms of right choice and action are longstanding in Western ethics. Some theorists argue that what is right is defined in terms of the goods attained by acting onthat norm (consequentialism), others contend that norms of right conduct pertain irrespective of

claims about the good (strict deontologists), and still other thinkers, like myself, argue for a "mixed" moral theory wherein the good is the necessary condition for the validity of norms of choice (the good – the integrity of life – tells us what we ought to respect and enhance) and yet acting on valid norms itself gives rise to a unique form of human goodness, the genuine ethical good.

10 There has recently been renewed interest in natural law ethics among theologians, legal theorists, and philosophers. Traditionally, natural law ethics specified both a claim about right reason (as Thomas Aquinas put it: natural law is the rational participation by humans in the eternal law of God) and an axiology (Aquinas: all things intend the flourishing of their nature). Recent discussions have tried to retain these two elements of natural law ethics without endorsing a static and reductionistic naturalism or the non-historical conception of "reason" found in too much Roman Catholic ethics. On this see Charles Curran, *Directions in Fundamental Moral Theology* (Notre Dame, IN: University of Notre Dame Press, 1985). Also see Lisa Sowle Cahill, *Sex, Gender and Christian Ethics* (Cambridge: Cambridge University Press, 1997) and Cristina L. H. Traina, *Feminist Ethics and Natural Law: The End of Anathemas* (Washington, DC: Georgetown University Press, 1999).

11 Mary Midgley, *Can't We Make Moral Judgements?* (New York: St. Martin's Press, 1991), p. 23.

12 Roland Robertson, "Globalization and the Future of 'Traditional Religion'" in *God and Globalization* vol. 1: *Religion and the Powers of the Common Life*, edited by Max L. Stackhouse with Peter J. Paris (Harrisburg, PA: Trinity Press International, 2000), pp. 53–4.

13 See Jürgen Habermas, *Moral Consciousness and Communicative Action*, translated by Christian Lenhardt and Shierry Weber Nicholsen (Cambridge, MA: MIT Press, 1990) and John Rawls, *Political Liberalism* (New York: Columbia University Press, 1993). Also see Franklin I. Gamwell, *The Meaning of Religious Freedom: Modern Politics and the Democratic Revolution* (Albany: State University of New York Press, 1995).

14 Niklas Luhmann, *Social Systems*, translated by John Bednarz, Jr. with Dirk Baecker (Stanford, CA: Stanford University Press, 1995).

15 David Tracy, *Plurality and Ambiguity: Hermeneutics, Religion, Hope* (San Francisco: Harper and Row, 1986).

16 Christoph Wolf, "Mimesis" in *Historische Anthropologie: Zum Problem der Humanwissenschaften heute oder Versuch einer Neubegründung*, hg. Gunter Gebauer et al. (Hamburg: Rowohlt Taschenbuch Verlag, 1989), p. 119. For afurther examination of this problem, see William Schweiker, *Mimetic Reflections: A Study in Hermeneutics, Theology and Ethics* (New York: Fordham University Press, 1990).

17 On the idea of "moral meaning," see William Schweiker, "Understanding Moral Meanings: On Philosophical Hermeneutics and Theological Ethics" in *Christian Ethics: Problems and Prospects*, edited by Lisa Sowle Cahill and James F. Childress (Cleveland, OH: Pilgrim Press, 1996), pp. 76–92.

18 See, for example, Elizabeth Johnson, *She Who Is: The Mystery of God in Feminist Theological Discourse* (New York: Crossroad, 1992). Also see *The Otherness of*

God, edited by Orrin F. Summerell (Charlottesville: University of Virginia Press, 1998).

19 Michael Welker, "Creation: Big Bang or the Work of Seven Days?" in *Theology Today* 52: 2 (1995): 183–4. Also see his *Gottes Geist: Theologie des Heiligen Gottes* (Neukirchn-Vluyn: Neukirchener Verlag, 1992).

20 I will return to this theme later and the place of so-called just war thinking in an account of political forgiveness (chapter 6) and then other responses to fanatical violence (chapter 9) and moral dualism (chapter 5).

21 There is a longstanding debate among Christian theologians about whether the Decalogue or the Sermon on the Mount best expresses the core of the Christian moral life. John Wesley, for instance, saw the Sermon on the Mount as the sum of the Christian religion, while others, such as John Calvin and many Roman Catholic thinkers, focus on the Decalogue. My move here is to connect a Wesley-like insight with the importance of "creation" as the horizon within which to understand Jesus's teaching. And these two claims are also linked to the idea of new creation as the renewal and transformation of conscience.

22 I disagree, in content and method, with thinkers like John Milbank and others who view the "secular" as rooted in an "ontology of violence" that is supposedly missing from the biblical and Christian worldview. See John Milbank, *Theology and Social Theory: Beyond Secular Reason* (Oxford: Blackwell, 1990). While it is the case that the biblical vision begins with harmony and abundance, that outlook is neither as idealistic nor unambiguous as these thinkers contend. In my formulation, what is at issue in claims about the divine is the transvaluation of power to respect and enhance the integrity of life. I take this to be the conceptual expression of Christian beliefs about the being of God as love.

23 Joseph Sittler, *The Structure of Christian Ethics*, foreword by Franklin Sherman. The Library of Theological Ethics (Louisville, KY: Westminster/John Knox Press, 1998), p. 49.

24 See Paul Ricoeur, *Interpretation Theory: Discourse and the Surplus of Meaning* (Fort Worth: Texas Christian University Press, 1976).

25 Welker, "Creation," in "Creation: Big Bang or the Work of Seven Days," p. 184.

26 This is sometimes call a "relational" and multidimensional theory of value. On this idea see H. Richard Niebuhr, *Radical Monotheism and Western Culture* (New York: Harper Torchbooks, 1960) and also James M. Gustafson, *A Sense of the Divine: The Natural Environment from a Theocentric Perspective* (Cleveland, OH: Pilgrim Press, 1994).

27 One sees this move most obviously in thinkers like Martin Heidegger and his claims about the retreat of the "gods" and also Friedrich Nietzsche and the philosophers of the future as well as the coming of the übermensch. The apocalyptic air of these positions should give us pause.

28 I am drawing an insight from John Wesley, who insisted that Christ's presence in the world had retroactive force, as it were. There is nothing and no one outside of the scope of Christ's redeeming action. This means that there is not something called "nature" outside of redemption. Wesley called this "prevenient grace": it enables and empowers the free response to Christ's life and work. On my reading,

the same point is made biblically through the ideas of creation/new creation. Reality itself – despite its brokenness – is always and already within the reach of God's care and mercy. A similar idea was developed much later by the twentieth-century Roman Catholic theologian Karl Rahner. I cannot explore these matters at this point.

CHAPTER 3

Reconsidering Greed

The previous chapters of this book outlined dimensions of the time of many worlds. These dimensions ranged from global dynamics to the moral challenge of pluralism. An ethics was proposed through a post-critical, explicative hermeneutics that links creation and "new creation" in the renewal of conscience. Realizing that any comprehensive account of the present global situation is beyond the scope of this or any other book, this chapter nevertheless takes another step in reflection. As many note, the spread of corporate, multinational capitalism is one of the most pressing issues in the time of many worlds. Around the planet, there is a sense that the "global market" is the major force shaping human lives, a force that seems well beyond our control. There is the danger of wanton consumption that drives an overhumanization of the world destructive of responsible human life. And there is also the fact that gross inequalities in access to material goods breed hostility, terrorism, and cycles of conflict. As a United Nations Development Program recently noted, "Global inequalities in income and living standards have reached grotesque proportions."[1]

This is not to suggest, as the United Nations report rightly continues, that competitive markets should somehow be eliminated. Markets have, in fact, stimulated growth. What is more, human beings have always engaged in patterns of exchange – barter, trade, and the like. Mythically speaking, Eden is "pre-commercial," but as soon as real human beings enter the world of history, exchange is present. Ancient "economies" were agrarian or nomadic and embedded in special social and cultural relations, often deeply religious and patriarchal in nature. In our situation, having traversed mercantile and industrial ages, we find highly differentiated and coordinated financial and credit systems as well as high-tech industries and even post-industrial information flows that influence all aspects of economic life. There is the emergence of new kinds of agencies (World Bank, International Monetary Fund, World Trade

Organization, as well as the North Atlantic Free Trade Agreement) and the collaboration of transnational corporations in the making of international law. How should we respond to this economic situation? What does it mean in the context of globalization?

For many thinkers the task in this situation is to explore and specify rules and institutions that will ensure that the market serves persons and communities. While essential, this chapter does not focus on solely political and economic analysis, nor, for that matter, important institutional questions about the global economy. Since we have explored some social and cultural developments in other chapters, it is important here to examine human sensibilities. What is the morality of motives for wealth? Can we probe felt reactions, the love of wealth and our revulsion, or lack of moral censure, over hideous inequalities in the distribution of the material necessities of life? More pointedly, we are addressing in this chapter a basic theme of the entire book, namely, the role of the imagination and its relation to moral sensibilities. From that angle, the "economy" is at root a dynamic of the social imaginary that shapes human desires. Children are constantly bombarded with images of new games, new toys, new fashions. Automobile companies talk of installing refrigerated glove compartments so that drivers can consume at will. By some reports, Americans snack virtually around the clock. An alarming percentage of the US population can be clinically defined as overweight. Our topic, then, is the complex connection between human desires and culturally mediated schemes of value as this impinges on facets of the moral life. One form that desire can take is best called by the old term "greed." Perhaps it is time to reconsider greed.

How then to begin? We must move back in time to philosophies of commercialism at the dawning of the modern West. And we can do this by turning to a work of the imagination rich in its analysis of human desire and the problems of social life. It was written during the explosive development of the modern industrial revolution. It is about a man who traveled between worlds.

Gulliver's Complaint

Recounting his visit to the land of the Houyhnhnms, the country of gracious and virtuous horses, Gulliver, in his *Travels*, notes how despicable and vicious the Yahoos, human beings, are in appearance and manner. Allowed to live among the Houyhnhnms, even to serve one as his master, Gulliver soon enjoyed a life mostly free of Yahoo vices. "I had no Occasion of bribing, flattering or pimping, to procure Favor of any great Man, or his Minion. I wanted no Fence against Fraud or Oppression."[2] But this was hardly a blissful "state of nature," as if the "horses" were more "natural" than human beings. The

Yahoos – ignorant, violent, petty, lustful – also lived out their "nature."[3] The land of the Houyhnhnms was actually a country of virtues that curtailed viciousness and cultivated peace for "rational creatures." This country required no "fences" because cool reason ruled social interaction.

Gulliver is expelled from the land by the Houyhnhnms. The cause of his expulsion is proper fear by the Houyhnhnms that the odd mixture in his person of "some Rudiments of Reason" and "the natural Pravity of those Animals" (Yahoos) would work ill in their country. Gulliver's very being, his seeming inability to live a life of reason and virtue, meant that he was a threat to the fragile bonds of rational society. Rejected and brokenhearted, Gulliver departs by makeshift craft and some time later arrives back in his native England. It took him years, he tells us, before he could tolerate the company of Yahoos, even his wife. At last he is able to take supper at the same table with his wife and son.

Gulliver is never fully reintegrated into human company. In the final pages of his travels he tells us why. "My Reconcilement to the Yahoo-kind in general might not be so difficult, if they would be content with those Vices and Follies only which Nature hath entitled them to." The vices naturally allotted to Yahoos are theft, whoremongering, lying, deception, and the like. But, Gulliver continues, "when I behold a Lump of Deformity, and Diseases both in Body and Mind, smitten with *Pride*, it immediately breaks all the Measures of my Patience, neither shall I be ever able to comprehend how such an Animal and such a Vice could tally together."[4] Jonathan Swift, author of *Gulliver's Travels*, thought, with good reason, that a certain dualism besets human beings, namely, our capacity for right action and our constant failure to do so. From this fact flows tragedy and comedy. The greatest tragedy, Swift insists, is willful self-deception and self-aggrandizement, that is, pride.

Gulliver's complaint against Yahoo vices, and especially pride, is brilliant and timely satire. Writing amid the economic and political expansion of the British empire, and mindful (no doubt) that John Locke, in the *Second Treatise on Government*, had insisted "In the beginning all the world was *America*," that is, a wasteland to be improved by human industry, Swift's satire joins interlocking debates in eighteenth-century Europe. Gulliver travels to strange and foreign lands and learns not about the supremacy of the English Yahoo, but the wisdom of the Houyhnhnms, the truly "other" – a rational creature seen by Europeans as mere "animal." Swift's picture of the Yahoos in their "state of nature" is part of the debate made famous by Jean-Jacques Rousseau about the conflict between nature and culture. Yahoos are hardly the free and peaceful "natural men" released from the corrupting force of society that Rousseau so dearly imagined. Gulliver's insistence that among the Houyhnhnms one needs no "Fence" against oppression and fraud dips into English political philosophy. He confirms Thomas Hobbes's judgment that political society is formed precisely to escape the war of each against each. Yet this is only true of Yahoos; one can imagine another creature, another way of social existence, not so brutish. Against Locke, Swift seems to be saying that the true "wasteland" is not untamed natural resources, but the human soul. The industry most needed is training in virtue, reason, and humility. And, finally, *Gulliver's Travels* advances a discussion among thinkers like Locke, Bernard Mandeville, and later David Hume and Adam Smith on the place of "vice" in the advance of culture and especially commercial society. Mandeville, one might recall, insisted that "Great Wealth and Foreign Treasure will ever scorn to come among Men, unless you'll admit their inseparable Companions, Avarice and Luxury."[5]

Are pride, greed, and want the engines of wealth? Is capitalism ignorant, violent, petty and lustful? Is capitalism Yahoo to the bone? Much current reflection on economic matters forgoes any discussion of how to assess the motives for wealth, a question deemed basic by Swift. There seem to be two reasons for this neglect. First, among Christian theologians in the twentieth century there was profound suspicion of market economies. From popes like Leo XIII and American Social Gospel thinkers such as Walter Rauschenbusch to Latin American liberation theologians, the market was usually viewed as a profound impediment to the just distribution of material goods. In its most extreme form, this perspective has virtually identified economic injustice with capitalism. For such thinkers, capitalism is Yahoo to the bone; capitalism is beyond the reach of Christian morals. There has been little interest among such theologians to take a new look at the market and human motivations.

During the 1980s this assessment changed somewhat, at least in the US. Protestant thinkers, like Max Stackhouse, David Krueger, and others, as well as Roman Catholic bishops and moral theologians Dennis McCann and David Hollenbach, reopened the question of the moral assessment of the market.[6] Even Pope John Paul II, in his encyclicals on labor, made proper, if limited, place for the growth and expansion of the market.[7] Yet while all of this has been a welcome development, there has still been little exploration of matters of human motivation. Questions of social justice, not moral anthropology and psychology, have been central in recent years. The discourse of institutional and political analysis has ruled the day.

What is interesting about Swift's century is that the focus was on how to account for the bonds of human society, and, especially, commercial culture. In order to understand those bonds rightly we must, Swift and others insisted, grasp the tenor and direction of human desires. This meant that economics was part of moral inquiry, and, further, that an ethics demands a robust psychology. The second reason for the present neglect of this topic is, then, that, unlike Swift or Adam Smith, political economy is no longer seen as part of the larger task of moral philosophy. The rise and differentiation of the "sciences" since the late eighteenth century has meant that economics and ethical reflection often move in rather diverse, even separate, orbits. Furthermore, too much contemporary ethics neglects work in psychology.[8] It is typically argued, for instance, that the marks of moral agency are "rationality" and "freedom." But surely any informed account of behavior needs to provide a richer, more textured and culturally saturated picture of human existence. It is time to reopen the discussion about vice and capitalism realizing that, at the level of validating claims, we are traversing disciplines. The target of criticism is a culture of consumption that works within and through the social imaginary and the market. And our purpose is to secure the integrity of life – especially human life – as the aim of, not the means, to economic activity. It is to insist on breaking economic overhumanization through a theological humanistic perspective.

On the way to that conclusion we must next outline in broad strokes traditional assessments of avarice in commercial life. That discussion forms the backdrop for an engagement with the question that vexed Swift, Mandeville and others, prompting complaints against or praise for Yahoo vices.

Assessing Avarice

Unless blinded by sheer ideology, most would admit that greed is a true and present reality. Many people on this planet are hungry; a minority of its inhabitants consume resources at an increasing and alarming rate. As R. L. Longworth reported in 1999, the three richest officers of Microsoft had more assets (approximately $140 billion) than the combined forty-three least developed countries with populations in excess of 600 million! In about half of the world's nations, per capita income is lower than it was ten or twenty years ago.[9] The desire for wealth and property is often mediated by a global media system, the flow of images that defines commercial hype. Furthermore, population is increasing at drastic rates in precisely those parts of the world with the least access to the earth's resources. This accentuates the division between "haves" and "have nots," even as it signals the possibility of an age of global migration, social violence, and international conflict as persons and nations scramble for scarce resources. We live in an age of scarcity and runaway consumption bent on eating up human beings and the earth. The cities and cultures we built, as well as our own sense of self, seem bound to property and consumption.

Greed is not only a present reality. It seems to be a constant feature of human life. It is hardly surprising, then, that voices of condemnation span the ages reaching from ancient prophets to current advocates of economic rights.

Buried deep within the moral imagination of the West is the assumption that greed enslaves and destroys persons and communities. But what is greed? Simply put, greed, or avarice (Latin: *avarus*, "greedy"; "to crave"; "to desire"), is the inordinate love for riches. It is the rapacious desire for more goods or wealth than one needs or deserves.[10] The term greed designates, then, the relation between human craving and a specific object of that desiring, namely, culturally determined "riches," if and only if such craving exceeds basic human need and also the rightful limits on consumption. This is why, we might imagine, the topic of greed has traditionally been located at the intersection between the ethics of exchange, and thus the demands of commutative justice, and matters of personal morality, the virtuous self.[11] Of course, it is a difficult question to determine "limits" and when they are exceeded; this seems, at least empirically, to be a matter of different social boundaries and projects. What counts as "greed" in one society might not in another.

Greed is an exceedingly complex human desire. Phenomenologically, we can describe "greed" as a culturally defined craving, in terms of "what is desired" and rightful limits of possession, even as it is an attack on the limits of individual satiation and social relations. The greedy person wants to possess all of a culture's highest riches and thus, implicitly, to have her or his own desires absorbed, inscribed into and defined by the society's value system even while exceeding the limits defined by that social system. Ironically, the life of the greedy person undercuts participation in the very social network that defines her or his desires. This is why the greedy person appears in books and films as isolated, friendless. It is also why in traditional virtue theory, greed is understood in relation to concupiscence and the demand for temperance. As Thomas Aquinas puts it, covetousness (hence greed or avarice) subjects the human will to a good lower than God, the true human end, and hence is sinful. Greed disorders the soul. Virtue puts the order of reason into passion, and, specifically, temperance curbs the passion that incites to anything against reason.[12] Greed is a passion, a human desire, to draw some socially defined material or ideal value (money, power, etc.) into the self and thereby to undercut the domain of social meaning. Greed works to isolate the self by breaking the necessary bonds of human community. One could see greed as a form of inverted narcissism in which the self is not elevated to the center of the world, but, rather, seeks to consume the world and lose itself in what is consumed. Greed is one of the engines of the overhumanization, the enfolding of all reality within human projects and desires.

Gulliver is an apt example of this rough and ready phenomenology of greed. At one point in his stay with the Houyhnhnms, he learns that the Yahoos have found a treasure of diamonds. While these stones are worthless in the land of the Houyhnhnms, Gulliver craves them, and, in fact, seeks them out in the dead of night. His craving, in other words, is culturally defined by European images of "riches" that pits him against the Houyhnhnms' society he (supposedly) wants to join. And his craving for the diamonds undercuts all his social relations: it involves theft from the Yahoos, and, for dread that he be seen as really Yahoo, the deception of the Houyhnhnms. Greed lives from while it also undermines social relations. It is a culturally formed craving riddled with excess. The excess is that the greedy person wants to subsume the socially defined wealth at the violation of the natural limits of satiation and normal communal bonds. Greed is rightly one of the traditional vices, both in terms of individual moral failing and also a violation of the demands of distributive justice. "Greed" is a vice that links the person's self-relation to her or his interaction with a community.

If this is at all right, then one can easily understand why greed has long been condemned in Christian ethics. The prohibition of covetousness is found in the Decalogue (Exodus 20:17) as well as New Testament texts (cf. Luke 12:15) and even lists of vices (Colossians 3:5). We are even told that "the love of money is the root of all evil" (1 Timothy 6:10), and, in the Sermon the Mount, Jesus insists that one cannot serve two masters, God and Mammon (Matthew 6:24). This augments the claim, in Matthew 6:21, that where one's treasure is, there the heart – the core of one's being – will also be. Personal and communal identity is bound to what is possessed, and, accordingly, it is of grave moral and spiritual import not to be possessed by what one owns. In a word, Jesus's teaching concerns a doubleness in the property relation: it is necessary for life and yet also potentially destructive of right self-understanding, social life, and relation to the divine.

Drawing on these biblical themes, traditional Christian thinkers taught that the malice of greed lies in the getting and keeping of money and possessions as the defining purpose of life. The greedy person does not see that these things are valuable only as instruments to an integral life. There is confusion within greed between what is to be used for the necessities of life and what is to be sought as a good in itself. Martin Luther, for instance, endorsed traditional Christian teaching against usury. Yet he also thought, in a treatise on the "Common Chest," that the drive for wealth through investment was idolatrous. The investor trusts in something other than God as the true sovereign over time and life; the investor has faith in economic powers as sovereign. This allows us to see why greed was called a capital vice. Given its object, avarice can be the cause of many other sins. As the Hebrew prophet Amos put it, God will not revoke punishment of the people since "they sell the righteous for silver and the needy for a pair of sandals . . . and in the house of their God they drink wine bought with fines they impose" (Amos 2:6–8). Idolatry, oppression, slavery, exploitation, and deception gather round and flow from greed. Furthermore, avarice can conceal itself as a virtue; it can commend itself under the pretext of making provision for future earthly life. The excessive desire of, or pleasure in, riches has been seen throughout the history of Christian ethics as ruinous of the moral life.

This judgment about greed has meant a decided ambivalence about trade within traditional Christian ethics. Aquinas, in line with Aristotle (*Politics* I.3), distinguishes, in *Summa Theologiae* II/II, q. 77, two kinds of exchange. One kind, so-called "natural exchange," aims at satisfying the needs of life. This is the work of householders and civil servants whose responsibility it is to care for home and state. The other kind of exchange, "profit exchange," aims not at satisfying the needs of life, but purely for profit. While natural exchange is commendable, the latter, in words similar to Luther's, "is justly deserving of blame, because, considered in itself, it satisfies the greed for gain, which knows no limit and tends to infinity." Importantly, Aquinas's argument centers on the "ends" sought through exchange (cf. ST II/II, q. 118). Since the end of greed is for infinite gain, rather than satisfying basic human needs, it is morally condemned. Trading only becomes "lawful" when it is turned to serve some necessary or virtuous end. In their judgments, Luther and Aquinas echo long-standing convictions held by Christians and "pagan" philosophers, like Aristotle and Plato. St. Ambrose put the matter well. In a letter to Bishop Constantius sometime in 379 CE, he wrote: "Woe to him who has a fortune amassed by deceit, and builds in blood a city, in other words, his soul. For it is the soul which is built like a city. Greed does not build it, but sets it on fire and burns it."[13] Greed crosses through social existence – the "city" and the ethics of exchange – and the integrity of personal life, the "soul." It is potentially destructive of person and community. Greed is a boundary phenomenon: it connects economics, politics, culture, self. It gathers around it a host of images: hunger, fire, destruction, a primal insatiability. The Christian can, at best, accommodate trade for the necessities of life. Interestingly enough, the idea that greed is socially and personally destructive continues to find expression among those people sensitive to the moral danger of the spread of overhumanization.

What classical thinkers like Ambrose or Aquinas and current critics are saying is that one must consider the reflexive connection between desire and commodification within the social imaginary; that is, how craving for things situated within patterns of economic exchange helps to shape and define the self and her or his desires. Greed is a culturally saturated desire. Some desires – if not all – are not simply "given"; they do not arise in human life fully born. What you love, as Jesus might say, shapes who you are, but our loves are also shaped by cultural forms and practices. We have to understand how property matters to people, and this is a more complex issue than simply meeting basic needs like hunger, sex, or shelter, although it includes those needs as well. From this perspective, many philosophies of commercialism are deficient because they fail to grasp how property is reflexively linked to the formation of a person's identity. The distinctly human fact is that "property" is a cultural form and thus entangled with a culture's sense about and arrangements for human identity, dignity, and worth. What is at issue is how we build souls and cities.

However, it is not at all clear that the moral designation "greed" is really apt for market-driven economies, or even the formation of moral desires and identities. This is the point of the debate that Swift so brilliantly helped to advance. The debate marks a decisive shift from the perspective of Aristotle, Ambrose, Aquinas, and Luther. There are, first, economic reasons why we might want to challenge an all too easy moral condemnation of human acquisitiveness, or desire for gain. After all, how is one to generate wealth, stimulate production, and enhance savings if a spirit of relentless acquisition is lacking? As Milton Friedman once put it, the social responsibility of business is to increase profits.[14] The idea that moral norms can and ought to bear on the market is wrongheaded and economically dangerous. The wholesale condemnation of "greed" is nothing less than misplaced moralism. Second, Friedrich Nietzsche would say that moralism bespeaks the resentment of the poor for the power of the rich. The weak invert the table of values established by the powerful and healthy to serve the purposes of the weak. While life, strength, and wealth are virtues for the powerful, in the eyes of the weak and outcast these "virtues" become vices that the powerful (i.e., evil) inflict on the innocent (i.e., weak).[15] So one might have not only Friedman-like economic suspicions about the old vice of greed, but also advance a Nietzschean, psychological denial of moralism.

In this history of Western ethics and even current discourse there seems to be little debate about how best to define and understand greed. Yet for much Christian discourse, "greed," associated with covetousness, seems to cover all forms of human acquisitiveness, making it difficult, if not impossible, to speak of a morally right search for gain and wealth. Conversely, a good deal of current economic thought mindful of the differentiation of social subsystems segregates the moral and the economic and thus banishes the very concept of greed from the domain of "exchange" to the realm of private life. The market requires the engine of human craving, but discourse about that desiring is oddly de-moralized. Mindful of this long condemnation of greed in Christian thought and the current economic reality, let us turn next, briefly to be sure, to earlier debates about avarice and commercial life. For the sake of brevity, consider Bernard Mandeville, in his *Fable of the Bees*, and David Hume's essays as decisive for the question of avarice and commerce. The larger question, once again, is how to understand the loss of the discourse of "greed," its virtual banishment from the moral lexicon, within reflection on economic life.[16]

The Vicious, yet Prosperous Hive

On Mandeville's account, in the *Fable of the Bees*, society is driven by greed, envy, and discontent. Commerce is a matter of exchange, not production, and because of this there is constant revolution in tastes going on to further the market. Society is like a beehive. And, as Alan Ryan has noted, "Nobody can exactly say the creatures in the hive are happy . . . they are permanently discontent with what they have already. But the hive prospers . . . they are well adapted to a peaceful and prosperous society."[17] Mandeville's point, and the force of his "fable," is to show that all the so-called vices – and only the vices – are in fact the foundation of a good social order. Private vices reap public good. While vice might mean moral ruin to the self, it is in fact economic salvation. Mandeville does not give wholesale endorsement of vice. Good results do not justify vicious conduct. His point, rather, is about the motivations necessary to run the market. Economics as well as the morality of exchange must be evaluated on terms other than the discourse of personal virtue or viciousness. The market demands, for instance, not only avarice and pride, but also that the poor be ever kept in want. "When Men shew such an extraordinary proclivity to Idleness and Pleasure, what reason have we to think that they would ever work, unless they were oblig'd to it by immediate Necessity?"[18] A rich nation must make sure that most of the poor are always at work, spend what they get, and are thus always provoked to labor by necessity.

Mandeville's argument rests on a particular anthropology. He puts it like this:

> Man never exerts himself but when he is rous'd by his Desires: Whilst they lie dormant, and there is nothing to raise them, his Excellence and Abilities will be for ever undiscover'd, and the lumpish machine, without the Influence of his Passions, may justly be compar'd to a huge Wind-mill without a breath of air.[19]

The spring of human action is desire, and thus, if one wants economic production, one must provoke those cravings. Pride, avarice, and want drive persons to labor. And these same "vices" also keep consumption growing, a growth necessary for economic flourishing. One cannot aggrandize or enrich a nation if the very motives for prosperity and consumption are morally censured. This is important to see. According to Mandeville, morality, in the strict sense of the term, aims at eradicating rather than directing the passions. His anthropology, in other words, undergirds what moral theorists call "non-naturalism" in ethics. Like Immanuel Kant after him and many Christian theologians before him, moral duty and virtue stand against natural desires and wants, and not as their proper fulfillment. Accordingly, Mandeville must "de-moralize" economics in order to release motivations necessary for the generation of wealth.

It is, then, this assumption about the character of morality that requires Mandeville to "de-moralize" economic life and give free reign to the vices as the engine of production and consumption. This move has two important consequences. First, it forces the question of morals inward upon the self and aids other modern impulses to rabid individualism, impulses like private religion, the growth of psychological inquiry, and the feeding of personal preference. Virtue and vice become disconnected from one's life as an economic agent. The self inhabits multiple roles, each ruled by its own logic, discourse, and values. This compartmentalization of life leads, one suspects, to a certain public muteness about the depth and meaning of personal existence. Second, once private and public life are so separated, economic activity and human exchange are ruled by no other value than simple utility. If the wealth of the nation requires the poor remain in want as a goad to labor and consumption, then poverty is a legitimate necessity of economic life. The principle of legitimation is no longer moral or even political, it is strictly economic in nature. One determines what is a tolerable degree of human depravation not in moral terms but on the grounds of economic calculation. The division of private and public not only bears on the individual, but also social exchange. The nation is straddled between two different value systems. In personal life, the demands of duty and virtue reign; in the life of the nation, strict utility guides decision and policy. In other words, the language of "greed," or avarice, no longer has relevance to economic life other than as a purely descriptive term about human motivation for wealth.

Patrick Murray has noted that by drawing a stark line between hard-working poor and greedy rich, Mandeville "avoids the . . . paradox that crops up in twentieth-century capitalism, where the same persons are counted on to work hard and consume hard."[20] But we need to see that this separation is built on a certain conception of morality and also an account of desire. The upshot is that commerce is not a humanizing force, even if it generates wealth. In this respect, Mandeville continues, somewhat ironically, the longstanding censure or reluctant accommodation of trade running from Amos and Aristotle to Luther and Pope John Paul II.

Utility and Social Virtues

David Hume departs from the condemnation and accommodation of trade in traditional Christian thought. Hume also differs from Mandeville. He was critical of the "irreclaimable" passion of unmixed greed. And he even held that "a sense of humor and virtue" alone is able to "restrain or regulate the love of money." In spite of this, "commerce," in Hume's view, "is the great humanizing force in history. Moral consideration, joined to a host of others, weigh heavily in favor of commerce."[21] Unlike Mandeville, commerce serves for Hume not only economic ends, but genuinely human ones. These human goods include increased knowledge, setting up law and order, softening human tempers, and even increased happiness. Against the hard and reductionistic vision of human beings and commerce, Hume presents a more capacious account of economic activity. How does Hume make this argument?

Hume's decisive move, with respect to Mandeville and some (but not all) traditional Christian morals, is to reject non-naturalism in ethics. For Hume, the point of morality is to direct and tame natural desires, not to negate or transcend them under the call of duty. Mandeville's brand of non-naturalism in ethics meant that "morality" was limited to the realm of the private. Hume insists that human beings have genuine sympathy for others. "The social virtues must, therefore, be allowed to have a natural beauty and amiableness, which, at first, antecedent to all precept or education, recommends them to the esteem of the uninstructed mankind, and engages their affections."[22] Human beings, uninstructed and natural, are hardly Swiftian Yahoos; they have some untutored sympathy for the common good, for utility, and thus an appreciation of the social virtues. Of course, persons need training in social virtuc. This training is with respect to moral principle.

> It appears to be matter of fact that the circumstance of *utility*, in all subjects, is a source of praise and approbation: That it is constantly appealed to in all moral decisions concerning the merit or demerit of Actions: That it is the *sole* source of that high regard paid to justice, fidelity, honour, allegiance, and chastity: That it is inseparable from all the other social virtues, humanity, generosity, charity, affability, lenity, mercy, and moderation: And, in a word, it is a foundation of the chief part of morals, which has a reference to mankind and our fellow-creatures.[23]

Having established the chief moral principle, utility, and its relation to fellow-feeling, the question Hume faced concerning commerce is whether or not it furthers utility and social virtues.

Hume's basic point is that commerce as such advances social virtue, since it aims at utility. "Industry and arts and trade increase the power of the sovereign as well as the happiness of the subjects; and that policy is violent, which aggrandizes the public by the poverty of the individual."[24] Two claims are asserted here. First, happiness, according to Hume, consists in action, pleasure, and indolence. "In times when industry and the arts flourish," Hume continues, "men are kept in perpetual occupation, and enjoy, as their reward, the occupation itself, as well as the pleasures which are the fruit of their labor . . . Banish those arts from society, you deprive men both of action and of pleasure; and leaving nothing but indolence in their place, you even destroy the relish of indolence."[25] The more commerce and the arts advance, the further social virtue and happiness are to be found in a nation. Second, Hume cannot conceive, as Mandeville did, a utilitarian justification for the poverty of the individual. A thoroughgoing naturalism, that is, a careful look at actual human desires and affections, shows that we cannot approve policies that demean and destroy our fellow citizens. The shape of human social affection means that utility and personal happiness must go hand in glove if a nation's policies are to meet with approval and human life to advance. It also requires, as Hume knew, local communities to foster virtue and identities. Since there seem to be limits to how far fellow-feeling can extend, local communities are far better at enlarging affections than larger and more complex collectives. In terms of sentiment and affection no one is a citizen of the world; such grand communities exist only at the level of principle.

Is this too optimistic a picture of economic life? Hume does consider "vicious gratifications." Any particular form of gratification can become vicious, he writes, "when it engrosses all of a man's expense, and leaves no ability for such acts of duty and generosity as are required by his situation and fortune." And he continues, no doubt with Mandeville in mind, "To say that, without a vicious luxury, the labour would not be employed at all, is only to say, that there is some other defect in human nature . . . for which luxury, in some measure, provides a remedy."[26] Hume argues, against Mandeville, that one can never see vice as "advantageous." But this judgment flows from a different moral anthropology, one built on fellow-feeling, and also a naturalistic ethics in which the purpose of morality, and social institutions like commerce, are to form and direct rather than thwart human desires. Precisely for this reason, social utility can never in any simple sense override personal happiness. Commercial society was to further virtue and, when coupled with a sense of humor, enlarge sentiments beyond the "monstrously absurd" desire of unmixed avarice.

What Hume introduces back into the discussion of commercial society is the connection between trade and the sentiments of self, the "soul" as St. Ambrose put it. Unlike in Mandeville's text, human sentiments can be tutored and enlarged; it is the special benefit of commerce to expand our fellow-feeling and love of utility. But of course this poses massive problems as well. As Murray has noted, "Hume had just an inkling of the question: Does the global economy erode the local conditions which form identities, loyalties, and virtues? Will the commercial 'enlargement' of our sentiments stretch them beyond the limits of their elasticity?"[27] More to the point, Hume seems to miss the force of Mandeville's real insight: that commercial society might need to foster "vice," greed, in order to balance production and consumption. How is it, we might ask, that "greed" itself is not a kind of enlargement of sentiment, not in terms of fellow-feeling but in the intensification of economic motive?

Is it so easy to claim that commercial society on a global scale transforms sentiments, inordinate desires, directing them to the proper end of happiness and social utility?

Conflict of Assessments

Our path of reflection has moved from an initial, and rather formal, phenomenological description of "greed," aided by Swift's wit and insight, through assessments of avarice by ancient Christian and "secular" moralists, and onward to the arguments of Mandeville and Hume, as modern philosophers of commercialism. There is a conflict of assessments about greed. The thinkers surveyed differ in their judgments about the Yahoo-nature of trading. Traditional Christian ethics denounces Yahoo vices that too easily dominate commerce. And yet thinkers like Luther and Aquinas also hold that we can become better. We are not condemned to remain Yahoo. Mandeville praises Yahoo vices for their economic impulse. Realistic in his assessment of actual economic life, Mandeville is rather pessimistic about the possibilities for transformation, human betterment. David Hume is quite optimistic about human betterment and that precisely through commerce. He believes that commerce is not Yahoo to the bone; somehow it transforms our vices into genuine virtues. We might put it like this: traditional Christian thought is more pessimistic than Hume about the motives driving commerce, even as it is more hopeful than Mandeville about moral betterment. The reason for this response is that Christian ethics must not only account for human vice and fault, but also the created goodness of human life. In terms of an analysis of any human motivation, Christian thought will, by its internal logic, weave a middle path between utter condemnation and simple endorsement of natural human capacities.

Two general conclusions can be drawn from our inquiry. First, it is clear that the meaning of commercial society differs among the various traditions of thought explored. For the traditional Christian, to live responsibly in a commercial society one must labor for the necessities of life, curtail greed, and seek the higher goods of the spiritual life. Mandevillians, conversely, would argue, like some current rational-choice theorists, that we ought to seek, and seek unrelentingly, the acquisition of wealth.[28] In the domain of commerce, the "vices" must be given free reign; virtue should pertain only to private relations. Finally, Humeans contend that the responsible life entails the cultivation of social virtues and that, properly conducted, commerce is precisely the means to live such a life. In other words, we have seen that the basic question of our present inquiry is not easily answered, since "a culture of consumption" admits of different construals with decidedly divergent implications for living morally. Little wonder, then, that societies deeply marked by these various traditions of thought, as well as others, seem at a loss for any coherent vision of responsibility in commercial life. Even if one understands life in (say) markedly Humean terms, the society in which one works, loves, and dies is nevertheless informed by different visions of life, populated by Mandevilleans, Christians, and many others. This is merely to say that the questions of moral diversity and pluralism explored in chapter 2 beset matters of commercial existence as much as any other aspect of social life.

Second, we have learned something else. Greed is a human craving informed by social conceptions of "wealth." Greed, as pictured here, is imaginatively shaped desire. A child might experience the pangs of greed for the latest video game; an adult wants great wealth, cars, clothes. Excessive craving is not in itself greed. It becomes greed if and only if the craving is imaginatively saturated with respect to social conventions about what counts as "wealth." "Wealth" designates a social end or purpose the desire for which can be the efficient cause of human action, of choice. But this is a unique kind of desire or cause of action. The greedy person, as noted before, is one who craves to have his or her desire so informed, wants to be absorbed into the social convention in the very act of consuming culturally defined goods. This was Aquinas's point in saying that avarice subjects the will to a good lower than the proper human end (ST II/II, q. 114, a. 5). Accordingly, we need to understand property and wealth not simply in terms of its use or exchange value, but also what Jean Baudrillard has called the "sign value" of commodities.[29] A teenager may crave a pair of GAP jeans not because of the market or exchange value of the pants, but, importantly, because the jeans have sign value among his friends, a value pertaining to status and social acceptance. Sign value operates within the social imaginary to saturate human desires.

Greed is the desire to have one's self and most basic passions inscribed within the semiotics of a culture, its sign values. The phenomenology of greed, as I have called it, takes seriously the sign value of commodities in the formation of a person's sense of self. Something like it seems manifest in traditional Christian discourse, Swift's biting satire, and Hume's sensitivity for the need to enlarge sentiments. Only Mandeville, it would appear, fails to grasp this point and that is because, given his non-naturalism in ethics, human passions are strictly untutorable. In other words, Mandeville does not grasp the reflexive structure of greed: how what is desired constitutes, through the mixing of imagination, sign value, and craving, a new order of desire best called greed. For him, passions are just given.

What then is the insight? How is this argument not simply a descriptive claim about the structure of one kind of human passion? The insight for ethics is that the odd dynamics of the passion called greed is such that it feeds on cultural values, especially sign values, while simultaneously endangering the tranquility and justice of social life. Greed inscribes a person within a culture's table of values and yet, in the drive to subsume them into the self, also threatens social bonds that require fairness, justice, and concern for the common good. This is why greed in personal life is analogous to forces behind overhumanization on a global scale. It is also why, one might imagine, Ambrose drew the connection between the "city" and the "soul"; it is why Hume had to conceive of the means to enlarge sentiments; it is why Mandeville tried to separate morality and economy; it is why Luther and Aquinas, despite other differences, saw that greed is idolatrous and an attack on the common good. The paradox is that commercial culture, through the power of its sign values, can and does foster excessive consumption and greed, but in the act of doing so threatens social stability and flourishing. Is it any wonder, then, that in advanced commercial cultures we see the breakdown of concern for the common good both among the wealthy, who consume at an alarming rate, and the poor, who desire that high level of consumption? Traditional Christian thought was right on this point: greed is a capital vice because it gathers around it other forms of viciousness that undercut sustainable social existence. What then are we to do?

Imagination, Desire, and Consumption

If the above reflections are at all convincing, then the line between, on the one hand, human aspiration and acquisitiveness that motives economic action, and, on the other hand, true greed in all of its destructiveness, must be drawn with greater care than often is done in ethics. One should distinguish greed from acquisitiveness in terms of how the sign value of wealth functions through the social imaginary in the formation of human desire. On this account, commercial society is Yahoo to the bone if and only if it aims to form desire solely through the sign value of commodities. This is a real and present possibility when the social imaginary is at a loss for any alternate symbolic scheme through which to shape desire. It is a possibility when the social imaginary is flooded only with commercial images. In that case, commodification becomes totalistic; it infests all other realms of life with a seemingly limitless desire. Body parts, children, love – everything becomes a commodity for sale. Now we see the reason to combat the banishment of the discourse of greed from social life. The language of "greed" presupposes some table of values and symbolic resources other than "commodities" and their sign value in the understanding and articulation of human desire and motivation. And this is so, since to call a desire "greedy" is to make a judgment about its destructiveness to individuals and society no matter how much new wealth desire might produce.

It is at this level of insight that Christian thought has a surprising contribution to make to reflection on economic life and even the social imaginary.

In the formation of human desires, the believer is bid to love what shatters, overturns, and transcends sign value. One is to love God with heart and soul and mind and the neighbor as one's self. God and other persons are realities that cannot be inscribed within any system of signs. This is why, in the Decalogue, one is not to make images of God and also why the only image of the divine on earth is a living one, human beings (cf. Exodus 20:1–6; Deuteronomy 5:6–21). The reality of God breaks form, as does the needs of others. The love of God that enlivens a sense of responsibility for others and this earth upends, shatters, the complete formation of desire by the images flowing within the culture. The love of God, we might say, can limit the desire of acquisition precisely because what is desired exceeds objectification and thereby escapes the grip of the imagination.

Of course, it is also the case – given the human heart – that "God" can become the ultimate sign value in relation to which all else is valued. The labor of the social imaginary, in the need to fix an object of desire, fabricates God-images which can and do legitimate other social structures and hierarchies. Race or gender or clan or nation or church or religion can become seen as the sole source of worth and thus function as the "god" of someone's life. The destructiveness of this "theologizing of desire" at the heart of overhumanization has been seen by many, ranging from the Hebrew prophets and their denunciation of the wealthy's exploitation of the poor, to current feminist theologians. But the paradox is that the demand to destroy idols can itself become an idol. Idolatry, that is, the reduction of the divine to our system of signs, is the inner meaning of greed theologically construed. This is what makes greed religiously dangerous, a "mortal" sin, and also a kind of moral madness. "Greed" is only checked when human desire seeks a non-consumable object. Is this really possible? Perhaps what is needed is not an idea that escapes the strange logic of iconoclasm so much as a discourse about inordinate and destructive desires. From this perspective, the loss of the discourse of greed means the triumph of commodification and the subsuming of persons within a society's system of sign values.

Taking a lead from Christian ideas about "greed," we are led to a profound moral and conceptual insight. At the very origins of human motivation is not a value-neutral set of blind impulses, but a complex, reflexive relation between desire and cultural, imaginative valuations. But this means that while human desires might be morally and psychologically recalcitrant, how they are culturally saturated, and thus rendered meaningful and understandable, depends on the "valuations" used to shape and inform desires. One must explore the imaginary and conceptual forms used to saturate desire in a culture that give rise to motivations. And this requires that there is some room for moral change, moral improvement, in and through the rigorous examination of the reflexive relation of desire and valuations. In making this claim about motivations, a bridge is made between "nature and nurture," simple naturalism and bald social construction, in an account of "greed." The discourse of greed is one of those forms of "cultural saturation" needed to assess and shape human desire. The rejection of this discourse in ethics is the loss of a crucial form of moral self-understanding.

There is irony in this, of course. The suggestion made here is that the contribution religious discourse can make to current economic life hinges on what is understood to exceed that discourse (i.e., "God") and yet is forever pulled into the circle of desire and cultural saturation. Theological reflection makes its contribution by keeping a language of human viciousness alive! Put differently, the contribution Christian moral philosophy can make to commercial society is to designate what is "outside" of commodification and how that "outside" might form human motivations and self-understandings as well as exposing moral failing, viciousness. Of course, Christian discourse is not the only means to check the commodification of desire, since, as just noted, it too continually falls into that enterprise. Like every moral tradition, lived Christian faith is ambiguous. The point is that such discourse opens up reflection on human desire in a surprising way that can and ought to inform our reflection on economic existence. It provides a way to "reconsider greed."

What does this mean for living responsibly? The focus of responsibility in the time of many worlds is the exercise of power.[30] In terms of commercial life, this means that we are enabled and required to assess and even transform our self-understandings in the direction of economic power, the power to produce and to consume. The language of greed is really a discourse about self-understanding at the level of human craving. By keeping this discourse in play within the social imaginary of commercial societies, we have one means to test self-understanding and the uses of economic power. The loss of this discourse can unleash a Yahoo world. It is against that possibility that the Christian tradition contributes a rich and complex moral discourse needed for a global future.

NOTES

1 Cited in the lead story "A 'grotesque' Gap" by R. C. Longworth in the *Chicago Tribune* 153, no. 193 (July 12, 1999) section I, page 1.

2 Jonathan Swift, *Gulliver's Travels and other writings*, edited by Ricardo Quintana (New York: Modern Library, 1958), p. 226.

3 I hasten to add that some connection here is surely true for "Yahoo," the popular Internet search engine!

4 Swift, *Gulliver's Travels*, p. 242.

5 Bernard Mandeville, *The Fable of the Bees* in *Reflections on Commercial Life: An Anthology of Classic Texts from Plato to the Present* edited by Patrick Murray (New York: Routledge, 1997), p. 150.
6 See Max L. Stackhouse, *Public Theology and Political Economy: Christian Stewardship in Modern Society* (Grand Rapids, MI: Eerdmans, 1987); *Christian Social Ethics in a Global Era*, edited by Max. L. Stackhouse, Dennis McCann, et al. (Nashville, TN: Abingdon Press, 1995); David Krueger, *The Business Corporation and Productive Justice* (Nashville, TN: Abingdon Press, 1997), and *Economic Justice for All*, US Roman Catholic Bishops.
7 See, for example, John Paul II, *Centesimus Annus*, 1991.
8 For recent work on ethics and psychology, see Ernest Wallwork, *Psychoanalysis and Ethics* (New Haven, CT: Yale University Press, 1991); Don S. Browning, *Religious Thought and the Modern Psychologies: A Critical Conversation in the Theology of Culture* (Philadelphia, PA: Fortress Press, 1987); Owen Flanagan, *Varieties of Moral Personality: Ethics and Psychological Realism* (Cambridge, MA: MIT Press, 1990); and *Identity, Character, and Morality: Essays in Moral Psychology*, edited by Owen Flanagan (Cambridge, MA: MIT Press, 1990).
9 See Longworth, "A 'grotesque' Gap," p. 1. For a graphic portrayal of this point, see Peter Menzel, *Material World: A Global Family Portrait* (San Francisco: Sierra Club Books, 1994).
10 On this see Richard Newhauser, *The Early History of Greed: The Sin of Avarice in Early Medieval Thought and Literature* (Cambridge: Cambridge University Press, 2000). This same point could be made comparatively, namely, other religious traditions have also noted the problem of inordinate craving in human life. For examples of this see, in Buddhism, Hammalawa Saddhatissa, *Buddhist Ethics*, introduction by Charles Hallisey (Boston, MA: Wisdom Publica-tions, 1997); also, in Hinduism, Radharkrishnan, *The Hindu View of Life* (London: Mandala Books, 1960). Matters of social justice and the criticism of greed are also found in the great Hebrew prophets (e.g., Micah, Jeremiah, etc.). Sadly, it is not possible to explore these comparisons in this chapter.
11 On the idea of commutative justice and the ethics of exchange, see Jon P. Gunneman, "Capitalism and Commutative Justice" in *The Annual of the Society of Christian Ethics* (Washington, DC: Georgetown University Press, 1985), pp. 101–23.
12 See Thomas Aquinas, *Summa Theologiae* II/II q. 118 (covetousness); I/II q. 61 (virtue).
13 St. Ambrose, *Saint Ambrose: Letters 1–91* in *Fathers of the Church*, translated by Mary Melchior Beyenka OP (New York: Fathers of the Church, 1954), p. 80.
14 Milton Friedman, "The Social Responsibility of Business is to Increase its Profits" in *New York Times Magazine* 13 (September 1970), 32ff. Also see Paul Weaver, "After Social Responsibility" in *The US Business Corporation: An Institution in Transition*, edited by John R. Meyer and James M. Gustafson (Cambridge, MA: Ballinger Publishing, 1988), pp. 133–48. Also see C. Edward Arrington and William Schweiker, "The Rhetoric and Rationality of Accounting Practice" in *Accounting, Organizations and Society* 17: 6 (1992): 511–33 and

William Schweiker, "Accounting for Ourselves: Accounting Practice and the Discourse of Ethics" in *Accounting, Organizations and Society* 18: 2/3 (1993): 231–52.

15 Friedrich Nietzsche, *The Birth of Tragedy and the Genealogy of Morals* translated by Francis Golffing (New York: Doubleday Anchor Books, 1956).

16 For a helpful history of economics, if not greed, see Lionel Robbins, *A History of Economic Thought*, edited by Steven G. Medema and Warren J. Samuels (Princeton, NJ: Princeton University Press, 1998).

17 Alan Ryan, *Property* (Minneapolis: University of Minnesota Press, 1987), pp. 99–100.

18 Mandeville, p. 151.

19 Ibid, p. 149.

20 Murray, *Reflections on Commercial Life*, p. 148.

21 Murray, "Introduction" in *Reflections on Commercial Life*, p. 155.

22 David Hume, *An Enquiry Concerning the Principle of Morals* (La Salle, IL: Open Court, 1966), p. 48.

23 Ibid, p. 66

24 David Hume, *Essays: Moral, Political and Literary*, Essay 1: On Commerce, in *Reflections on Commercial Life*, p. 159.

25 Ibid, Essay II: On Refinement in the Arts, pp. 164–5.

26 Ibid, p. 170.

27 Murray, "Introduction" in *Reflections on Commercial Life*, p. 156.

28 For an analysis of these arguments, see Margaret Jane Radin, *Reinterpreting Property* (Chicago, IL: University of Chicago Press, 1993).

29 See Jean Baudrillard, "Consumer Society" in Murray, *Reflections on Commercial Life*, pp. 447–73.

30 On this see Hans Jonas, *The Imperative of Responsibility: In Search for an Ethics of the Technological Age* translated by Hans Jonas and David Herr (Chicago, IL: University of Chicago Press, 1984) and also William Schweiker, *Responsibility and Christian Ethics* (Cambridge: Cambridge University Press, 1985), esp. ch. 7.

PART II

Time and Responsibility

CHAPTER 4

Timing Moral Cosmologies

Part I of this book examined aspects of the time of many worlds, specifically the press of global dynamics (chapter 1), the reality of moral diversity and human power (chapter 2), and the spread of economic forces around the world to the point that they saturate human desire (chapter 3). In the course of those chapters we have also been developing ideas and convictions needed for an adequate ethics; ideas like overhumanization, the place of the imagination in cultural processes, and also the demand of responsibility for the integrity of life. In Part II we shift our attention in order to explore in more detail beliefs about time and responsibility. Having considered some of the problems that arise because of the reality of many "worlds" on our planet, we need at this juncture to think about the "time" of many worlds. This is the case because beliefs about time are really beliefs about the medium for moving between worlds.

Timely Matters and Human Concern

We live in a time-obsessed world. Among advanced, late-modern societies driven by the whirl of globalization, the speed of travel and communication as well as production and consumption spells an unrelenting demand for instantaneous satisfaction of human desires and wants. The rhythms of nature – the facts of light and dark, dawn and dusk – are lost in the immediacy of an electronic world. This is part of what we have called overhumanization. It is a reality in which human power and technology increasingly enfolds everything within itself. And there is irony in this fact: time now seems to be compressed into the present, and, yet, we also witness the expansion of time-consciousness. Young children readily speak of the life of galaxies and stars in terms of billions of years. We understand the evolution of our species as short term in relation to the long geological history of the earth. The anomie and anxiety seen in the time of many worlds is due in part to the fact that human life in high modern societies is rocked between the demand for satiation and consumption and a deep awareness that we seem lost in a cosmic, eternal ocean of endless time.

However, no one experiences time as a brute fact. Human beings endow their timeliness with meaning. Every culture, and even individuals, configure time – pull together the fleeting present, the ever fading past, and the anticipated future – through memory, hope, and the narratives we tell about our lives.[1] Oddly enough, people inhabit time like a space in which they must orient themselves by what is deemed worth seeking in life. If one views the future with fear, imagines that entropy, decay, or doom are the final word, then the "space" of temporal life takes on a specific meaning. Conversely, to meet the future with zest and some confidence that genuine triumphs are possible, implies a view of the world, a coloration of existence. In contemporary Western societies, apocalyptic fear – say of ecological disaster or random acts of terrorism – mixes and conflicts with confidence in technological progress. How are we to understand the twilight mood of the day, especially as it is manifest in moral beliefs and practices?

For Christian theologians, the question about the moral meaning of time comes to focus on the extent to which ancient eschatological texts, Christian beliefs about the end times, can and should inform present ethics. Three answers to this question dominated twentieth-century thought. First, some scholars, drawing inspiration from Albert Schweitzer's work on the historical Jesus, held that the eschatology of the New Testament meant its virtual irrelevance for contemporary life. Insofar as the end of the world does not seem immediately at hand, then the eschatology of early Christian texts marked by the expectation of Christ's imminent return is false and profoundly out of step with a scientific age. Others insisted, second, that Christians encounter the Word of God in the present as an eschatological event. Karl Barth and Rudolf Bultmann variously argued that the command of God or the claims of Christ on life encountered in the present are irruptions of the end of time in the middle of history. For these thinkers, what is unique and distinctive about Christian ethics is its eschatological meaning. Third, there were theologians, especially political theologians like Johann Baptist Metz and Jürgen Moltmann, who insisted on the already-not yet character of Christian eschatology. Christ's life and teaching provide direction for Christian existence even though the final realization of the reign of God, disclosed in the resurrection, is not yet fully realized in history.[2]

This debate in Christian ethics continues today. Yet since the debate is often confined to the question of the contemporary, practical relevance of eschatological beliefs, theologians too often fail to probe deeply enough into the relation between conceptions of time and morality. There is, at least in the West, a surprising connection between ideas about time and convictions about the moral space of human life. The moral worldview, or moral cosmology, configured in divergent beliefs about time is the subject of this chapter. We can excavate divergent strata of Western thought, specifically modern beliefs about time and ancient apocalyptic beliefs, which collide and coalesce in contemporary consciousness. The final aim of the chapter is to show how Christian convictions about time and time's end serve to respect and enhance the integrity of life.

The crux of the argument that follows is to recast the relation of claims about reality and those of morality around the idea of new creation as a regeneration of conscience and its meaning for the moral life (cf. 2 Corinthians 5:17; Galatians 6:15). In this respect, we add to the discussion in Part I of this book about the origins of the world, extending them into reflection on the moral meaning of the end of time. The idea of new creation will be used to render productive, rather than destructive, the tension between modern scientific and ancient eschatological modes of thought.

Comparing Moral Cosmologies

In order to explore the relation between beliefs about time and moral outlooks in diverse cultural contexts, consider the idea of moral cosmology.[3] A moral cosmology is a set of beliefs and valuations, often tacit in a culture, about how human beings are to orient themselves rightly and meaningfully in the texture of the physical cosmos. The point of focusing on cosmology – as opposed to "moral worldview" – is to stress the fact that beliefs about the moral space of life also have to do with beginnings and endings, the whence and whither of existence. In this book we are developing interlocking ways of speaking about the context of the moral life: a moral world (a formal designation); moral space (the relation of people and some environment as a conglomerate of reasons for action); and moral cosmology (an account of moral space attentive to beliefs about the structure, origin, and end of existence). The "cosmological" aspect of moral reflection is the focus of concern in this chapter.

Why speak of a "moral" cosmology? A moral cosmology configures the intersection of two other accounts of reality: (1) *physical cosmologies* aimed at understanding, explaining, and controlling physical processes (paradigmatically seen in the natural sciences) and (2) *speculative cosmologies* that provide frameworks of meaning about what exceeds, but includes, the domain of human behavior and natural processes (seen, for instance, in mythologies and metaphysical systems).[4] Explaining the possible entropy of the universe is the stuff of physics; asking about "God" in relation to a universe so explained and experienced vexes a speculative cosmology. A moral cosmology, conversely, explicates how human agents can and ought to inhabit a universe open to these other ways of construing the way things are.

However, a moral cosmology is not simply built on physical or speculative cosmologies. It actually helps to provide criteria for what can count in other ways of construing reality. This fact is most obviously true about so-called pre-scientific worldviews. For instance, the Egyptologist Jan Assmann has shown that for the ancient Egyptians the world "is ambiguous and has to be constantly disambiguated by the imposition of moral distinctions." And what is more, the "moral sphere in which gods and men cooperate to institute and maintain prevails over 'natural' distinctions."[5] At the deepest level, the present argument must focus on the relation between moral distinctions and the domain of intelligibility in the face of the ambiguities of life.

The need to clarify the world morally is easily shown. The most primordial forms of what we can call *moral terror* are surely chaos and tyranny.[6] Moral chaos, which can take various forms, is any situation where the fabric of a culture has been rent asunder such that it is impossible meaningfully to orient life. The Greek term "chaos" simply means "empty space." This is contrasted, again in classical thought, with the idea of "cosmos," or an ordered realm. Ancient themes like the fear of banishment (say, Cain's fear of being banished from God's sight, as we will see later in chapter 9), to contemporary experiences of cultural breakdown in war, anomie, and meaninglessness, all testify – mythically and experientially – to the fact that moral chaos is a genuine human terror. So too with *moral tyranny*. This is a situation, again taking many forms, in which there is the wrongful imposition of markers of worth such that human life becomes distorted and destructive. Racism, sexism, and other ideologies are examples of precisely this kind of tyrannous imposition of distinctions of value. Later, in chapter 6, we will see the need for restorative justice to overcome legacies of tyranny. While chaos bespeaks the terror of the loss of a coherent moral space, tyranny is characterized by the fact that wrongful authority has defined one's moral universe. In each case, one must disambiguate the world within the limits and possibilities of a specific moral cosmology.

The ambiguity of life, and so moral tyranny and chaos, is why a conflict between good and evil is depicted in so many of the world's mythologies and religions. This conflict is often conceived as warring "gods," or in apocalyptic discourse the conflict between "ages." We have already seen this ambiguity in an earlier chapter by drawing on the myth of the Titans and also Christian discourse. One could explore other myths, say ones from the Ancient Near East, like the Enuma Elish or the Gilgamesh Epic, to make the same point. What is at stake in all these cases, is, imaginatively, the struggle to define the moral space of life, to create a moral cosmology. The struggle at the origin of the world is imagined as supra-human, beyond the playing field of human action; it is also, as Assmann noted, not simply a matter of "nature." This is so because at issue is the very definition of the context within which distinctly human action can meaningfully take place. The social imagination grasps how central and radical the question of defining the moral space is for human life. Outlooks breed diverse attitudes and dispositions to life: resignation, hope, courage, despair, joy. The life we actually live is given substance by an operative moral cosmology expressed in the beliefs, practices, and institutions of a culture.

The kinds of classical Christian and modern moral cosmologies we will explore shortly hinge on quite divergent assessments about time's content. In each of these cases, a conception of time's end has fostered a moral cosmology in which worth is bound to norms of right and wrong conduct separated from reflection on patterns and processes in the natural world.[7] We will investigate outlooks that sever the connection between a moral cosmology and accounts of existence attentive to physical processes (physical cosmology). These positions insist on discontinuity, rather than continuity, between time morally understood and the structure of the physical universe. Inquiry into the natural world – the domain of the natural sciences – is banished from providing valid content to our understanding of the human dilemma in time. The resulting moral cosmologies warrant non-naturalism in ethics.

Any viable engagement with the theme of eschatology in our age of ecological endangerment requires attending to the vitalities and limits, the processes and patterns, of actual life. In terms of ethics this means showing how naturalistic claims about the complex integrity of life in its diverse forms rightly fund concepts of moral worth.[8] The sciences have something to teach us about the possibilities and limitations of human existence, even if, as is also the case, such knowledge informs but does not determine conceptions of good and evil, right and wrong. Happily, some scientists now insist that there is a confluence between eschatological beliefs and the fact that "physical process is open to the future. We live in a world of true becoming."[9] It would seem that "reality" is not so closed or "block-like" as modern physics often imagined. Endorsing an integrated cosmology that traces continuity between the present and the eschaton has radical moral implications.

Eschatological reflection within ethics consistent with an integrated cosmology means that the moral meaning of Christian faith cannot be a hidden "no" to finite existence in all of its limitation, wonder, and travail. Christian faith, if it is to be a real power in the world, must be a transformation of human existence and thus a real regeneration of human life. The idea of the new creation reaching back to St. Paul's writings is a way to think about faith's transformation of life within an integrated cosmology. The moral meaning of eschatological faith is the love of life and love of the living God amid the pressing facts of finitude and its limitations. The new creation is a moral transformation by God's grace that enables and empowers one to respect and enhance the integrity of life. This disposition is not stoic resignation, false consolation for a better world, or a relentless pursuit of present goods. It is real joy.[10] The term "real joy" designates joy in the real, a yes-saying to existence, and also genuine (real) joy, true human happiness, grounded in a delight in the divine. This kind of joy is a response to the finitude, brokenness, violence, and suffering of life without a fall into despair or the hatred of life. Real joy enables a proper respect and enhancement of life without the temptation to demean or idolize any finite reality.

What would a moral cosmology look like that understood real joy to be basic in responsible human life? With that question in hand, let us turn now to comparative analysis. The analysis of representative modern and ancient moral cosmologies will be a step towards constructive claims about new creation in ethics. We are, again, excavating and comparing strands of thought that have deeply informed Western civilization, mindful of the fact that we now exist within the time of many worlds.

Empty Time and the Creation of Value

While we do not often notice it, one distinctive feature of the modern West is that "time" is understood to be empty. People assume that tomorrow is neither determined, and thus necessarily going to happen in some way, nor full of some reality to which they must respond. To be sure, we have many cares, demands, and obligations that trouble us, but basically "time" is believed to be empty. One might imagine that at some point everything will come to an end in a cosmic crunch. But on a more human scale, most people believe, and believe heartily, that in a genuine sense they make the future. This disconnection in the contemporary Western mind between a moral cosmology expressed in beliefs about making the future and current physical cosmology, with its debates about a cold or hot death for the universe, is what we need to understand. To do so requires some digging into modern thought about the connection between time and morality.

Modern philosophers like Immanuel Kant noted that we cannot see or touch time. Time is not a direct object of the senses. Whatever we do experience (like the sun streaming in the window) takes place in time, but time itself is not directly sensed. I experience the warmth of the sun in the morning. Later in the day, I can recollect its radiance and the shadows it cast across my office walls. These experiences take place "in" time, as we say. Yet time itself is empty. Given this, time must be defined differently; it must be understood as a *form* of all possible experiences. As Kant puts it, "time" is a form the mind gives to any possible intuition.[11] This is important. It means that a basic *form* in which people organize experience is without content. Further, there are two perspectives on time so defined, a fact that shows us that "time" is a boundary phenomenon at the interface of nature and culture: clock time (the perspective of non-personal markers of temporal succession) and experienced time. I see the sun "in the morning" (clock time) but can also recall its warmth later in the day (experienced time). This doubleness in how to mark time, the fact that any idea of time is a boundary idea, is why, for instance, the very same lecture lasting fifty minutes can be experienced by one person as dragging on boring moment after boring moment, while for another the experience of the lecture might be a flash. Our experience of time is not the same as tools – like clocks – used to measure moments. In their timeliness, human beings are poised between natural and experiential processes.

This understanding of time as a form of intuition open to contrasting perspectives (mechanical; experiential) has a liberating effect. It means that the way the human mind organizes experience is free from the material conditions that fund, make possible, and limit human life. Neither the clock nor the lecturer determines how one experiences the event. I can decide to experience the event differently, say by focusing my attention on other ideas. If this is so about time, then we ought to be able to explore other ways in which the mind supplies "forms" for experience. That simple but radical point is basic to much modern ethics. Kant, one of the great modern moral thinkers, reformulated the Golden Rule (cf. Matthew 7:12; Luke 6:31) along these lines. The moral law, he insisted, is that we ought always to treat persons with respect, that is, we ought to treat others and ourselves as ends and never only as a means to some other end (say, pleasure, power, or prestige). This law given by reason is the "form" which is to direct all morally right actions. Whatever course of action I choose – my vocation, hobbies, whatever – must, if it is to be moral, comport with the law given by reason. The moral law is free from, but determinative of, our embeddedness in the natural order as sentient, desiring, social beings. The moral law of respect for persons is something we bring to our encounters with others. The moral law is not found in nature or experienced like something we touch or see. It is the work of reason giving "form" to our actions, relations, and inclinations if they are to be truly moral. In the terms of ethics, this is "moral formalism."[12]

One must grasp the significance of the connection between moral formalism and a conception of time as empty. The moral law is defined on purely rational grounds; it is not funded or limited by claims about the natural world or our lives as sentient creatures. Further, reason is best conceived as legislative, as a rule giving power. "Reason" legislates the forms in which any possible experience or maxim for action is to be grasped. In this way, the emptiness of time and the formality of the moral law bespeaks the power of the human mind to organize its world and determine norms for action. Time is empty, but it is also a moral space: it is the space for the law-giving work of reason. The future is open, something we make, and the only laws for our making are moral, rational ones. The point is that, oddly enough, in much modern ethics there is a connection between how morality is understood and how "time" is defined. Morality is about how the human mind legislates maxims, laws, for actions; time is about how the same mind gives "form" to its experienced world. These are simply different ways in which the mind works to order existence and to assert its irreducible autonomy. It also shows us that both time and morality are boundary phenomena: time connects natural processes with the power of the mind to form experience; morality connects our existence as sensible beings with the capacity of reason to give laws for our behavior.

Importantly, this connection between empty time and moral formalism combats what we called above moral terror. The moral law rooted in reason means that, at least in terms of moral principle, human life is never devoid of moral order. Moral conflict and ambiguity can be overcome because human beings all possess the same power of reason.[13] Moral tyranny is also countered. Insofar as I am acting on the moral law that my reason provides, I am genuinely free. I am autonomous. I need not bow to any power foreign to my will: the state, parents, religious authorities. I have the grounds to criticize and to revise any appeal to authority that challenges the rational moral law. The very formality of the moral law intertwined with a conception of time as "empty" is a bulwark against moral tyranny and chaos.

The legacy of modernity in the West is the working out of some of the ideas just noted. We hear those who insist that communities have their own moral worlds, construct their own identities, because it is their languages, patterns of social power relations, narratives – that is, the socially contingent "forms" of experience – that give order to experience. The moral implication of this is not hard to imagine. Moral value is not findable; there is no meaning to human existence outside our making. As Irving Singer puts it, meaning in life simply is the creation of value with respect to human needs and inclinations. And this is true even of death, the seemingly most powerful counterexample to the claim that we give form to human time. In Singer's words, "Death is so great a problem for human beings only because it intrudes upon our search for a meaningful life."[14] Here is the final triumph of the self's power to create value as a bulwark against chaos and tyranny, even the ravages of death.

The current mood in high modern societies is marked by developments in philosophy and the pervasive cultural assumption, voiced by Singer, that the job of human life is about making, not finding, meaning in existence. The shared point of contact between all of these developments is that time is a moral space, but in the uniquely modern sense that it is "empty," awaiting us

– as individuals and communities – to give it form and content.[15] The right to create value is ours and ours alone simply because moral values are not "out there" to be found. Not only cosmic death but even individual death does not count against this human power to create value. How then are we to take seriously the embeddedness of human life in processes of reality not open to manipulation? The modern conception of time as empty waiting to be "filled" by human power is the heart of global overhumanization.

Full Time and the Coming of the Lord

The basic features of the moral cosmology of the modern, scientific West just explored stand in radical contrast to many ancient Christian conceptions. This is most clear if we explore ideas of time that bind eschatological thinking to an apocalyptic outlook in terms of "final judgment."[16] We will return to the theme of eschatology in the next chapter, but for now take as an example Mark 13:24–7.

> But in those days, after that suffering, the sun will be darkened, and the moon will not give its light, and the stars will be falling from heaven, and the power in the heavens will be shaken. Then they will see "the Son of Man coming in clouds" with great power and glory. Then he will send out the angels, and gather his elect from the four winds, from the ends of the earth to the ends of heaven.

This is, admittedly, extravagant, excessive discourse. The text undoes virtually every aspect of the Genesis creation narrative, light and dark, heavens and winds. The text pictures the end time as a cataclysmic, final judgment in which the elect will be saved. The divine is construed as moral judge; the one who rewards the righteous and punishes the wicked. Further, the point of the "final judgment" is to relieve moral ambiguity. Moral order has been established to which "nature" adheres and follows. The "elect," while scattered around the globe, are gathered into the divine reign. The ambiguity of life is overcome by God's judgment. The discourse presents a moral cosmology under the sovereign authority of the divine, an authority exercised in judgment.

The passage relates to Mark 13:3–8, in which Jesus speaks of the signs before the end time. Along with 13:14–20, the so-called "desolating abomination," the apocalyptic discourse is tied to the opening of the chapter and the destruction of the Temple in Jerusalem. And this means, of course, that the sayings about the coming of the Son of Man are linked to the destruction of the ancient "Temple State" (i.e., the social order of ancient Israel defined by the complex relation between state and temple, king and priest). One might easily imagine that Jesus's challenge to that social order would lead to his death.

The social, political, and religious reality of the Temple State, while itself an answer to the problem of moral chaos, was seen as tyrannous. The destruction of the Jerusalem Temple (70 CE), and with it the moral universe of Second Temple Jews, is set within a wider compass, specifically a claim about the end of time. Of course, there are complex historical-critical questions about Q, the developing discourse about the Christ, and the relation between the text and the Roman Jewish war. All of those matters are beyond the scope of this inquiry.[17]

From a literary perspective, Mark 13 reinterprets Hebraic prophetic discourse in stressing the authority of Jesus over all the world. The vision of the Son of Man is the crucial affirmation of this passage. Reflecting Daniel 7:13 – and thus imaginatively inscribing past prophecy in future events – the text is about the coming of the Son to inherit his kingdom. In the book of Daniel the "coming" of someone "like a human being" is towards the Ancient of Days. "To him was given dominion and glory and kingship" (Daniel 7:14). The direction of the "coming" is quite distinct. In Mark, the Son of Man *comes to* the elect, from the winds, the earth, and the heavens. In this sense, his coming is not only about dominion and the Ancient One; it also draws together in a unique event domains of creation (heaven, earth, winds) and differentiates the elect from others.

In ancient texts, the Son of Man was thought to be an individual, superhuman person possessing heavenly power and glory. His coming constitutes a new reality defined by (1) a differentiation of the elect from others, (2) the intersection of domains of creation (earth, heaven, the winds) manifesting his "power and glory," (3) signaled by cosmic events (stars will be falling . . .), and (4) overturning the Temple State while inscribing previous Jewish expectation into the future. A moral cosmology is thus defined in terms of the Son of Man. To accept this cosmology is difficult for people living in the time of many worlds! And one of the root difficulties is that rather than answering problems of chaos and tyranny, the text seems to the contemporary person set to enact them. Nature tumbles into confusion at the Son of Man's coming. The division of humanity into elect and non-elect could be an act of moral tyranny. Fear and pessimism seem to be the only plausible attitudes towards such a conception of time.

Of course, it may be, historically speaking, that much apocalyptic discourse is a defensive move on the part of some people to protect a threatened way of life. When a people's world is endangered, as in the Roman–Jewish war, many need to imagine a situation in which, in highly dualistic ways, the "good" are rewarded (gathered from the ends of the earth) and the "bad" punished (cf. chapter 5). But that sociological observation, while pertinent, is not the whole story. We are interested in how apocalyptic discourse presents a cosmology that links time and morality. The biblical scholar P. D. Hanson is surely right:

> Apocalyptic eschatology, then, is neither a genre, nor a socio-religious movement, nor a system of thought, but rather a religious perspective, a way of viewing divine plans in relation to mundane realities . . . In its view toward the future as the context of divine saving and judging activity, apocalyptic eschatology can be seen as a continuation of prophetic eschatology.[18]

It is clear that this apocalyptic outlook is one in which all institutions and structures are subjected to a cosmic order of justice. The order of justice, cosmically understood, is not an end (*finis*) striven for, but a fullness (*telos*) that is "coming to" earth in power and glory. The moral space of life is created from the fullness of cosmic justice, God's saving and judging acts. The future is not something people strive for and fill with meaning, as it is for moderns. This future comes to the present, interrupts the course of life. This seems to answer the principal social fact that spawns apocalyptic thinking, namely, the disintegration of socio-religious structures and their supporting myths. The threat of chaos and tyranny provokes the articulation of a new moral universe. But it is a vision in which the conditions for life are reassured not through human action. God rules. That is the primordial fact creating the moral space of life.

Assessment of Moral Cosmologies

The accounts of time and time's end we have been exploring have helped to shape the moral outlook of Western cultures. There are profound differences and similarities between the kind of apocalyptic eschatology found in Mark 13 and the modern idea of "empty time." What are these similarities and differences? In each case, a conception of time and time's end is an answer to moral chaos and tyranny. The question of power and authority is taken as *the* defining fact of the moral cosmos: the power and authority of reason or the sovereignty of God. Much is at stake, accordingly, for determining the rightful or legitimate power to create the moral cosmos. Strategies for what validates claims to legitimacy differ: in the apocalyptic eschatology we explored there is an appeal to a vision of cosmic justice; in modern, formalist ethics it is what, abstractly or concretely, fosters negotiation of moral differences, supports equality, and maximizes human freedom. Yet despite these differences in patterns of legitimation, our comparison has shown that strands of tradition shaping contemporary Western life are defined by the exercise of power to create value and order, the mind's legislative power or God's sovereign power.

That is not all, however. Despite the similarities between a modern outlook and apocalyptic eschatologies, there are profound differences. In Mark's text the implied legitimation of Jesus as Son of Man is messianic hope and a vision of cosmic justice. Insofar as Jesus meets that hope and enacts that vision, he is the legitimate Son of Man. In terms of the modern moral vision, typically expressed by Kant, one cannot appeal to God or nature, divinity or cosmic justice, since such appeals would be heteronomous, tyrannous. The validation of the moral law must be in terms of its formal characteristics and rational necessity. While the discourse of Mark 13 was dependent for its legitimacy on the reality of an implied, if not articulate, cosmic justice, such is not the case in modern conceptions of empty time. There is no moral order outside human beings making time meaningful. This is the deepest implication of the contrast between full and empty time.

Comparing these moral cosmologies exposes the weakness of each. The modern conception of empty time and human sovereignty in the creation of value is a bulwark against tyranny. Yet the danger is that the human search for freedom will tyrannize its environment, since that environment has no moral standing or worth independent of human aspiration. The modern outlook, by disconnecting morality from the whole domain of natural reality, might actually be nihilistic, that is, it is a denial of finite and contingent life in order to maximize human power. Witness, for instance, the growing ecological crisis. This is, again, part of overhumanization: all reality, even time, is enfolded into cultural projects. The form of apocalyptic eschatology found in Mark's Gospel is a bulwark against moral chaos through its implied affirmation of a larger cosmic/moral order in which human life is set. And yet the fusion between moral authority and cosmic order can devolve into a new form of tyranny (what is called moral madness later in chapter 9). This possibility has of course actualized itself all too often within apocalyptic movements and fanaticism around the world. It is seen in religiously motivated forms of terrorism. Mark's apocalypse portrays a situation of confusion about the sustaining structure of creation: the sun will be dark, the moon will give no light, and the stars will fall from the sky. Ironically, a discourse that was aimed at countering moral chaos could in its zeal to assert the absolute, free, sovereign judgment of God reduce all else to chaos.

There are points of instability in these moral cosmologies: the modern outlook aimed at combating moral tyranny can endorse a tyrannous relation between humans and the rest of the world; apocalyptic discourse, in no less an ironic way, seeks to overcome moral chaos and yet can lead to just that condition. These points of instability are not merely logical possibilities; they have manifested themselves in the historical legacy of Christian fanatical movements and modern societies. Modesty requires that we acknowledge that a fail-safe position is beyond our grasp. Still, comparative labor does provide some direction for constructive reflection aimed at avoiding these problems.

The Time of New Creation

Conceptions of time are interpretive prisms through which a culture understands its moral world. How time is construed shapes a culture and its moral outlook even as that outlook (e.g., human freedom; God's will) shapes beliefs about time. Conceptions of time are, furthermore, articulated in a variety of discourses. As an interpretive framework, any form of discourse about time presents a view of the world and orientation for how to live in it; it expresses *in nuce* a moral cosmology. Yet we have also seen, through brief comparison, that ancient apocalyptic eschatology and modern accounts are internally unstable. They too easily breed attitudes that are troubling and dangerous for actual life. The twin terrors of chaos and tyranny are unleashed when it is clear, as it surely is now, that limited resources, increasing demand, and unjust patterns of distribution mark each and every nation and culture on this planet. Indeed, the single most pressing fact of our global age may well be the realization that, despite technological progress, the ecosystem is limited; it is not completely malleable to our purposes. The modern dream of an open future and unending progress is pitifully naive. Any form of ethics, like apocalyptic thought, that in principle undercuts the input of the natural and social sciences in our assessment of courses of action and the limits on human desire, is dangerous. Ancient hopes in God's coming to separate the elect from the damned, to cast the stars from their course, are morally problematic when they feed religious and ethnic conflict or ecological abuse.

The eschatological mood of our day, a mood of twilight, skepticism, despair, and fear, bespeaks a deep quest for renewal. There is a quest for the renewal of the human heart, human orientation, so that we might live rightly amid realms of reality that sustain and make possible life and its flourishing. Do we have symbolic resources to explore this possibility for life? New creation as an eschatological discourse for a rich moral cosmology might speak to the mood of the day. It might help articulate for us a transformation of life. Can we make sense of this discourse?

These are complex matters. First, we must take from modern thought the insight that forms of perception and sensibility are not simply given in what is apprehended. Cultural practices are always at work in rendering life meaningful. Forms of experience are not the empty categories of "reason" but, rather, complex linguistic and imaginative media that work to shape perceptions for good or ill.[19] The discourse of "new creation" is the symbolic means Christians can use to form sensibilities and understanding. New creation is bound, scripturally, to the renewal of covenant between God and humans.

The Hebrew understanding of the "new covenant" is about God's righteousness; it is, as one author notes, "a new creation event that sets things right *for* creation and *between* creation and God."[20] Creation and God's acts of justice and righteousness are fused. In the prophets this is further bound to a conception of the heart, conscience. So we read in Jeremiah 31:31ff.:

> The days are surely coming, says the Lord, when I will make a new covenant with the house of Israel and the house of Judah . . . I will put my law within them, and I will write it on their hearts; and I will be their God, and they shall be my people. No longer shall they teach one another, or say to each other, "Know the Lord," for they shall all know me, from the least of them to the greatest, says the Lord; for I will forgive their iniquity, and remember their sin no more.

The same remarkable connection between God's act of forgiveness, justice and righteousness as a "creation event" even to the depth of human existence continues in the New Testament. Specifically, Paul writes: "Do not be conformed to this world, but be transformed by the renewing of your minds, so that you may discern what is the will of God – what is good and acceptable and perfect" (Romans 12:2). This is linked to Paul's ideas about the "law written on the heart" and thus ideas about "conscience" (Romans 2). In other words, the divine will resonates in the depth of human life (the "heart") and this is the condition for a "perception" of what is good and perfect. In this way, the discourse of new creation is nothing less than a "form" of experience; it is a symbolic prism through which one can see the world. For Christians, the form of new creation through which one sees the world is manifest in Christ. As St. Paul and later Protestant Reformers put it, one lives *in* Christ. Unlike the modern turn to the formal structure of the moral law, a form which is empty and correlates to a conception of time, this form – the law written in the heart and manifest in Christ – is not empty. It provides the way to participate in God's good creation, to see the good and perfect, rather than a form for the projection of our purposes onto all of reality.

Persons and communities touched by this transformation of life, this new creation, are saved from moral chaos but in such a way that the moral law – the good and perfect – is anything but tyrannous. The new creation – God's gracious renewal of conscience and a right relation between God and creation – is a way of life in the world marked by a realistic affirmation of finite existence as good. This combats despair and fear and pessimism without false consolation. It is a primal yes-saying to reality as God's creation; it is real joy. Humanly speaking, this renewal of mind and heart (conscience) is not simply a claim about the nature of reason; it is also about participating in the covenantal community. The transformed conscience that enables a perception of the good and perfect is not a "point" in the self; it is not the biblical version of pure practical reason! The "conscience" is a way of living in the world within the discursive, ritual, and communicative patterns of a community defined by faith in the new creation. It is a way of life in which reality is apprehended through the good and perfect.

This brings us to a second important thing to note. We learn from modern moral cosmologies the need to explore "forms" of experience. One can also reclaim, but transform, an insight from apocalyptic beliefs about "full time." This will lend a note of realism to cosmological inquiry, avoiding the impression that "new creation" is simply a matter of how we decide to interpret the world. What is at stake are beliefs about *the way things are*. The idea of new creation as an eschatological belief does not bespeak apocalyptic judgment wherein the stars fall from the sky.[21] It is, rather, about the renewal and enlivening of conscience and creation in relation to God. Insofar as creation is more than nature, that is, "creation" designates the bringing into being and sustaining the right integration of diverse realms of "natural" existence (earth, wind, heaven; animals, humans, culture), then what is being renewed is not simply natural resources or how we see the world, but, rather, the human capacity to live with justice, with integrity or the right relations, among these domains of reality. The new creation is not about renewable natural resources: we cannot imagine that it can be used to endorse the ecological naïveté and thirst for unending consumption that blatantly disregards the real and present limits on human activity. Rather, new creation is about a renewed "mind," a new conscience, empowered to seek the integration (just relations) between domains of reality so that life, with its specific finite limits, might flourish. It is also and at the same time a new covenant between God and creation. Human beings are empowered to participate in this renewed integrity; enlivened by a transformed mind to be participants in God's good creation. There is continuity and discontinuity between creation and new creation.

Time is not empty; it is full. Yet the fullness of time is not linked to apocalyptic judgment; it is not about how the sovereign Lord passes judgment on the world. The new creation is a judgment in which creation is not negated, swept away, transcended; creation is endorsed as good. Christian faith affirms human finitude and the finitude of the world as good (cf. Genesis 1:31). Wherever there are signs of dynamic integrity, the right confluence of patterns and processes of life, that enable the furtherance of life, then there are "signs" of God's good creation, signs experienced by a transformed conscience as nothing else than grace. Time is not an empty form of experience; it is not the simple movement of physical reality; it is not the event of final judgment. For Christian faith, time is understood as part of the renewal of life and also as one of God's good creatures. Orienting life rightly within God's good creation requires in the face of human violence and folly the renewal of the conscience to perceive the good and perfect. The task of human life so understood is to respect and enhance the integrity of life.

The interpretation of new creation offered here, an interpretation that traces the continuities in "creation" and assigns "newness" to a regeneration of conscience and a renewed covenant between God and creation, opens the possibility for dialogue between the natural sciences and ethics, nature and morality. "Creation," we might say, is the domain of worth; "new" is a transvaluation of the conscience and what we value, how we are enabled to respond to the goodness of existence and God's transformation of patterns of life. The new creation is an ongoing revolution in sensibilities and attitudes set within God's respect for and enhancement of all creation.[22] Theologically stated, an adequate account of the new creation as the final judgment about finite life demands that we move – at long last – beyond the conflict between revealed and natural theology. It is, to use terms introduced above, a moral cosmology that mediates physical and speculative cosmologies. Like traditional natural theology, the image of new creation opens a space for reflection on the patterns and processes of reality as providing some indication of God's will and way for human beings. Like standard revealed theology, new creation is not something we infer from the "facts" of nature; it is a divine gift, a renewal of heart, mind, and covenant with life, which cannot be achieved but only graciously received.

This vision, crossing through natural and revealed theologies as well as physical and speculative cosmologies, is consistent with the real joy that is the root and fruit of Christian life. Real joy is the genuine freedom of the Christian to live and work within the created order. One does not deny the obvious sinfulness, brokenness, and horrors of life. People of good will can and may and must work to end forms of injustice and suffering. What it does mean is that Christian faith – as a kind of real joy – can see through the brokenness of the world to the good that shines in reality. To live the new creation is to dedicate one's life to combat all that unjustly demeans and destroys life out of a profound love of life and in the name of divine goodness.

NOTES

1 For the hermeneutical issues involved in this claim, see Hans Weder, "Metaphor and Reality" in *The End of the World and the Ends of God: Science and Theology on Eschatology* edited by John Polkinghorne and Michael Welker (Harrisburg, PA: Trinity Press International, 2000), pp. 290–7. Also see Paul Ricoeur, *Time and Narrative*, 3 vols., translated by K. Blaney and D. Pellauer (Chicago, IL: University of Chicago Press, 1984–7) and *Meanings in Texts and Action: Questioning Paul Ricoeur*, edited by David E. Klemm and William Schweiker (Charlottesville: University of Virginia Press, 1993).

2 See Albert Schweitzer, *The Quest for the Historical Jesus*, edited by John Bowden (Minneapolis, MN: Fortress Press, 2001); Karl Barth, *The Word of God and the*

Word of Man (New York: Harper and Row, 1957); Rudolf Bultmann, *Jesus and the Word* (New York: Scribner, 1958); Johann Baptist Metz, *Faith in History and Society: Toward a Practical Fundamental Theology*, translated by David Smith (New York: Crossroad/Seabury, 1980); and Jürgen Moltmann, *The Crucified God: The Cross of Christ as Foundation and Criticism of Christian Theology* (New York: Harper and Row, 1974).

3 My idea of a moral cosmology is also related to, but distinct from, the account of cosmogony and ethical order outlined by Robin Lovin and Frank Reynolds. See their essay "In the Beginning" in *Cosmogony and Ethical Order: New Studies in Comparative Ethics*, edited by Robin W. Lovin and Frank E. Reynolds (Chicago, IL: University of Chicago Press, 1985). By speaking of cosmology, rather than cosmogony, I mean to signal a wider interest in ethical order than simply its origin. For the idea of "cultural cosmologies," see William Stoeger, "Cultural Cosmology and the Impact of the Natural Sciences in Philosophy and Culture" in Polkinghorne and Welker, *The End of the World and the Ends of God*, pp. 65–77. I think it is important to speak of "moral cosmologies" to signal the fact that every human culture is marked by basic moral convictions and distinctions necessary for human life to have meaning, worth, and direction. For a similar argument about the importance of diverse ways of "construing the world," see James M. Gustafson, *Ethics from a Theocentric Perspective*, 2 vols. (Chicago, IL: University of Chicago Press, 1981, 1984).

4 For a summary of the religious import of current physical cosmologies, see Paul Davies, *God and the New Physics* (New York: Simon and Schuster, 1983). In our time the most radical speculative cosmology, as I am calling it, is found in "process philosophy." See A. N. Whitehead, *Process and Reality: An Essay in Cosmology*, edited by D. R. Griffin and D. W. Sherburne (New York: Free Press, 1978).

5 Jan Assmann, *Moses the Egyptian: The Memory of Egypt in Western Monotheism* (Cambridge, MA: Harvard University Press, 1997), p. 190.

6 For a recent discussion of the problem of terrorism from the perspective of Christian thought, see *Surviving Terror: Hope and Justice in a World of Violence*, edited by Victoria Lee Erickson and Michelle Lin Jones (Grand Rapids, MI: Brazos Press, 2002).

7 By the term "worth" (or value) all that is meant is the complex way things matter to human beings, kinds of importance. Some things are *esteemed* as ends or good in themselves; others are *assigned* importance within a scheme of other purposes. Esteeming and assigning are acts of valuation, a power that is absolutely basic in human existence and culture. The root problem of eschatology, I contend, is about the rightful power or authority to create a scale of values (what is to be esteemed; what assigned value), thereby defining the moral space of life.

8 For a discussion of naturalism in ethics, see Philippa Foot, *Natural Goodness* (Oxford: Clarendon Press, 2001).

9 John Polkinghorne, *The Faith of a Physicist* (Minneapolis, MN: Fortress Press, 1996), p. 25.

10 My argument is related to (but distinct from) other positions that see the prime religious question for the moral life as focusing on how we respond to the facts of finite existence. Paul Tillich spoke of the "courage to be" in the face of anxiety

and he contrasted this courage to stoic resignation. Yet Tillich could hardly speak of joy. Friedrich Nietzsche did speak of joy, a "yes-saying" to reality. For Nietzsche, this "joy" was about the increase of power in self to overcome resistance. He could not imagine a joy that delights in another, in (say) God. James M. Gustafson insists on a piety that consents to the powers bearing down and sustaining us. Consent is an apprehension of our place in reality consigned by God. While close to Albert Schweitzer's "reverence for life," my account of faithful existence is not keyed to a pessimistic cosmology. Schweitzer, after all, read too much Schopenhauer. Likewise, I do not think – but cannot argue here – that responsibility for life means that all we face are "tragic" choices when life confronts and competes with life. Tragedy there is, and enough of it for all! Yet tragedy is not the whole (moral) story. On these positions see Paul Tillich, *The Courage to Be* (New Haven, CT: Yale University Press, 1952); Friedrich Nietzsche, *Thus Spoke Zarathustra*, translated by R. J. Hollingdale (New York: Penguin Books, 1961); Gustafson, *Ethics from a Theocentric Perspective*; and Albert Schweitzer, *The Philosophy of Civilization* (New York: Prometheus Books, 1987).

11 Kant's argument is, of course, set forth in the famous *Critique of Pure Reason*. We will return to this problem of "form" later in the book, especially in chapter 7.

12 See Immanuel Kant, *Fundamental Principles of the Metaphysics of Morals*, translated by Thomas K. Abbot (New York: Liberal Arts Press, 1949).

13 This claim, we might note, is stressed by present day Kantians like Jürgen Habermas. See his *Moral Consciousness and Communicative Action* (Cambridge, MA: MIT Press, 1990).

14 Irving Singer, *Meaning in Life: The Creation of Value* (New York: Free Press, 1992), p. 71.

15 This point was made forcefully, if unintentionally, in President George W. Bush's speech to Congress and the nation on September 20, 2001 in the aftermath of the terrorist attacks on the USA. Bush remarked: "Some speak of an age of terror. I know there are struggles ahead and dangers to face. But this country will define our times, not be defined by them. As long as the United States of America is determined and strong, this will not be an age of terror; this will be an age of liberty, here and across the world." See the *New York Times*, September 21, 2001, B4. Of course, the president's concern was about the struggle to retain and advance human freedom, but the point about time is striking.

16 For another examination of apocalyptic discourse, see Patrick D. Miller, "Judgment and Joy" in Polkinghorne and Welker, *The End of the World and the Ends of God*, pp. 155–70 and "Creation and Covenant" in *Biblical Theology: Problems and Perspectives* (Nashville, TN: Abingdon Press, 1995), pp. 155–68.

17 On the Jesus movement and Temple State, see Burton Mack, *Who Wrote the New Testament? The Making of the Christian Myth* (New York: HarperCollins, 1995).

18 P. D. Hanson, "Apocalypticism" in *Interpreter's Dictionary of the Bible: Supplementary Volume* (Nashville, TN: Abingdon Press, 1976), pp. 29–30.

19 In this respect, constructive moral cosmological reflection is post-critical or hermeneutical in nature. On this see William Schweiker, *Power, Value and Con-*

viction: Theological Ethics in the Postmodern Age (Cleveland, OH: Pilgrim Press, 1998), esp. ch. 4, "Understanding Moral Meanings."

20 Frank D. Macchia, "Justification through New Creation: The Holy Spirit and the Doctrine by Which the Church Stands or Falls" in *Theology Today* 52: 2 (2001): 207. Also see Brevard Childs, *Biblical Theology of the Old and New Testaments: Theological Reflection on the Christian Bible* (Minneapolis, MN: Fortress Press, 1992).

21 On this see, for example, Michael Welker, *God the Spirit*, translated by John F. Hoffmeyer (Minneapolis, MN: Fortress Press, 1994) and also Jürgen Moltmann, *The Coming God: Christian Eschatology* (Minneapolis, MN: Fortress Press, 1996).

22 On the idea of "revelation" as an ongoing revolution in human faith, see H. Richard Niebuhr, *The Meaning of Revelation* (New York: Macmillian, 1941).

CHAPTER 5

Love in the End Times

The last chapter presented a rather complex argument about the depth of value in the time of many worlds.[1] This chapter continues the inquiry into the moral meaning of conceptions of time within Christian faith. We will focus on a text that paints a stark line between the saved and the damned and thereby risks fostering dangerous moral attitudes in a time of global diversity. The demand now is that we reclaim within early Christian beliefs a connection between eschatology and neighbor regard in such a way as to curtail the potential danger of apocalyptic beliefs. The next chapter will continue the discussion of the "time" of many worlds by turning to toleration and forgiveness as political acts in the face of historical *legacies* of violence. But for now, we must return to ancient Christian beliefs and practices about love in the end times.

Eschatology and Ethics

It has long been known that the early Christian movement tied beliefs about good and evil, right and wrong, to a dualism of time, specifically, the present age and the coming reign of God. Christian existence seemed to transpire in a gap or cleavage within time, and, further, time's end was soon to come. This eschatological outlook could warrant markedly divergent moral stances: a strict morality with no concern for consequences found in the so-called hard sayings of Jesus, or, conversely, the possibility of moral accommodation to the surrounding culture given the ambiguity of living between the times. There is, for instance, a striking difference between Jesus's hard injunction, at Matthew 5:29, to pluck out your eye if it causes you to sin, and Clement of Alexandria's claim over a century later that the Rich Man can be saved if he has the right spiritual attitude towards wealth.[2]

Time is configured by early Christian thinkers by picturing it within moral beliefs basic to their faith, especially beliefs about perfection and the reign or Kingdom of God. This continues the theme addressed before, namely, that ideas about time are boundary ideas in the sense that they are a crossing point between natural processes and cultural beliefs. We can examine these matters by looking to an exemplary text. In the early Christian text called the *Didache* all of nature and all of reality are enfolded, inscribed, in a dualistic logic of the way of life versus the way of death. The problem of the "other" is taken into a picture of reality in ways not unlike the myth of the Titans explored earlier in this book (see chapter 1). The moral life is about "reading" life within a specific view of time. That is how life became Christianly "textured."

There are several reasons to look at the *Didache* as an exemplary early Christian text. First, it will allow us to isolate and to identify a moral and hermeneutical practice, what we can call the practice of *inscription*. This idea designates a kind of myth-making found in strands of Christian ethics, one that presents an account of the world and time by interweaving strata of an inherited textual tradition. But the aim of inscription is not simply to give a picture of reality; its aim is moral and social formation. In the case of the *Didache*, inscription interweaves moral, epistemic, and metaphysical dualism. And this fact relates to the second reason to look at this text. We can show how the linking of metaphysical and moral dualism can lead to a kind of moral madness, as it is called in chapter 9, wherein sharp lines are drawn between the saved and the damned. Beyond identifying a unique moral practice of identity formation, the practice of inscription, the other reason to explore this text is to make good on the claim announced in the introduction to this book, namely, that we must draw on and yet also test our moral traditions, even those most dear to us.

The act of inscription is a unique signifying act and moral pedagogy; it is not "philosophy" as conceived in the ancient world or what comes to be called Christian philosophy. Yet inscription is also different than the moral practice associated with Jesus's teaching and the proclamation of the church centering on the call to discipleship in the coming of the Kingdom of God (*kerygma*). I hope to explain and to defend this thesis about the act of inscription as a moral practice.[3] But more than that, the third reason to explore this work is to isolate within the *Didache* a claim that allows for the transformation of the practice of inscription. That claim is found in the double love command (love God and love neighbor as yourself) nestled within the text of the *Didache*. In this sense, we will be reading the text in terms of a moral claim, the double love command, that requires one to transform the moral practice the text itself enacts (inscription). This insight requires a return within Christian moral thinking to the importance of more general norms beyond their banishment by narrative ethics, the most recent example of inscription (cf. chapter 7).

If persuasive, this reading of the *Didache* means that we must drop the idea that early Christian ethics was simply an "interim ethics," that is, a morality for "between the times," defined solely by conceptions of the end of the world.[4] We can begin with a brief account of the *Didache* as a text and then move through layers of reflection aimed at grasping the moral significance of eschatological beliefs.

Didache as Text

The *Didache*, or "teaching," was long attributed to the twelve Apostles.[5] It is a handbook to introduce new Christians to the faith. A much disputed text, coming either from Alexandria or Antioch in the mid-second century CE, it talks about the community and its internal ordering and direction of life. The text is part of "church order literature," which included moral instruction and direction for church order but, in fact, had no immediate apostolic sanction. Clearly, calling the text the "teaching of the twelve apostles" was an attempt to provide legitimacy to its moral and religious vision. Parts of the text as we now have it were discovered in 1883. Yet the *Didache* draws on earlier material, like the *Epistle of Barnabas*. In this respect the *Didache* provides us with a "snap-shot" in the development of a tradition.

Two concerns dominate the text. One is the matter of church order. The other, and more gripping, is to distinguish virtue and vice and to instruct members in a way of life that is pleasing to God. In this respect, the *Didache* expresses common forms of moral *parenesis* (exhortation) found in the New Testament (cf. Matthew 5–7). Most strikingly, the text draws on a distinction between the way of life and death found in Jeremiah 21 and Deuteronomy 30 to depict the relation between the community and the rest of the world. Those in the church are in the Way of Life, everyone else is in the Way of Death. The task of the believer, accordingly, is to live a life worthy of the church amid a godforsaken world poised on the brink of destruction. This is also why church order is important. The twofold concern (church order; *parenesis*) actually structures the work: the tropological distinction of the two ways (Life; Death) is explored in chapters 1–5; church order material then runs from chapters 6 through 16. The text is a "compilation" of materials, even as there is a rough ordering of issues around commandments.

Of most import for the present argument is the powerful use of the rhetorical figure or trope of the two ways. As Abraham Malherbe notes, this was a conventional rhetorical device. It is the "image of a man at a crossroads, challenged to choose between the life of virtue and one of vice."[6] As Robert Frost put it much later in "The Road Not Taken,"

> Two roads diverged in the woods, and I –
> I took the one less traveled by,
> And that has made all the difference.[7]

Within the rhetoric of a decision between two "roads," there is the tendency found in the *Didache* to list duties of the members of the household (*Haustafeln*). So we read: "Do not be harsh in giving orders to your slaves and slave girls" (4:10) and "At the church meeting you must confess your sin and not approach prayer with a bad conscience" (4:14). Thus the difference of the way of life and way of death is detailed through some common moral topics and conventional rules for behavior.

So, as a text, the *Didache* is a compilation of church teachings drawing on a specific rhetorical trope in order to engage in *parenetic* discourse: to exhort a certain way of life. The work begins, importantly, with the twofold command of love of God and neighbor as definitive of the way of life. The ground of obligation is God "who made you" (4:12), even as the concern will be with the neighbor – however that "neighbor" is understood. And this relates to the trope of the two ways, the way of life versus the way of death. The novice and the reader are confronted with a crisis of decision. We see the gravity of the moral life and its decisions. The moral life entails one's eternal destiny and also the way of one's life in this world regarding the community to which one belongs. Not surprisingly, the text is intensely concerned with the character of the agent and links this to a kind of perfectionism. We read: "My child, do not *be* lustful . . . do not *be* a diviner . . . do not *be* a liar . . . do not *be* a grumbler" (3:3ff.). This emphasis coheres with the demand to be in the way of life and to follow the commands. The center of the ethic is the character of the moral agent and the community. Wayne Meeks observes: "the catechumen is already being trained to participate in the community's process of mutual admonition and discipline."[8]

The *Didache* presents then an ethic concerned about ongoing participation in a community and its process of life. And this helps explain why the demand for perfection is finally attenuated. At the transition from the *parenesis* built on the trope of the two ways to the material on church order we read: "If you can bear the Lord's full yoke, you will be perfect. But if you cannot, then do what you can" (6:2). The task of the Christian life is knowing the right thing to do, what one's responsibilities are in the church, and the moral formation of character. And in this respect, the text seems somewhat at odds with itself. It seems filled with a tension between the radical claim about the two ways and the demand for perfection, set aside a rather modest, community based ethics. That alone is enough to make the *Didache* an interesting text for understanding early Christian ethics.

More importantly, the *Didache* represents a type of moral reflection that leaves genuine ethical problems to theologians. What is the relation between the Christian community and the "world," especially regarding the command to love one's neighbor? What is the principle of choice to follow the way of life and can it be given any rational determination, or is it to be accepted on blind faith and authority? In order to address some of these concerns, we turn next to a deeper engagement with the thought world of the *Didache* by isolating concepts important for understanding what is at stake ethically in this text and the practice of "inscription."

Kinds of Dualism

In order to understand the *Didache* and the practice of inscription, we need to clarify the meanings of dualism, myth, and philosophy as conceived in the ancient world. We can begin with dualism, since it is most important for understanding the thought of the *Didache*. The trouble is that dualism is an ambiguous concept, especially in current thought. Indeed, the fact that there are different kinds of dualism is often missed insofar as many contemporary theorists take dualism simply to mean any dyadic structure of thought in which there is a hierarchical ordering of terms, say soul over flesh, or, in patriarchal societies, men over women.[9] Mindful of these rather global accounts of dualism, we must begin more modestly.

The first kind of dualism important for this inquiry is metaphysical dualism. By this is meant the claim that in any domain of reality there are at least two independent and irreducible substances. For instance, in Plato's *Phaedrus*, Socrates tells a story, uses a myth, that depicts the human as a composite of body and soul, wherein neither body nor soul are reducible to the other. The soul is pictured as a chariot driven by a charioteer (reason) and drawn by a pair of winged horses, desire (ill-tempered and hard to control) and the other noble part. "Soul" can only be defined dualistically, that is, in terms of the distinction between charioteer and the two horses. We see an instance of metaphysical dualism in the *Didache*. The texts begin on a dramatic note: "There are two ways, one way of life and one of death, and between the two ways there is a great difference" (1:1). Reality is defined through the opposition between the two ways. The point is made more stark by the use of the singular: one way of life; one way of death. The "ways" are non-reducible modalities of social existence found in history. But other forms of metaphysical dualism are possible. One can also think of Cartesian dualism (the difference between thinking beings and extended reality), or Immanuel Kant's distinction between the noumena (the *Ding an Sich*) and phenomena.

Dualism in this metaphysical sense is the claim that reality, or some of the things in reality, cannot be explained or defined with reference to one underlying principle. Put more simply, metaphysical dualism is opposed to any form of monism, whether that is materialism (reality is only matter in motion) or idealism (the real is an expression of mind). On this score, Jewish, Christian, and Islamic thought is complex.[10] As forms of radical monotheism, Jews, Christians, and Muslims assert that there is only one ultimate principle definitive of reality, that is, God. Yet God and creation are not reducible to each other and even within the domain of finite being, within creation, certain beings, like human beings, are composite creatures. The Abrahamic religions give a complex account of reality that is neither simple monism nor simple dualism.

The second form of dualism is epistemological. This is the claim, or any theory used to sustain the claim, that in perception, memory, and other types of non-inferential cognition (e.g., intuition) there is nonetheless a distinction between the content known to the mind and the real object known. In other words, an epistemological dualist thinks that there is a difference between our ideas and what our ideas are about. Given this fact there is a possible incongruity between idea and reality: we can be mistaken. Plato is a good example. In various dialogues, Plato examines theories of language and how words refer to something as well as to our ideas. He shows the shortcoming of strict imitative theories, where words simply reflect reality, and also ideas of language as the product of social convention. Insofar as human knowing is bound to language it is also open to error and deception. For Plato, it is only in ecstatic insight that the tension between idea and reality is transcended. The knower just sees.

In the context of early Christianity, and much inter-testamental Judaism as well, there is also some form of epistemological dualism. This is because scripture demands interpretation insofar as the ultimate referent of the text, the way and will of God, is not identifiable with any act of human cognition. God is not human ideas about God. The deity transcends the conceptual and linguistic means used to speak of the divine, including those revealed in scripture. This is the epistemic meaning of the prohibition of idolatry. Only mystical insight or divine epiphany could possibly escape this problematic. Again, this epistemic point is made in the *Didache*. Those in the way of death do not know their own creator (5:2). But even those in the way of life must learn from the apostolic teaching, not be tempted by the way of death, and hold fast to the revealed word of God.

Again, a dualistic epistemology stands in contrast to various forms of epistemological monism. For the dualist, the human mind, while perhaps aiming at conformity with its cognitive objects, is nonetheless distinct from those objects. Mind and what the mind grasps are distinct and non-reducible one to the other. This is why dualists like Plato were so deeply aware of the problem of illusion. The mind can mistake its products, its ideas, for what are real things. Yet epistemological dualism is also different than epistemological idealism, where the object of knowledge must conform to the mind's content. For the dualist, it is simply not the case that the knowable world is constituted by our categories of knowing. This is what makes Kant, ironically, some kind of dualist. While he thinks that what we can know (phenomena) must conform to our cognitive capacities, it is also the case that reality (phenomena plus noumena) exceeds our capacities. On this score, one might note, parenthetically, that much postmodern theory is actually a form of epistemological monism. The claim is that what can be known is dependent on their means of expression. Sign systems create meaning. There is nothing outside the text, as Jacques Derrida once famously stated.[11] The labor of overhumanization is found in the structure of language.

Rather than exploring current thought, we can isolate the third kind of dualism germane to the present inquiry, that is, moral dualism. Moral dualism means that the domain of beliefs about the values human beings seek and the rules they live by is a matter of choice between two opposite values. Things, actions, or persons are good or evil, right or wrong, real or illusory. Of course, thinkers and even whole traditions will differ on the meaning of these basic distinctions. The *Didache*, for instance, defines good with respect to obedience to the commands of God insofar as God is creator, and, also, with respect to the demand to imitate God's action of generosity. As we read in chapter 1:5: "Give to everybody who begs from you, and ask for no return. For the Father wants his own gifts to be universally shared."

In the *Didache* a conception of moral goodness is rooted in divine commandments. This has its deep roots in Hebraic thought and is a mark of Jewish influence on the text. As one scholar notes,

> From the Hebrew people there entered into the Christian tradition the fundamental conviction that God has given man a supernaturally revealed law wherein all man's duties are made known. What the law enjoins is right, what it forbids is wrong. Morality is summed up as essentially righteousness, obedience to this supreme law of God.[12]

This claim no doubt requires some nuance, since, as seen in other chapters, beliefs about creation and new creation, not just divine commands, are central in Christian and Jewish conceptions of moral existence. Nevertheless, it is clear that a vision of the moral life bound to the will of God, however known or expressed, differs radically from the work of, say, an ancient Stoic philosopher like Epictetus, who claims that one must live according to nature. And each of these stands in contrast to modern, Western conceptions of freedom and human rights. Still, it is hard to imagine a viable human society that would not have some means of ranking values and distinguishing between forms of behavior. Moral pluralism, the fact that societies have different moral worldviews, does not negate this point about moral dualism.

These are then the three basic kinds of dualism, at least as we will use the concept "dualism." What becomes interesting for ethics is when kinds of dualism are linked. The *Didache* asserts that the domain of history is defined by an opposition between moral good and evil, where these distinctions are not simply evaluations of behavior, but, in fact, conflicting realities, specifically, the way of life and the way of death. The way of death are those "who persecute good people, who hate truth, who love lies" (5:2). Further, these conflicting metaphysical realities – as two ways of living and being persons – find sociological manifestation in the church and the world as distinct realms. The wedding of moral and metaphysical dualism, accordingly, grants ontological standing to an evaluative distinction (good/evil) and in doing so pits the righteous against those seen as sinful. Here we find not only a powerful moral realism, but also the possible roots of what I call moral madness, that is, devotion to a moral cause to the point of destruction. Taken seriously, the Christian community, if the *Didache* is read in a certain way, must utterly remove itself from the "sinful" world or must pass judgment, even violent judgment, on the way of death. In order for either possibility to be realized the religious community must come to see itself, to have its identity, formed by a vision that binds together moral and metaphysical dualism. What kind of practice could form identity in that way? Drawing on the *Didache*, we can isolate at least one kind of practice that so constitutes identity. One might call this the work of "inscription" insofar as life is "inscribed," for good or ill, within the layers of a text.

The act of inscription in the *Didache* is a signifying and moral practice aimed at social formation, at the creation of community, through an oppositional logic that is at once metaphysical and moral. This kind of mixed dualism is also found in much apocalyptic discourse, as well as certain Ancient Near Eastern cosmogonic myths like the Gilgamesh Epic.[13] And to be sure, there are also epistemological dimensions to these texts. The *Didache*, for instance, relies on revelation to specify the way of life. In fact, after the dramatic opening of the text, it follows immediately with the twofold great command and also the so-called Golden Rule: "Now this is the way of life: 'First, you must love God who made you, and second, your neighbor as yourself.' And whatever you want people to refrain from doing to you, you must not do to them" (1:2). This is the case, presumably, because human reason, trapped in sin and death, cannot know even the most basic moral truths (e.g., the demands of respect, reciprocity, and equal regard). Here an epistemological point about the nature of valid knowledge is made by the interweaving of texts (cf. Matthew 22:37–9; Leviticus 19:18; Matthew 5:44–7; Luke 6:27–8,

32–3); that is, by inscription. In the *Didache* we see, then, a mixed form of dualism.

On Myth and Philosophy

This brings us to another aspect of the world of the *Didache*, namely, the connection between myth and philosophy in ancient thought. The connection is a rather complex one. At one level all ancient thinkers agreed that some picture of reality is needed for the proper guidance of life. These pictures of reality, that is, rational or traditional myths, are not value neutral; they articulate beliefs about the moral texture of reality, they provide a moral cosmology. This meant that virtually all forms of ancient ethics were versions of *moral realism.* What is morally right and good was linked to the nature of a vision of reality, whether that reality is imagined as an ordered cosmos (Stoicism), defined by the form of the Good (Platonism), a collection of atoms (Epicureanism), or dependent on the will and being of God. The moral life is about conformity to the real, say by living according to the *logos* in Stoicism or obeying the will of God among Christians and Jews.

In ancient philosophy morality and metaphysics are linked in ways many people, especially modern moral philosophers, now find baffling. If we use "myth" in the contemporary scholarly sense of the term as simply a story that accounts for the world in which people find themselves and must orient their lives, then there simply was no opposition between myth and philosophy in ancient thought. The ancients understood that how "we see and describe the world is moral too – and the relation of this to our conduct may be complicated."[14] It might be the oddity of modern Western ethics that we have tried to get along morally without orienting myths.

That is not the whole story. In the Greek context, Socrates initiated an enterprise in which accepted myths and their use in education are submitted to rational examination. Socrates brings philosophy down to earth, and that means, at least in part, mediating between a transcendent ideal of wisdom and the messiness of actual life. More pointedly, Socrates summons his interlocutors to existence; he confronts them with the question of their destiny and thus the state of their souls.[15] In this sense, as Plato notes, philosophy is learning to die. It is learning how to confront one's destiny through rigorous moral self-criticism, and philosophy is also, cognitively speaking, learning to separate body and soul, sensation from the intellectual grasp of pure ideas; that is, to "die" to the material, sensual world. The traditional myths, as Plato saw, too easily become comforting illusions that lessen the moral demand of existence, and, further, they wrongly impute moral failure to the gods. In the name of the soul and justice, Plato held that one must exile the poets from the city.

Gregory Vlastos observes that, for Socrates, "what is necessary and sufficient for moral reformation is intellectual enlightenment."[16] This insight is won through the spiritual practice of philosophy called dialectic. Socrates and others do not abandon myth so much as transform it with respect to the demands of philosophy. Centuries later, Seneca the Stoic would capture this very same idea of philosophy. In Epistle XVI, Seneca writes that philosophy "molds and constructs the soul; it orders our life, guides our conduct, shows us what we should do and what we should leave undone; it sits at the helm and directs our course as we waver amid uncertainties. Without it, no one can live fearlessly and in peace of mind."[17] In living a life of reason, the myths will not help. Peace and courage come from meeting life through the "philosophic" exercise of reason.

If the demand for intellectual enlightenment characterized the move from myth to philosophy in Greek and Roman thought, then in the biblical context the shift must be seen in terms of the importance of history for knowing God. Already with the eighth-century BCE Hebrew prophets there is a concern for justice as opposed to purely cultic worship of God. Insofar as cult always seeks to stabilize the social order with respect to beliefs about the world, then it is, we might say, the practice of myth. But with the prophets, righteousness and not blood sacrifice is central to a right relation to the God of Israel (see Amos 5:21–4). The world is disambiguated, not in cultic sacrifice, but through works of justice and righteousness. This critique of cult, as many scholars note, is a moral revolution that asserts the moral being of the deity.[18] To conform to the real, to seek goodness, is to live in obedience to God and God's will. It is to seek justice, love mercy, and walk humbly with God (Micah 6:8). Of course, the idea of "ethics" as a spiritual practice and rational inquiry into how we ought to live is foreign to the biblical texts. But something analogous to the Socratic critique of myth in the name of morals is seen in the prophetic message, a message deeply woven into the teaching of Jesus. The demand to "choose life and not death" (cf. Jeremiah 21) by following the ways of the Lord, a demand, we will see, inscribed in the *Didache*, is not unlike the philosophic concern to confront one's own existence before the transcendent ideal of wisdom. The difference, of course, is that the ways of the Lord are known historically, not through a pure intellectual grasp of ideas. Nevertheless, with the prophets a form of moral critique is brought to bear on the worldview and values of their nation. This does not negate cult or myth, it morally transforms them.

By myth, then, is meant a story used to situate and orient human life in the world. We have been exploring them and their moral meanings throughout this book. Granting that rather general point, it is important to see that in the period we are exploring in this chapter traditional myths are being interpreted and even conceived anew with respect to moral demands. And that interpretive and conceptual work was part and parcel of various moral practices. The best known of such practices was "philosophy." But when we try to grasp what was meant by "philosophy," we also confront problems of comprehension. Philosophy in the ancient world, as Pierre Hadot reminds us, was a love of wisdom. It was a spiritual practice of self-transformation. And this means that "to philosophize is to choose a school, to convert to its way of life, and accept its dogmas."[19] Philosophy is a way of life; it is, as Seneca insisted, practical and moral in character. To explore ancient "philosophy" is then nothing less than to explore divergent ways of life. What these "ways of life" share that makes them "philosophic" in the strict sense is the demand to live according to reason or *logos*. The "myths" are submitted to critique, since goodness philosophically understood requires a rational life. Yet the life of reason is a form of spiritual practice.

It is within this intricate framework of dualism–myth–philosophy that we must explore the thought of the *Didache*. This text expresses a moral practice, "inscription," that is distinct from the church's proclamation (*kerygma*) and yet is not what comes to be called Christian philosophy, that is, living by the *logos* incarnate in Christ. The decisive difference in these moral practices is between moral formation through a type of myth-making (inscription) versus the fellowship gathered around Jesus and the proclamation about him (*kerygma*) and the discipline of loving wisdom manifest in Christ (Christian philosophy). The tension between these strands of Christian ethics, like those explored later in chapter 7, betray the fact that *kerygma*, inscription, and philosophy remain distinct options even to this day. In this book, we are practicing a form of "Christian philosophy," informed by these other positions, in order to show how it centers on respecting and enhancing the integrity of life.[20] At this juncture in our argument, the point is that the practice of inscription aims at moral formation by way of a new articulation of the founding "myth." The practice has been unidentified by historians of Christian ethics. So distinctive is this practice that recognizing its presence in the Christian movement requires recasting our conceptions about early Christian ethics. But it also allows us to identify some problems that inscription puts to ongoing moral reflection.

The Problems of Inscription

There seems little doubt that the core of the early Christian movement's belief system was the reign of God proclaimed by Jesus. It is also clear that in exploring the *kerygma* about the Kingdom, one must examine the connection between the *nature* of the Kingdom – that is, the reign of God's will – and what can be called its *manner of arrival*, how God's reign is in time or in fact makes time. I realize that this is formally stated. In fact, differences about how to conceive the connection between the nature and mode of arrival of the Kingdom run through Jewish and the early Christian texts.

For instance, in Isaiah 10:1–4 the divine is pictured as coming with an outstretched arm, with judgment and then mercy. This is an imaginative metaphor for the *manner* in which the divine reign arrives. In apocalyptic discourse (cf. Mark 13), as we saw in chapter 4, the mode of the Kingdom's arrival is depicted in terms of judgment as a way to defend or protect the community. In the Apocalypse of John or even the Book of Daniel, time and reality are understood from their end, an end of cataclysmic judgment.[21] But this apocalyptic conception of *how* the Kingdom comes differs from forms of eschatological thinking wherein, as some scholars argue, the mode of arrival is the messianic acts of Jesus. The words and works of Jesus and the community formed around him manifest the kind of fellowship definitive of the Kingdom. Jesus's ministry *is* the mode of the Kingdom's arrival. This has led some theologians to argue that the present Christian community is the eschatological reality.[22] Yet other scholars have argued that the "Kingdom of God in the teaching of Jesus was not an apocalyptic or heavenly projection of an otherworldly desire. It was driven by the desire to think that there must be a better way to live together than the present state of affairs."[23] The manner of the Kingdom's arrival on this account is indeterminate and not focused on cataclysm or Jesus; all that is needed is the desire of persons to live together in a new way.

The sheer diversity of pictures about how the Kingdom of God arrives and the scholarly disputes over them should help us to escape a presupposition that has dominated too much thinking about early Christian morality. The claim, in brief, has been that metaphysical beliefs are the *grounds* of substantive moral concepts like good, evil, justice, righteousness, and love. In other words, moral beliefs supposedly rest on non-moral convictions about reality, especially about time. Early Christian ethics, on this reading, faced the problem of how to apply Jesus's radical teachings to actual life when the Kingdom did not immediately arrive with or shortly after his resurrection. Christian morality is for the interim between the presence of Jesus and the arrival of the Kingdom. Attention to the complex connections between forms of dualism, myth, and philosophy gives a more complex picture of early Christian ethics. We see a variety of forms that understand the manner of the Kingdom's arrival in different terms. The practice of inscription and its formation of identity through mythmaking is a distinctive account of the connection between the Kingdom and the Christian community.

We can now note two problems the *Didache* and its practice of inscription bequeath to later Christian thinkers. The first is that the act of inscription is one in which Jewish texts are Christianized, and, thus, Israel is relativized and superseded by the church. This is of course a strategy already present in the

New Testament, say in Matthew's Gospel in the use of the Sermon on the Mount material, but in the *Didache* it is most striking. The relation to Jewish thought and life must continually be addressed in Christian moral thinking.[24] The desire to pull all the world within the biblical story, as many narrative theologians put it, risks the reduction of other traditions that lay claim to these same texts. In other words, the practice of inscription is too easily a Christianized version of overhumanization, the enfolding of life within one symbolic horizon and framework. Inscription as a moral practice is below the level of complexity of life in the time of many worlds, an odd fascination with the unity of "form."

The second problem with the kind of inscription found in an early Christian text like the *Didache* is related to the first, but bears directly on the link between moral and metaphysical dualism. It moves us in the direction not of "form" but of moral madness, a theme, as noted, addressed later in the book (chapter 9). Insofar as the *Didache* defines the moral space of life oppositionally, that is, as a battle between the way of life and the way of death, then it pits church against the world. To be sure, there are safeguards within the text against a crusader-like spirit. Along with the distinction between the way of life and the way of death the text insists that one must love God "who made you," the creator, and the neighbor as oneself. As I noted above, this command is central to the *parenesis* of the work as a whole. How are we to understand the norm embedded in the *Didache*?

Only by insisting on the centrality of this norm can the practice of inscription and its narrative form be redeemed from the worst expression of its own oppositional logic. Contrary to what many contemporary theologians hold, the wisdom of the early church was to test its narrative inscription of life by more basic and more general norms. We can further this inquiry into the practice of inscription by exploring this basic norm of the double love command in Christian existence and its import for the world in which we now live. This demands that we dig deeper into early Christian beliefs beyond ideas about myth, dualism, and philosophy. We need to read the *Didache* against itself; pit the double love command against the rhetorical trope of the two ways.

Moral Norms and the Practice of Inscription

The connection between the "first" and the "second" great love commands given by Christ continues a long line of Jewish teaching.[25] When asked, by a non-Jew, to teach the entire Torah while standing on one foot, Hillel replied: "What you dislike don't do to others; that is the whole Torah. The rest is commentary. Go and learn" (B. T. Shabbat 31a). Further, the first command, the love of God, is violated if not accompanied by a life marked by the second. In this respect, a much later epistle, 1 John 4:19–21, captures an essential feature of Jewish practice and Jesus's teaching and fellowship: anyone who claims to love God but hates the other is patently wrong. To be sure, the command of neighbor love is ambiguous.[26] What is meant by "love"? Who is the "neighbor"? Just how far does the principle of reciprocity, signified by the little word "as," really reach? Am I really commanded to love a child in a distant land as much as I love my own son?

Ambiguity abounds. Still, Christians have always understood the command of neighbor love to be about how to treat and relate rightly to others. The presence of the double love command within the dualistic logic of the *Didache* can be used to block destructive tendencies in inscription and turn that practice to more humane purposes. It does so by shattering the domination of one dualistic form, namely, the way of life and the way of death. But to make this case in the contemporary context requires that we progress through elements of the "second command" correlate to the theme of "otherness."

Proximity and love of neighbor

One challenge to Christian ethics is not unlike the criticism leveled against the practice of inscription when it links moral and metaphysical dualism. Currently, there are many thinkers, religious and non-religious, who believe that injunctions like the second of the love commands actually miss the core of morality. Their argument is that the demand to love others *as* ourselves, requires that the "other" become like us in order to be worthy of moral respect and love. Neighbor love is a veiled imperialism of the self or the local community. On this reading, the love command fits all too well with the practice of inscription and the enfolding of all reality within one narrative form. Mindful of pluralism and difference, these thinkers demand a turn away from the idea of neighbor love and toward claims about the moral priority of the "other." In the name of respect and care, Christians and Jews ought to abandon their traditional ways of thinking about how to relate to others.

The theme of the "other" dominated much twentieth-century theology, and with good reason. In the face of tyrannous and idolatrous political machines, like National Socialism in Germany, as well as the failure of classical liberal Protestant theology to provide strong lines of demarcation between "Christ" and "culture," theologians like Karl Barth insisted that God is "totally other." But nowadays, if one asks, "who is the other?" answers tend immediately to focus on the human and not the divine other.[27] The air is buzzing with debates about how best to acknowledge openly and honestly difference among peoples. As noted in chapter 1, around this planet "enemies" are forced to live together, the fact of proximity. From the West Bank to Los Angeles, Tokyo to Bosnia, the shifts in political power and the movement of peoples have evoked renewed and bloody cycles of violence. We need an ethics fit for a world in which diverse and different peoples, usually former enemies, live side by side.[28]

It is at this level that the distinctive nature of the second great command begins to appear. We can explore this beyond the limitations of the *Didache*'s own position. If we look to the text, Jesus's interpretation of this commandment is given parabolic and imperative forms. Immediately after uttering the double love command and in response to a question about how to inherit eternal life, Jesus is asked "who is my neighbor?" (Luke 10:25–8). He answers with the parable of the Good Samaritan (Luke 10:29–37). In that parable the question of the "neighbor" is reversed. The Samaritan, someone despised by the Jews of Jesus's day after untold years of conflict, had compassion on a man beset by robbers. There is absolutely no suggestion that Jesus thinks the Samaritan must become Jewish in order to act as a neighbor; the loving act of the Samaritan is what constitutes him as a neighbor. This rests upon Jewish beliefs about the relation between righteous action and the human being as the image of God. "Since human beings are created in the image of God, it is obvious that one achieves the highest possible level of perfection or self-realization by becoming as similar to God as humanly possible. This is the basis for what may be the single most important ethical doctrine of the Hebrew Bible, that of the *imitatio Dei*, the imitation of God."[29] The *imago dei* is hardly an attribute of the mind or soul, as many early and medieval theologians thought. It is manifest in actions that imitate God. "Neighbor" is defined not by likeness but by the work of compassion.

The second great command tears asunder any constriction on who the neighbor is, any limitation of compassion, respect, and justice to members of one's own clan, race, gender, community, or religion. In this respect, the presence of the command within the *Didache* overturns the dualism of the way of life and the way of death. Just how far this destruction of any limitation on compassion goes in the double love command is seen in Jesus offering two further injunctions that interpret the second part of the command: the demand to love others as he loved and also the injunction to love even the enemy. Not only a parabolic extension of the command (the story of the Good Samaritan) but also further conceptual elaboration is given. At Luke 6:35–6 we read: "But love your enemies, do good, and lend, expecting nothing in return. Your reward will be great, and you will be children of the Most High; for he is kind to the ungrateful and the wicked. Be merciful, just as your Father is merciful."[30] This command is grounded in God as creator, the one who sustains all life. Just as in the parable, the meaning of "neighbor" is shattered, expanded. And this is explained not in the direction of an abstract "other" but with respect to the actual problem of how to live beyond cycles of violence and conflict.[31] "Neighbor" is not someone near to us, but anyone who acts righteously and, more radically, loves like Christ, loves even the enemy.

Of course, it might be the case that given Christ's interpretation of the command no one is really able to be a neighbor! All have sinned and fall short of God's glory. And, further, it might also be the case, as I believe it is, that love of enemy requires that demands of justice remain in order to protect the innocent. In the face of terrorism and fanaticism, the demands of justice, even some measures of corrective justice, are pressing (see chapter 6). Still, it seems clear that the point of the second great command is to guide action in response to those radically different than self. The command should be interpreted in the direction of the Good Samaritan and the love of Christ. This is vitally important in an age of globalization and the problem of proximity. In order to have a viable future, societies riddled by the reality of multiculturalism must find resources for breaking seemingly unending cycles of revenge and violence. Even in cases of justifiable warfare (I believe there are such cases), one must still develop ways beyond retribution. Knowledge of this fact is hardly unique to Christians. In the Hebrew bible, the so-called *lex talionis*, an "eye for an eye" (Exodus 21:23–5), was meant, originally, to place strict limits on retributive violence. The world's other religions make an analogous point in their praise of compassion, mercy, and justice.

The commentaries on the second love command given in Jesus's actions and parables introduce forgiveness into human affairs in a way that seems required by the reality of what we have called "proximity," that is, the problem of enemies having to live together. Without some notion of forgiveness conjoined to the demands of justice, it is hard to imagine how societies composed of diverse peoples broken by violence and suffering at each other's hands will long endure. But this is precisely what the second great command does: it links justice and forgiveness, forging a life imitative of God's good action. It explodes the *Didache* from inside the text itself and thus overturns the separation of humanity into the saved and the damned. Within the text of the *Didache* the second command is like "new wine" that bursts the "old wine-skins" of dualistic thinking.

Self, totality, and other

Part of the concern for otherness in current ethics arises from the deep problem of how to orient life in a world of pluralism and multiculturalism. Yet the second command insists that love of others can and must reflect love of self.

Does this mean that the "other" is reduced to a reflection of myself? The question is about the grounds for care and respect of others.

Early modern thinkers (Kant no less than Hume, Rousseau just as Voltaire) argued that in virtue of simple and basic humanity, persons command respect, sympathy, the rights of liberty, happiness, and "fraternity." Persons have worth irrespective of religious commitment, nationality, race, or gender. There are, as Thomas Paine put it, "rights of man." In the face of a long legacy of religious and political conflict (the Thirty Years War) and uncertainty about how to ground political rights, these theorists ventured a host of different political theories. The whole edifice of modern democracy no less than beliefs about human rights owes much to the passionate and yet rational vision of these prophets of humanity. We deny these moral aspirations at our peril. In fact, human rights have roots in Jewish and Christian faith.[32]

It must also be admitted that the idea of "humanity" that commends respect and demands these rights is a thin creature. The suspicion of critics is that it conceals deep religious, racial, and gender biases. For Immanuel Kant, "humanity" is defined in terms of the idea of rational freedom (i.e., will) that commands our respect. But this idea of "will" is deeply Western in character. Jean-Jacques Rousseau championed the "noble savage," a kind of pre-social being somehow free of the corrupting force of cultural life. But as feminist ethicists enjoy noting, we are embodied, social creatures whose freedom is deeply entangled and also empowered by our many relations. While celebrating freedom and rights, the picture of human existence found in these early modern thinkers is one stripped of the relations, characteristics, and social aspirations that make any person an actual person. What we really encounter in life is not "humanity" or "noble savages," but, in the apt words of Seyla Benhabib, "concrete others."[33] Our lives are saturated with relations and affections that give us meaning and particularity – ethnicities, sexuality, pieties, political relations, on and on. The discourse of "otherness" rivets attention on the uniqueness of persons rather than abstract modern ideas of "humanity."

Modern ideas about "humanity" are not the only targets of contemporary criticism. More profoundly, the challenge is to a long tradition of thought in the West about the self. The tradition of a reflexive philosophy of consciousness, running from Plato to Søren Kierkegaard, St. Augustine to Paul Tillich, René Descartes to Iris Murdoch, insists that within our self-awareness, the chaos and confusion of human inwardness, is to be found some relation, no matter how tenuous, to the sacred, to the ultimate good, to God. In virtue of our conscious self-relations, each and every human being has unique dignity and worth precisely in their embodied particularity. To love others as self means that I acknowledge in the other the unique human fact of self-relation as a medium of dignity and worth. While fantastically complex, the basic claim of any reflexive philosophy is seemingly undeniable. In all actions, feelings, and moods (acts of thinking or willing, feelings of joy or sorrow, moods of anxiety or confidence) there is, implicitly, an undeniable sense of self at one with and also at odds with itself. Further, there is a recursive nature to human activity: we are able to "act back upon" ourselves, observe ourselves, and to adjust to valuations and information about our acting and living. Without reflexivity, learning would be impossible for us, as would self-criticism and intentional moral change.

These two facts of human life (self-relation and reflexivity) command respect, testify to human worth and dignity. St. Augustine claimed that reflection on consciousness directs us through the self and towards God. He reasoned that we cannot deny the fact that when we think, we ourselves are thinking. The self so understood, he insisted, is found to be restless for another, desiring God. René Descartes, making much the same point about the activity of thinking, denied the longing for God.[34] "I think, therefore I am," he insisted. On this ground, we learn not of our desire for goodness or God, but rather a sure and necessary philosophical foundation for claims to truth. Others focused not on thinking, but willing (Kant, Kierkegaard), feeling (Schleiermacher), concern (Tillich), or valuing (H. Richard Niebuhr, Murdoch). In each case, reflexive thinking aims at critical self-knowledge. Mindful of the wild ways we can be deceived about ourselves, the banner line for these thinkers is the ancient dictum: "Know thyself."

Does reflection on self mean a reduction of the other to self; does it make God into a fact of our consciousness? Christian philosophers have never believed that self-knowledge alone is enough or that it can redeem us from alienation with God. Only God saves us. Yet thinkers from Augustine to Tillich and beyond insist that God reveals Godself and saves us respectful of the complexity of our existence. For a Christian interpretation of the double love command, the clause "as yourself" does not mean that we love others as we naturally care for ourselves. The command does not warrant some kind of extended egoism or benevolent self-interest! Rather, one is to love as one has first been loved by God, a love manifest in creation, in Christ, and in the reign of God. Christian self-love is grounded not in the self but in God. One's being as a Christian is *in* Christ. There is an "otherness" at the very core of any Christian conception of consciousness and the self.

The most ardent critic of reflexive philosophy in the name of the human other was the Jewish philosopher Emmanuel Lévinas.[35] Even more than Martin Buber, Lévinas stresses the heteronomous relation of the other over the self. He argues that depictions of consciousness in Western thought, far from opening the self to the other, trap the self within its acting, feeling, and thinking. Consciousness aspires to what Lévinas calls "totality," that is, an integrated system that subordinates everything to a common principle expressive of the self. Ironically, this drive to "totality" can even be seen in universalizable moral maxims. The command to love others *as* self means that the "other" is totalized within self-conception. The other is simply an object within my self-understanding, something that exists in some odd analogy to myself. Lévinas sought a way beyond totality in and through the encounter with the face of the other. This encounter, marked by the imperative "thou shall not murder me," is definitive of the self. We exist before the infinite, inescapable demand of the other. The other is heteronomous to the self; the other stands in relation of height and lordship over me. Lévinas speaks of this encounter with the other as a virtual Sinai experience. Coming to self-awareness is always awareness of being on trial, accused.

One must admire and commend the moral passion of Lévinas's critique of consciousness. Yet it is not without difficulties. Oddly, Lévinas must present a rather abstract conception of the "other" for his argument to hold. The "other" is simply a "face" void of all historical, social, sexual, religious, and cultural particularity that commands me not to "murder." As soon as one considers concrete, specific persons, that is, human beings in all their maddening complexity, it is doubtful that we would want to say that the other unquestionably commands me. What if the other is actually a violently abusive parent or a sexually abusive priest? Must we simply accept as unquestionable the command of the other? Moreover, the image of the self existing in a relation of obedience and subjugation has rightly been criticized by feminist thinkers. For too long self-determination and self-realization have been denied women precisely through demands to tend to the other.[36] Right self-love is a bulwark against dehumanization on the part of those without power. To answer these questions about the concrete other, Lévinas turns to an idea of justice built on equality and fairness.[37] Yet his idea of justice misses the link to forgiveness we have already found in the command of neighbor love.

It would seem that the double love command, when interpreted through some idea of reflexivity, is open to the charge of "totality," the denial of otherness, by Lévinas and like minded thinkers. Does this criticism stand? Ideas about the "image of God" mean that who one is, the very nature of our selfhood, is constituted in relation to what is other than the self, that is, to God. To love the neighbor as the self requires one, as St. Augustine first noted, to love others *in God*. That kind of love hardly reduces others to pale reflections of ourselves. Furthermore, by insisting on the recognition of the image of God in self as well as other, the double love command guards against a naive obedience to the other. It warrants proper self-love. Not only does the command avoid the charge of "totality," but it also enables us to think about moral relations in a more subtle way than the demand of the other. The discourse of "otherness" signals a proper concern for the problem of "totality" and "proximity." It is hardly obvious that

Christians, or for that matter Jews, should abandon their native moral language, the language of great commands, and adopt the discourse of "otherness."

God and the claim of the other

We have seen that elements of the double love command are intrinsically related to faith in the living God. Love of neighbor articulates at the level of a directive for action beliefs about the *imitatio Dei* basic to Jewish and Christian ethics. The imitation of God as interpreted by Jesus's actions and parables links justice and forgiveness (God is righteous) in a way sorely needed in a world torn asunder by violence. The second portion of the command gives the practical interpretation of loving God.

Read in the direction of how we can and should live, the double love command conjoins beliefs about human dignity (the image of God) with a directive for action in relation even to the enemy (the imitation of God). These two concerns are ethically demanded in an age of globalization and concern for the other. But this also means that the command of neighbor love is essentially related to the love of God. The great commands are interlocking perspectives on the same vision of life and faith. If faith in God fails or ideas about the divine are tyrannous, then the very meaning of the second command becomes unintelligible. Sadly, some ideas about God have fostered intolerance, hatred, oppression, and violence. One need only recall the "German Christians" and their complicity with fascism or the ways in which devout Christians promoted and protected slavery in the United States. This chapter has shown how this is a present possibility even in an ancient text like the *Didache*, the so-called Teaching of the Twelve Apostles. Mindful of these manifold legacies of suffering, it is hardly surprising that so much contemporary Christian theology is seeking new images and models of God: God as triune and relational; God as liberator; God the Mother and Father; God the soul of the world.

The explosion of new ideas about the divine rests upon an insight deeply embedded in strata of biblical faith. Advances in moral understanding and sensibility necessarily exert pressure on ideas about faith and God, even as beliefs about the divine are at heart convictions of ultimate goodness. In a world in which the major religions must contribute to social flourishing and stability rather than fuel ongoing hatred, suspicion and violence, some ideas about the divine are no longer morally plausible. But Jews and Christians have always insisted in their religious thinking on just such a principle of moral plausibility. Hillel believed that Torah is found in a negative version of the Golden Rule. All the rest is commentary. Christ places on par neighbor love with the love of God. No conception or idea of God or any form of piety and worship can rightly be held or practiced if it does not undergird and serve a life reflective of righteousness. The current concern for the other (the demand to escape "totality" and the imperative to meet the challenge of "proximity") is nothing less than an advance in moral sensibility which, in principle, ought to generate revisions in our conceptions of the divine.

How then ought we to think of the God whom we are commanded to love? Piety requires many images and ideas about God better to nourish and challenge the life of faith. Yet our analysis of the double love command has shown that it presents a criterion of moral plausibility that breaks the trap found in the practice of inscription. The God whom one rightly worships is none other than the power that endows each and every living thing with worth and human beings with intrinsic dignity, the image of Godself. The moral meaning of faith in God as creator is that what is other than God, non-divine, fleeting, fragile, and finite, bears immeasurable worth. So radical is this gift of life that God treats God's own enemies as still bearing worth. The God of Christ and Israel seeks to convert and not destroy the enemy; God bestows the sustenance of life, sun and rain, on the just and the unjust (cf. Matthew 5:43–8). The imitation of this God is precisely a life dedicated to respecting and enhancing the integrity of life in all its forms. It is to live amid a world of diversity and otherness, not in vengeance or tyranny or anxiety, but in a realistic gratitude for the wild and rich diversity of life. It is to oppose the destruction and demeaning of existence, not with cycles of violence, but through creative strategies of resistance. In these acts of imitation, faith enacts the image of God.

Love in Time

Christians now living in the time of many worlds shoulder the painful legacy of the wars and violence of the present and last century and an even longer history of conflict, imperialism, and anti-Semitism. We are in the midst of a moral revolution in ideas about God. Yet that revolution might surprisingly be the working out in existence of the full meaning of Jesus's word and deed. For the God of Christian faith requires and empowers one to draw near like the Samaritan and love as Christ loved. The challenge is to live within the vision of life opened by the double love command and its interpretation in the life and teaching of Christ. It is to live beyond the dangerous logic of the way of life and the way of death, the saved and the damned, that runs from the days of the *Didache* to the fanatical terrorism of the present time.

NOTES

1 This chapter was originally given in lecture form as "The End of Time and the Texture of Reality" at the International Conference, "The Beginnings of Christianity," held at the University of Tel Aviv on January 6–8, 1997.
2 On early Christian ethics, see Srvais Pinckaers, *The Sources of Christian Ethics*, translated by Sr. Mary Thomas Noble, PP (Washington, DC: Catholic University of America Press, 1995) and R. E. O. White, *Christian Ethics* (Macon, GA: Mercer University Press, 1994).
3 Two caveats must be noted. First, I am interested in "early Christian ethics" and not the whole field of so-called New Testament ethics. This is important, since in the early church we see the collision of distinctly biblical life with the wider world of Hellenistic and Roman modes of thought. Second, it is impossible to speak of "the" early church as a unified historical phenomenon. One need only compare the *Didache* and its stark contrast between the way of life found in the church and the way of death in the world with the Alexandrian fathers, say Clement, to sense the radically different forms of early Christianity. I do not purport to capture all of early Christian ethics in this inquiry.
4 There are of course counter-examples. See, for instance, Wayne A. Meeks, *The Moral World of the First Christians* (Philadelphia, PA: Westminster Press, 1988) and Christopher Stead, *Philosophy in Christian Antiquity* (Cambridge: Cambridge University Press, 1994).
5 *The Didache* in *Early Christian Fathers*, translated and edited by Cyril C. Richardson, Library of Christian Classics vol. 1 (New York: Macmillan, 1970). All citations will be given in the text by the chapter and paragraph numbers.
6 Abraham J. Malherbe, *Moral Exhortation: A Greco-Roman Sourcebook* (Philadelphia, PA: Westminster Press, 1986), p. 135.
7 Robert Frost, "The Road Not Taken" in *The Britannica Library of Great American Writing* vol. 2, edited by Louis Untermeyer (Chicago, IL: Britannica Press, 1960), pp. 1221–2.
8 Meeks, *The Moral World of the First Christians*, p. 153.
9 In poststructuralist philosophy, dualism identifies the inherent tyranny of certain traditional modes of Western thought or what Jacques Derrida calls "logocentrism." "Meaning," it is argued, is not about a relation between language and "reality;" it is, rather, a function of differences within the sign system and their use in signifying practices. Western discourse cannot articulate the "difference" that is productive of meaning within sign systems. To deconstruct this mechanism of difference and deferral, what Derrida calls *différance*, is to overturn the structuring principle of Western metaphysics and its dream of a final system by isolating the mechanism of meaning creation. On this see Jacques Derrida, *Dissemination*, translated by Barbara Johnson (Chicago, IL: University of Chicago Press, 1981). For a feminist position, see Rosemary Radford Reuther, *Sexism and God-Talk: Toward a Feminist Theology* (Boston, MA: Beacon Press, 1983). Also see William Schweiker, *Mimetic Reflections: A Study in Hermeneutics, Theology and Ethics* (New York: Fordham University Press, 1990).

10 Christian thinkers would conceptualize this point in trinitarian terms, whereas in Jewish thought the focus would presumably be on the many names of God. I cannot explore these matters in this chapter.

11 See Jacques Derrida, *The Margins of Philosophy,* translated by Alan Bass (Chicago, IL: University of Chicago Press, 1982).

12 John Herman Randall, *The Making of the Modern Mind* 50th edn. (New York: Columbia University Press, 1976), p. 39.

13 See *Myths of Mesopotamia: Creation, The Flood, Gilgamesh, and Others*, translated with introduction and notes by Stephanie Dalley (Oxford: Oxford University Press, 1989).

14 See Iris Murdoch, "Metaphysics and Ethics" in *Iris Murdoch and the Search for Human Goodness*, edited by Maria Antonaccio and William Schweiker (Chicago, IL: University of Chicago Press, 1996), p. 250. Also see Maria Antonaccio, *Picturing the Human: The Moral Thought of Iris Murdoch* (Oxford: Oxford University Press, 2000).

15 For a fine discussion of this point, see Laszlo Versényi, *Socratic Humanism* (New Haven, CT: Yale University Press, 1963). Also see Hans-Georg Gadamer, *Der Anfang der Philosophie* (Stuttgart: Philipp Reclaim, 1996).

16 Gregory Vlastos, *Socrates: Ironist and Moral Philosopher* (Ithaca, NY: Cornell University Press, 1991), p. 88. For an attack on the Socratic–Platonic position, see Martha C. Nussbaum, *Love's Knowledge: Essays on Philosophy and Literature* (Oxford: Oxford University Press, 1990).

17 Seneca, Epistle XVI, "On Philosophy, the Guide of Life" in Seneca, *Epistulae Morales I*, Loeb Classical Library (Cambridge, MA: Harvard University Press, 1977), p. 105.

18 Of course, there are many issues, exegetically and in the history of religions, about the relation of "cult" and "prophecy." I cannot enter those debates here. For a general account of the matter, see T. B. Maston, *Biblical Ethics* (Macon, GA: Mercer University Press, 1982).

19 Pierre Hadot, *Philosophy as a Way of Life: Spiritual Exercises from Socrates to Foucault*, edited with introduction by Arnold I. Davidson, translated by Michael Chase (Oxford: Blackwell, 1995), p. 60.

20 One should note the stark contrast with classical Greek and Roman thought, wherein philosophy was usually defined, beginning with Plato's depiction of Socrates, as learning to die. My claim throughout is that Christian philosophy is learning to live in the light of creation and Christ's life and death and resurrection. This makes the affirmation of the integrity of life basic for thought and action.

21 On this see Jürgen Moltmann, *The Coming of God: Christian Eschatology*, translated by Margaret Kohl (Minneapolis, MN: Fortress Press, 1996).

22 See, for instance, James W. McClendon, Jr., *Ethics: Systematic Theology*, vol. 1 (Nashville, TN: Abingdon Press, 1986).

23 Burton L. Mack, *Who Wrote the New Testament: The Making of the Christian Myth* (San Francisco: HarperSanFrancisco, 1996), p. 40.

24 On this see *Christianity in Jewish Terms*, edited by David F. Sandmel (Boulder, CO: Westview Press, 2000).

25 The difference between a negative formulation (Hillel) and a positive one (Jesus) has been much debated. For a discussion see Alan Donagan, *The Theory of Morality* (Chicago, IL: University of Chicago Press, 1977). Some of the following discussion has been published as "And a Second is Like It: Christian Faith and the Claim of the Other" in *Quarterly Review* 20: 3 (2000): 233–47.

26 See Jeffrey Wattles, *The Golden Rule* (Oxford: Oxford University Press, 1996). Also see Hermann Deuser, *Die Zehn Gebote: Kleine Einführung in die theologische Ethik* (Stuttgart: Philipp Reclaim, 2002).

27 Niklas Luhmann has noted that consciousness is always marked by self-reference and hetero-reference, relation to another other. See his *Theories of Distinction: Redescribing the Descriptions of Modernity*, edited with introduction by William Rasch (Stanford, CA: Stanford University Press, 2002).

28 Donald W. Shriver, Jr., *An Ethic for Enemies: Forgiveness in Politics* (Oxford: Oxford University Press, 1995).

29 Menachem Kellner, "Jewish Ethics" in *A Companion to Ethics*, edited by Peter Singer (Oxford: Blackwell, 1991), p. 84.

30 Parallel to Luke, Matthew 5:43–8, amid the Sermon on the Mount, has Christ link perfection and "sonship" to God in heaven with the demand to "love your enemies and pray for those who persecute you."

31 See Hans-Dieter Betz, *Sermon on the Mount* (Minneapolis, MN: Fortress Press, 1995). Also see Jürgen Becker, "Feindesliebe-Nächstenliebe-Bruderliebe. Exegetische Beobachtungen als Anfange an ein ethisches Problemfeld" in *Zietschrift für Evangelische Ethik* (1981): 5–17.

32 See Michael J. Perry, *The Idea of Human Rights: Four Inquiries* (Oxford: Oxford University Press, 1998) and Stephen Toulmin, *Cosmopolis: The Hidden Agenda of Modernity* (New York: Free Press, 1990).

33 Seyla Benhabib, *Situating the Self: Gender, Community and Postmodernism in Contemporary Ethics* (New York: Routledge, 1992).

34 See Augustine, *The City of God*, Book 11, 26 and *On the Trinity*, Book 15, 12.21–2. Also see Descartes, *Meditations on First Philosophy*, translated by Laurence J. LaFleur (New York: Liberal Arts Library, 1951).

35 See Emmanuel Lévinas, *Totality and Infinity: An Essay on Exteriority*, translated by A. Lingis (Pittsburgh, PA: Duquesne University Press, 1969). Also see Martin Buber, *I and Thou* (Edinburgh: T. & T. Clark, 1937) and Paul Ricoeur, *Oneself as Another*, translated by Kathleen Blamey (Chicago, IL: University of Chicago Press, 1992).

36 See Anne Patrick, *Liberating Conscience: Feminist Explorations in Catholic Moral Theology* (New York: Continuum, 1997); Cristina L. H. Traina, *Feminist Ethics and Natural Law: The End of Anathemas* (Washington, DC: Georgetown University Press, 1999); and Darlene Fozard Weaver, *Self-Love and Christian Ethics* (Cambridge: Cambridge University Press, 2002).

37 Emmanuel Lévinas, *Alterity and Transcendence* (New York: Columbia University Press, 1999).

CHAPTER 6

From Toleration to Political Forgiveness

The events are too well known. A mother cradles her raped and murdered child; she cries to heaven for help, for mercy. A bomb rips through a bus station in an act of terrorism and retaliation for injustice. In some town somewhere a protest march breaks into physical conflict because groups are locked in rounds of suspicion and hatred that can no longer be contained. Around the world a central problem of politics confronts us: how can human communities endure in the face of conflict? In the time of many worlds, the level of violent conflict and the horrible legacy of too many forms of suffering strain even the best hopes for peaceful existence. Little wonder, then, that cynicism and despair and a sense of twilight characterize so much political life.[1]

This chapter considers these dilemmas of contemporary politics in terms of the demands of responsibility and the challenge of reconciliation. In the two previous chapters we isolated how a moral space can be constituted in and through the social imaginary. In chapter 4 we found that various pictures of "time" help to found a moral cosmology and can lead to various assessments of the moral claim of others upon us. That inquiry was deepened in chapter 5. We examined a classic Christian text, the *Didache*, and how a specific moral practice, "inscription," aimed at rendering time meaningful, can lead to the drawing of moral boundaries that set one community (the Way of Life) over-against all others (the Way of Death). But through a strong post-critical, explicative reading one can isolate in the text the double love command as a way to thwart the possible viciousness of the moral practice of inscription. This chapter shifts from textual analysis and the examination of moral motivations to matters of responsibility in the face of social density and actual legacies of suffering. The *time* of many worlds is also the time of *legacies*, the memory of endurance of past suffering, and also the hope for a just future.

Interlocking Problems

What is the place of reconciliation in politics? If it were not for the facts all around us, this might seem an odd question. Indeed, for much of Western thought, reconciliation, especially in the form of forgiveness, was outside of politics; it was seen as a supra-political human act best spoken about in religious and moral terms. But in the twentieth century, with all its horror and suffering, things began to change. Theologians, religious thinkers, philosophers, and political theorists started to reconsider the place of forgiveness in politics. War crimes tribunals, the United Nations, commissions on truth and reconciliation in South Africa and elsewhere, even the World Council of Churches, bespeak awareness that past suffering and present conflict must be addressed in new ways.

Years ago, Hannah Arendt pointedly stated a basic insight. Arendt argued that forgiveness, as the ability to begin anew after ruinous human action, is basic to politics. And she even insisted that the "discoverer of the role of forgiveness in the realm of human affairs was Jesus of Nazareth."[2] Arendt understood this discovery in purely philosophical terms and thus without reference to the divine. And, of course, she acknowledged acts of mercy, the sparing of the vanquished, and even the right to commute a death sentence found in other traditions, especially among the ancient Romans. But the biblical message, Arendt noted, is unique in that the power to forgive is a "human power" in which God forgives those who themselves show mercy (cf. the Lord's Prayer). This shows, as we know, the surprising link between responsibility and redemption in the double love command (chapter 5) and the Golden Rule (chapter 9). Of course, Arendt was not the only one to insist on the importance of reconciliation in politics. The great movements of liberation in the twentieth century inspired by Gandhi, Martin Luther King, Jr., and Nelson Mandela, insisted on reconciliation. One must think about political existence differently in light of the realities now confronting societies in the time of many worlds.

When we explore reconciliation in politics it is important to see that it does not designate a single political problem or agenda. One needs to consider reconciliation in terms of moral and political responses to a host of problems ranging from, at one extreme, toleration in pluralistic societies, to, at the other extreme, ways of surmounting cycles of violence born of legacies of hurt and hatred. *Toleration* signals the need to reconcile, but not homogenize, divergent beliefs and values if we are to have sustainable yet pluralistic political communities. It is a response to the fact of moral diversity and multiculturalism that marks the compression of the world. *Political forgiveness*, or what is sometimes called restorative justice, is the path to reconciliation in the full light of the truth about intolerable acts. It is a response to legacies of suffering that attempts to restore political integrity. It is a response to the challenge of proximity. There are, of course, many problems found between the extremes of toleration and response to the intolerable.[3] There are questions of economic justice, debates about the common good, debates about property and international relations. Many problems indeed!

We focus on these interlocking problems (toleration; forgiveness) that represent the extremes on a spectrum of current political challenges. If a nation is unable to navigate responsibly human diversity, as well as surmount patterns of (ethnic, racial, religious, etc.) violence, it will not endure long upon this earth. Intolerance and revenge are responses to human conflict that negate political life; they finally destroy community. This is increasingly the case as we enter more fully the reality of globalized societies. Will the fires of hatred merely increase until they engulf the world? Reconciliation, far from being a supra-political act, is at the heart of politics. Of course, a wholesale toleration of all moral and political beliefs might threaten the coherence and mutual recognition of persons needed to overcome legacies of retribution. Some policies, some actions, some ideas, are simply intolerable, namely, those policies, actions, and ideas which wantonly and intentionally demean and destroy people's lives and, in principle, foreclose the possibility of life beyond cycles of violence. The "intolerable," as a moral and political idea, is definable in part by whatever action, institution, or policy is destructive of the very possibility of political existence and thus the social cooperation human beings need to exist and flourish. If we are to secure stable societies with some measure of tranquility, we must, politically speaking, navigate cultural diversity and foster cultures of toleration, but also overcome cycles of recrimination and thereby confront forms of the intolerable. In an age riddled by moral and cultural diversity and plagued by legacies of suffering and violence, is genuine political existence possible? Put as a maxim, we will argue this: reconciliation without politics is impotent; politics without reconciliation is impossible.

With some sense of the challenge to political life in hand, we can specify in more detail matters of responsibility and reconciliation. These are political problems, that is, problems of how human beings are to distribute social goods and also get along in their social life in spite of conflicts. Of course, political matters are deeply intertwined with economic, legal, and cultural processes and relations. For the sake of this chapter, attention remains on politics. In a similar way, we are considering reconciliation only as a human possibility, a matter of moral and political responsibility. At the horizon of the inquiry will arise theological questions about the source of that human possibility.

Toleration and Responsible Politics

There is of course a long tradition of reflection on tolerance in the West, a tradition bound to the aspirations of democratic politics. As a host of thinkers have noted, commitment to toleration rests on a belief about the nature of human understanding and also the requirements of validating claims. Concerning human understanding, toleration requires the admission of fallibility. No one has an undistorted and certain knowledge of the truth. "For nothing happens in this world which isn't full of folly, performed by fools amongst fools," the great Christian humanist Erasmus has lady Folly say.[4] And given the fallibility and foolishness of human existence, we must admit, Erasmus insists, that we hardly have a clean and clear grasp of the truth. From that admission – so difficult to win from the human heart! – flows a commitment to debate and discussion where all views can be expressed and the force of the better argument secured. Engaging with the beliefs of others is the path of genuine learning and attaining truthful ideas. As John Stuart Mill famously put it:

> However unwilling a person who has a strong opinion may admit the possibility that his opinion may be false, he ought to be moved by the consideration that however true it may be, if it is not fully, frequently, and fearlessly discussed, it will be heard as dead dogma, not a living truth.[5]

The rough and tumble of public debate is a way to curtail the partiality of our opinions, but also to vivify those truths we understand to endure. In this way, humility about the extent of our cognitive powers and a commitment to free and open debate about matters of deepest human concern happily travel together.

One must admit that the religions have been reluctant to make these admissions. Beliefs about divine revelation and the presence of the Holy Spirit in the church have made it difficult to say that Christians might be wrong. Contemporary liberation and feminist theologians rightly insist on the epistemic priority of the poor or women with respect to oppressive systems.[6] But that conviction does not *necessarily* entail the denial of fallibility; it merely means that some perspectives, rooted in unjust and oppressive structures of power, are most likely more systematically distorted than others. Some thinkers, especially within forms of religious fundamentalism found in all the world's traditions, believe that only certain people see the truth and hold this truth completely. We have encountered that belief in the last chapter while exploring the early Christian text called the *Didache* and its practice of identity formation through inscription. But let us be honest: the presumption of infallibility is found in other traditions as well.

Happily, there are strands of the Christian tradition that do admit the fallibility of our grasp of truth. As John Wesley insisted in the "preface" to his published sermons,

> For, how far is love, even with many wrong opinions, to be preferred before truth itself without love! We may die without the knowledge of many truths, and yet be carried into Abraham's bosom. But, if we die without love, what will knowledge avail? Just as much as it avails the devil and his angels.[7]

This is the venerable legacy of Christian humanism represented by thinkers running from Clement of Alexandria, to Erasmus, to Wesley, and to current voices. If people are to navigate the moral diversity of current political existence, a tolerance born of an honest admission of cognitive fallibility seems required. Without this conviction, beliefs harden into battle standards and conflict quickly follows. Intolerance is an attack on politics itself insofar as it disallows the negotiation of conflict in common life. Toleration is a way to respond rightly to others; it seeks to respect and enhance the integrity of common life. Toleration is a form of responsibility in politics at the level of beliefs, values, and ideals.

Toleration as a type of reconciliation, and so responsible politics, does not mean that all beliefs are of equal validity. We are not advocating a version of what some have rightly called "repressive tolerance," in which nothing matters too much and social life is reduced to the lowest common denominator. The moral diversity of multicultural nations need not lead to an easy relativism. Rather, admission of fallibility means that any claim to truth about common life, any belief about how we can and ought to organize our political existence, must be established by open and public debate. From thinkers like J. S. Mill to others such as Jürgen Habermas, claims are validated in the arena of open debate and discussion.[8] And this is a high standard indeed. It means that one cannot flee to authority or special appeals to establish the truth of beliefs. Political claims must make their way in open, public, and uncoerced debate. Put differently, fallibility as an epistemic principle requires liberal democracy as the social condition for establishing valid truth claims, at least claims about political existence. In this way, the least troubling expression of the problem of proximity, that is, moral and cultural diversity, is rendered politically productive rather than destructive in social existence. One needs complex and diverse societies in order to validate political ideas and beliefs. This is so if and only if there is the admission of cognitive fallibility of all participants and the need for the public, intersubjective validation of claims. This does not mean that we are not justified in being certain about some beliefs and values.[9] Most of the time we are justified, and rightly so. An admission of fallibility just means that no matter the degree of our certainty, we can also be wrong and, in any case, always stand in need of learning.[10]

The question then arises: why should groups – ethnic, racial, cultural, religious – adopt a fallibilist stance and consent to the public validation of claims? Is this not simply the imposition of Western democratic ideals on others? Is there not a hidden intolerance in the rhetoric of toleration, namely, that what cannot be tolerated is any belief held with dogmatic certainty? Does the demand for the public validation of claims deny as a viable epistemic possibility belief in a revealed divine truth and thus the task of evangelism, the need to preach conversion? Can religious people – Jews and Christians and Muslims and others – really submit to demands for the public validation of all political claims?[11] Is this not the mistaken agenda of modern philosophy from Descartes through Nietzsche and beyond, wherein radical doubt of all belief eventually leads to skepticism? To be sure, these worries are genuine and well taken. And, in fact, one ought to question any attempt to establish a necessary requirement to adopt fallibilism as a response to cultural and moral diversity. It would be strange to force others to accept toleration!

In the time of many worlds, things are taking a different shape. The question of fallibility is not only an academic one and not just a matter of theories about human knowledge. The sheer fact of global social diversity is placing pressure on all groups to assess their own beliefs. If one is to respond to the current world situation, then particular groups and communities must find within their own resources reasons to qualify claims, at least their political claims, and to enter fully democratic practices. Each community must find within its tradition, symbols, beliefs, and practices the grounds for genuine responsiveness to the other. For what is toleration but responsibility at the level of beliefs and values? More to the point, for Christians and for nations and cultures deeply shaped by the biblical witness, the reason to affirm fallibility is readily grasped. We are finite creatures. That finitude is no detraction from human dignity. Creation, as we have argued repeatedly, is good, but it is also finite and limited. Additionally, human fault, "sin," is too often crouching at the door, driving us to intolerance and intolerable acts. Stated otherwise, Christian theologians have long asserted that things are known according to the mode of the knower.[12] A belief about the limitation and yet worth of human beings is at the root of Christian beliefs about religious perception, experience, and knowledge. Finite creatures can only know through the troubled and joyous structure of finitude. So deep is this conviction within Christian faith and so deep is finitude valued, that one confesses God has been made known in those very structures of existence, that is, in Christ. One can admit human fallibility because God does not shun our condition. After all, as Erasmus finally shows, Christian faith is about the folly of the Cross. Other traditions and communities can and must find reasons for adopting the stance necessary to deal rightly with cultural, cognitive, and moral diversity.

The theme of responsibility and reconciliation must address, at its simplest level, the problem of how to reconcile diverse beliefs and values if we are to sustain viable political communities. This is all the more pressing as multiculturalism becomes a fact of most nations. But what if we shift now to the other problem of proximity, that is, how can groups scarred by legacies of suffering, conflict, and cycles of retribution, abide? The problem is then no longer tolerance, but how to address the intolerable.

Restorative Justice and Responsible Politics

Examples of the intolerable are burned into the very face of the last centuries. Whether we speak of the sad and horrible legacy of racism in the United States, the pain of anti-Semitism and the horror of the Holocaust, the scars of apartheid, survivors of killing fields, victims of sexual violence and rape camps, or children orphaned by terrorist attacks and political repression in the Middle East, the problem of the victim and perpetrator endures. As Donald Shriver has aptly put it, we need an ethic for enemies.[13] This becomes pressing when global forces spread hatred and compel hostile communities to share the same territory. Of course, we know that one option is simply to continue the legacies of recrimination. An eye for an eye, the famous *lex talionis*, might limit disproportionate violent response, as it was intended to do, but can it stop cycles of violence?[14] This is why chapter 9 takes a different strategy in looking at moral madness by turning, perhaps surprisingly, to the story of Cain and Abel. As we will see then, what is required are strategies of restorative justice or, same thing said, responsible forgiveness. This is the most difficult challenge of reconciliation besetting peoples around the world.

One must understand the full extent of this problem. Histories of unjust suffering are etched into cultural or ethnic memories, and, furthermore, they seem to call for a restoration of moral order in debt to those who have suffered. The memories of suffering require that one disambiguate the world. Yet some of the strategies for doing so explored in this book are no longer viable (apocalyptic discourse; dualistic visions; moral madness). Acts of recrimination are not necessarily irrational outbursts of violence. They can also be a response to the demand felt by survivors that justice be done and so the moral structure of viable human existence be honored and restored. Failure to grasp the depth of cycles of recrimination shows an inability or an unwillingness to understand the full scope of what is at stake. Restorative justice is the human, political act of reconciling victims and perpetrators aimed at reclaiming political integrity. It seeks to address and not sidestep the moral demands involved.

Social ethicists, like Shriver, and also psychologists note that forgiveness is a complex and long process. Demands of truthfulness are required even as the basic claims of social justice and the common good must be sustained. This is why truth and reconciliation commissions are found in many nations. Some might think it odd that restorative justice means that "forgiveness" comes with a moral price tag rather than being utterly gratuitous, sheer gift. But this must be the case, at least in the domain of politics. It makes perfectly good sense to speak of absolute forgiveness religiously, say, God's act of forgiveness in Christ's life, death, and resurrection. But it is not clear that this should hold in political existence.

There are longstanding reasons to back this distinction and yet connection between political and religious forgiveness. Theologically, one must avoid what Dietrich Bonhoeffer called "cheap grace." Even God's grace exacts a cost, namely, the demand to manifest the love of God and so a radical transformation of life and action, the new creation. Restorative justice cannot mean the healing of wounds and placating the memory of suffering without an enforceable demand for fundamental political change. Forgiveness does not leave the world as it is. Restorative justice is precisely – or must be – about respecting and enhancing a moral order of existence as the necessary precondition for viable political existence. That was the force of Hannah Arendt's insight that forgiveness is linked to the unique human power of natality, of forging new beginnings. Genuine restorative justice begins the political world anew; it comes with a specific moral demand to respect and enhance the integrity of political life.

It is important to avoid a naive and even dangerous liberality of acceptance that tries to sustain the common good while forgetting the demands of justice. In classical Protestant thought the way to avoid cheap political grace was formulated as the idea of the "two realms" or "two kingdoms." As Martin Luther might put it in his famous treatise "On Secular Authority the Extent to Which it Should be Obeyed," one must not attempt to rule the political order by love even as the church should be a realm of love and not coercive force. Of course, the history of the effects of this distinction is highly ambiguous.[15] It has backed the virtual removal of any idea of forgiveness from politics, as noted before. Likewise, the two kingdoms doctrine too often, especially in the twentieth century, fostered forms of quietism on the part of Christians, thereby leaving political regimes free from moral and religious criticism. The realities of our day require us to move beyond these old forms of relating forgiveness and political existence.[16]

However, the insight of the classical Protestant doctrine should not be forgotten in a realistic ethics. The political order must forever sustain the demands of justice; this is true even of political forgiveness. Not only is reconciliation costly, but also its specific cost is that it must further the claims of justice. And that is the point of speaking of restorative justice as responsible forgiveness. It is in this light that two strategies of restorative justice can be noted.

One strategy addresses the question of reparations for legacies of suffering, say the evil of hundreds of years of slavery and the trade in human beings. As became clear at the International Conference on Racism in the summer of 2001, posing the question of reparations in the international arena is exceedingly difficult. Not only did some nations, like the US and Israel, withdraw from the conference for cloudy reasons, but other nations were far more willing to confess guilt than to undertake real steps to meet this demand of restorative justice. Of course, there are exceedingly complex questions involved in the matter of reparations. Who should pay whom? How much? What is the scope and depth of guilt in terms of present generations? What is enough reparation? These questions, and many more, would necessarily have to be addressed. Without trying to enter the thicket of these issues, the point to be made is that the question of reparations can and must be raised insofar as genuine restorative justice must be just that: restorative and just. Only in this way is the political equivalent of "cheap grace" avoided, namely, the willingness of people to "confess" past wrongs while continuing to live within a political, economic, and social structure that perpetuates injustice.

Another strategy of restorative justice in the face of human suffering is beliefs about justified war, the so-called "Just War" tradition. This mode of thought is found in many religious traditions, including Christianity. It seeks to determine when, if at all, it is justifiable to use lethal violence against an aggressor for the defense of the innocent and also to restore peace.[17] This tradition of reflection is exceedingly complex, specifying criteria for the justice of entering conflict (*jus ad bellum*) and also for the just conduct of war (*jus in bello*). It is not possible here to enter into a discussion of these criteria, the varieties of their interpretations, or even a comparison with pacificism. While sharing with pacificism a presumption against violence, the Just War tradition argues that in certain specific and limited cases it is justifiable, it is morally right and required, to counter an aggressor to preserve the life of a community and to reestablish peace. Christians who advocate Just War thinking admit that an individual must turn the other cheek; they must be willing to suffer wrong rather than to do wrong. But in a violent world, the innocent must not be left as prey before forces of viciousness. As Luther once famously observed, "If the lion lies down with the lamb, the lamb must be replaced frequently."[18]

In a way similar to claims about reparations, admitting the possibility of a justifiable war to restore peace and protect the innocent underscores the costliness of political responsibility. The time of many worlds is not the time of the Kingdom of God where peace rules; in our world the lion and lamb cannot easily rest together. It is the time when people of good will must let justice flow down like waters (Amos 5:24). Tragically, this may require profound sacrifices in order to sustain social tranquility and to safeguard the innocent. This discourse of Just War, I suggest, must be seen as a strategy for considering the demands and possibility of responsible politics and, more specifically, restorative justice. This means that justified lethal conflict can never be about retribution or revenge; it must restore right conditions of social life.

If we have at least clarified the idea of restorative justice and how, in specific situations, it might lead to matters of reparation or even the possibility of justifiable warfare, the question becomes the warrant for a commitment to restorative justice. For Christians, as Paul Ramsey saw, this is actually a matter deeply linked to the second great command, the command of neighbor love, and also the Golden Rule.[19] Of course, some might find it odd that love of neighbor could lead to the demand for reparations or even justified war! Often it is thought that "Christian love," radical *agape*, is freely bestowed acceptance of others without demand or cost. But that is, again, simply "cheap grace." Previous chapters showed that the connection between creation and new creation is best understood not in terms of an abstract imperative but as commentary on God's action. And we have seen that the divine, while upholding justice, does not withdraw human worth or the conditions necessary to participate anew in the ongoing task of world-creation. This is why, in terms used earlier in this book, God's righteousness is a creation event. In other words, if God's action is the clue to the meaning of responsibility, and, for Christians, this is exemplified in the life and actions of Christ, then the command to love and the Golden Rule are anything but a blanket acceptance of all wrongs. It is, rather, a way to restore the world in and through meeting threats to a just and peaceful social order. In that light, a proper understanding of the commands shows that they are fit for the political demands facing us.

Consider the love of neighbor. The second great command ("love your neighbor as yourself") is meant to structure memory and thereby free persons from the domination of their hearts and imaginations by legacies of hatred and suffering. Jesus's interpretation of the commandment of neighbor love is given parabolic and also imperative forms. Immediately after uttering the love command and in response to a question about how to inherit eternal life, Jesus is asked: "Who is my neighbor?" (Luke 10:25–8). He answers with the parable of the Good Samaritan (Luke 10:29–37). As we know from earlier chapters, in that parable the question of the "neighbor" is reversed. The act of the Samaritan is what constitutes him as a neighbor. Cultural and religious memory is no longer the defining structure of religious and moral identity. This radical insight rests upon Jewish beliefs about the relation between righteous action and the human being as the image of God. "Neighbor" is defined not by likeness grounded in community or memory, but by compassion. The Samaritan disambiguates a moral situation – can a Samaritan and Jew relate? – by enacting a wider moral order reaching from shared humanity to beliefs about God. Jesus's parable, surprisingly and radically, pictures the Samaritan as imitating the divine, a God who loves when despised and sustains the reach of human worth. Even in situations of conflict – such as the human rebellion against God – the "enemy" is not excluded from the domain of worth.

The love command shatters any constriction on who is the neighbor, any limitation of compassion, respect, and justice to members of one's own clan, race, gender, community, or religion. Recall too that Matthew 5:43–8, amid the Sermon on the Mount, has Christ link perfection and "sonship" to God in heaven with the demand to "love your enemies and pray for those who persecute you." Just as in the parable, what is meant by "neighbor" is pushed beyond any simple constriction of concern. It is explained with respect to the actual, concrete problem of how to live with others beyond cycles of violence and conflict.[20]

The command should be interpreted in the direction of the Good Samaritan and the love of Christ. This is vitally important in the time of many worlds facing the problem of proximity. In order to have a viable future, societies riddled by the reality of conflict and hatred must find resources for breaking seemingly unending revenge and violence. Even in cases of justifiable warfare, one must still develop ways beyond retribution. Neighbor love breaks the memory of suffering, of injustice done, as the sole determination of moral identity and order. It founds the world anew by respecting and enhancing the integrity of life. And this is costly. Restorative justice is an extreme political act; it requires courage, vigilance in truth, and a profound trust in the possibility of reenacting the bonds of communal existence. It redefines the lives of those who exercise this unique human possibility; it constitutes one's life as a neighbor. No one ever imagined that these actions were easy, without cost and demands.

The love command institutes forgiveness rather than cycles of retribution as the necessary condition for the continuation of human life together. It means that while politics deals with human conflict, it is not defined by conflict. The origin of political existence is not to be found in a war of each against each, as Thomas Hobbes and some ancient myths contend (cf. chapter 2). This is a reason why civil rights leaders like Martin Luther King, Jr. looked to the love command even in the midst of the struggle for civil rights. Without some notion of forgiveness conjoined to the demands of justice, it is hard to imagine how societies composed of diverse peoples and scarred by suffering will long endure. But this is precisely what the command does: it links justice and forgiveness, forging a life imitative of God's good action. It is, politically speaking, about restorative justice as a form of reconciliation in politics.

Forms of Reconciliation in Politics

The extremes on a scale of political problems found in the present global situation confront us with the need for reconciliation as basic to political existence. Toleration is the responsible reconciliation of divergent beliefs and values required for social tranquility. It entails an acknowledgment of fallibility on the part of everyone, even as it demands some form of democratic polity and open public debate for validating political claims. Restorative justice is responsible forgiveness needed to sustain the demands for justice to protect the innocent, promote the common good, and to overcome legacies of suffering. As the various truth and reconciliation commissions around the world, and especially in the new South Africa, have tried to show, restorative justice comes with a demand for truth, namely, the public statement and recognition of the violence and injustice done. Toleration makes ongoing political existence possible by suspending the assumption of the *a priori* validity of any accepted tradition of belief; restorative justice founds anew the social world on grounds other than the memory of suffering and cycles of violence. This is why toleration and restorative justice are responses to the ends of a scale of current political problems. As forms of responsibility, these human actions make possible and insure the continuance of political existence by means of the negotiation of human social life in the face of conflict.

One must admit of course that there is nothing essential to political existence that necessitates toleration or restorative justice. Again, as Hannah Arendt noted, there are analogies to forgiveness found in non-biblical forms of political thought. And it is certainly the case that toleration has not been an enduring virtue of the religions or most political institutions. Given a frank realism about that fact, we have tried to uncover some sustaining convictions in Christian faith that warrant the formation of a culture of toleration and restorative justice. Parallel commitments could be found in other traditions.[21]

We now confront a question that moves us beyond the argument of Arendt and other political philosophers. It forces upon us once again the question of moral perspective in an age of expanding consciousness about the world. If forms of reconciliation, ranging from toleration to restorative justice, are needed to sustain our political existence, can those forms of reconciliation really be understood and practiced without some religious commitment or outlook? Stated otherwise, is the form of moral consciousness needed for an age of globalized political existence necessarily religious in depth and reach? There are of course many ways to answer this question, depending on how one defines "religious" and "political." It is also the case that this question poses massive legal and political issues, especially for nations that rightly insist on a separation of church and state. I do not want to enter these thorny issues at this time. And, in fact, one does not need to do so. The question asked is about the religious–moral outlook that informs political thinking rather than specific questions in law, church, and state. As the last step in this inquiry, we turn to address the question of background convictions needed to sustain responsibility in politics.

Background Convictions

The possibilities of toleration and restorative justice in political life rest on the very same conviction. What is that conviction? It is the ardent belief that human beings have some worth, some claim to respect and enhancement, not reducible to the acceptability of their opinions or the rightness of their actions or their place within ethnic or cultural memory. Toleration and forgiveness rely upon the recognition of the worth of human life that sustains epistemic capacities, historical memories, and actual conduct. In other words, commitments to human worth, and so the warrant for human rights and the demands of justice, require a construal of the world in which the source of goodness is not reducible to our capacities, cultural memories, or the products of human cultural labor and power. It requires a trans-human source of worth that exceeds the drive of overhumanization.

Of course, it is the case that a particular person or group can advocate horribly anti-human ideas; they can demean and destroy human life. Communities might tell racist or nationalistic or exclusive narratives of their supremacy. Yet if a human being's moral worth were in fact dependent on the veracity of her or his opinion, then those in error could rightly be compelled to accept some defined doctrine. If a person's moral value were in fact dependent on conduct – say, on what she or he produced – or even the moral rectitude of action, then the poor no less than the wrongdoer could make no claim to justice. If the meaning of those who suffered negates the worth of those living or even the unborn, then the very future of memory itself is endangered. Toleration and restorative justice as political actions are understandable if and only if human beings have some non-instrumental value, if persons are in some important sense of the term ends in themselves. Responsible politics requires beliefs about intrinsic worth. That idea, I submit, merely expresses a wider and more encompassing construal of reality, a construal in which what makes a claim to moral and political recognition is not reducible to human power, purposes, or projects.

Moral worth is not abstract equality. The Good Samaritan did not respond to some "abstract other" or to "rational freedom." He acted on the claim of responsibility uttered in the very life of a specific, suffering person. He answered the call of conscience. An ethics for the time of many worlds must insist on the dignity of individuals in all of their oddity, fallibility, and specificity. This further means that moral worth is not reducible to political processes. Human worth cannot be only an endowment of the political order, otherwise it would cease to be intrinsic and become instrumental. This follows, since, as the navigation of human conflict, the political order is defined precisely by human acts of thinking and acting of worth to the community. If the twentieth century taught us anything, it is that the wholesale politicization of life leads all too easily to death camps, ethnic cleansing, calculated terrorism, and the banalization of life. When political communities are believed to be the sole source of human worth, persons tend to suffer. An ardent conviction about the irreducible worth of the individual disrupts tyranny. This is also the deeper insight of the classical Protestant claim that the "earthly realm" is of penultimate importance. Ultimate worth is not the product of the "earthly kingdom," the reign of overhumanization. Insisting on the reality of human worth as not reducible to human power or project is not, I judge, some imposition of Western ideas. As Iris Murdoch has rightly noted, "our sort of democracy cannot at present live everywhere (and we cannot know how or whether it will survive into the more than ever unpredictable future) but humane ideas and enlightened axioms and conceptions of human rights can."[22] The moral challenge of the present age and also the expansion of consciousness is precisely to let these humane ideas come alive in political existence everywhere.

The two forms of reconciliation we have explored are basic to political existence and yet are not grounded in political activity. Despite what some may think, the principles of toleration and restorative justice are not just political; they are, in fact, religious and metaphysical in depth and reach.[23] Insofar as we recognize the claim to respect others in acts of toleration aimed at democratic existence and imagine the possibility, no matter how weak or difficult, of actual forgiveness, then convictions other than political ones are in play. In this respect, references to Christian beliefs about human worth – our lives as finite creatures endowed with value – and love of neighbor were meant not simply to show the contribution of Christian thought to political existence. They were meant to suggest that belief in the non-reducible worth of human beings is itself religious in nature. Better put, a conviction about the irreducible worth of human beings needed to sustain toleration and restorative justice articulates the moral meaning of distinctly religious ideas. We ignore those religious meanings at great peril. If we do not continually sustain belief in the dignity of human life by fostering democratic cultures of toleration and patterns of restorative justice, then that belief will surely wither and with it much of the capacity to escape unending conflict.

Notice the argument being made about politics. Specific political activities – toleration in democratic practices and acts of restorative justice – express a sustaining belief, a background conviction, about the non-instrumental worth of human beings. The source of human worth is often, in fact usually, expressed in religious terms: the human being as the image of God for Christians and Jews; universal compassion for all who suffer in Buddhism; the will of Allah in Islam; and so on. The expression of that belief is not presented in confessional, articulate form, and thus as religious doctrine, but in actual political action. The political order is the indirect, practical expression of wider and sustaining religious and moral convictions. Political life always shows, for good or ill, the operative convictions of a people. Insofar as toleration and restorative justice seem essential for viable political existence in the age of globalization, then we must admit and seek to sustain a belief in the irreducible worth of human beings. Making sense of that background belief is the contribution of religious thinking to political reconciliation. The work of reconciliation in politics is finally and ultimately about a commitment to respect and enhance the integrity of life. It is about true political responsibility.

Concluding Reversal

These reflections on reconciliation and politics have shown the need in the age of globalization to address the challenge of proximity. Meeting that challenge requires that one address a host of problems between the extremes of how to reconcile divergent beliefs in a peaceable manner and also how to overcome legacies of suffering and retribution. Exploring the questions of toleration and restorative justice, we have seen how they require fallibilism, democratic practices, the hard work of just forgiveness, and also a background conviction about the non-instrumental worth of human beings not limited to cultural memories of suffering and violence. Seen in this light, reconciliation is basic to political existence in our time. This does not determine what institutions should make up a nation's life. That is a question of policy. We have been exploring basic ideas and practices. Yet certain requirements have been isolated about the institutional forms a nation's political life should take. Insofar as reconciliation is basic to the continued viability of political existence, then we can, may, and must foster convictions about respecting and enhancing the integrity of life. Only in this way can a people successfully navigate the political task of how to enable persons to live together despite conflict.

In concluding, we should forestall a grave misunderstanding, and, interestingly, reverse the flow of the argument. By arguing that reconciliation in politics enacts background beliefs about human worth that are deeply religious, one might be taken to mean that the religions themselves, and in this case Christian communities, are and have been and will be unambiguous champions of human value and genuine reconciliation. Such a claim would be gravely mistaken. The religions have all too often fostered intolerance, endorsed cycles of revenge, and warranted dehumanizing acts ranging from slavery to infanticide and sexism. Remember South Africa. The story of that nation, it seems, is in part the story of the terrible ambiguity of Christianity on precisely the matter of human worth. Some Christians died to sustain the evils of apartheid; others struggled for freedom and human dignity.[24]

The force of this argument is thereby clear. By isolating the challenges of proximity and the background belief in human worth needed to sustain forms of reconciliation, we see how the present world situation and basic political problems are placing pressure on the religious for their own reconciliation. We need an expansion of religious consciousness. Once we see our own faith traditions in the context of global realities and the terrible sufferings of persons, can we any longer live as if the cry of human dignity should remain unheard? Is it not time to make our religious traditions responsible to their own best insights? In this light, we ought to look for the "Good Samaritans" found in other people's religions – the exemplars of humility, forgiveness, and vigilance of commitment to the integrity of life – to expose to us the possibilities of our own traditions. In this way, interreligious dialogue becomes the crucial venue of reflexivity and public debate needed for the reformation of the traditions and the vitalizing of political existence. Put simply, not only do the religions contribute to political existence, but also the political challenges of our day demand truthfulness of conviction. As much as reconciliation cannot be seen a supra-political, so too the religions must acknowledge the political expression of their sustaining beliefs. As political realities, it is time for the religions to become cultures of toleration and communities of restorative justice.

NOTES

1 This chapter was originally given as a lecture titled "Responsibility and Reconciliation: Toleration and the Travail of Forgiveness in Political Existence" in April 2000 for the Conference "The Foundation of Society" sponsored by the Center of Theological Inquiry (Princeton, NJ) and the University of the Western Cape, South Africa.

2 Hannah Arendt, *The Human Condition* (Chicago, IL: University of Chicago Press, 1968), p. 238. Also see Jeffrie G. Murphy and Jean Hampton, *Forgiveness and Mercy* (Cambridge: Cambridge University Press, 1988) and *Doing Justice to Mercy*, edited by Mathew Boulton, Kevin Jung, and Jonathan Rothchild (Notre Dame, IN: University of Notre Dame Press, forthcoming).

3 I am mindful that there are thorny issues here about how to define what is intolerable and from what perspective. For present purposes, these formal claims must suffice. For a helpful discussion, see *Die religiosen Wurzeln der Toleranz*, edited by Christoph Schwöbel und Dorothee von Tippelskirch (Freiburg: Herder, 2002).

4 Erasmus, *In Praise of Folly*, translated by Betty Radice (London: Penguin Books, 1971), p. 99.

5 John Stuart Mill, *On Liberty and Other Essays*, edited with introduction by John Gray (Oxford: Oxford University Press, 1991), p. 40.

6 The literature on this topic is extensive. See, for example, Paulo Freire, *The Pedagogy of the Oppressed* (New York: Continuum, 1970) and Beverly Wildung Harrison, *Making the Connections: Essays in Feminist Social Ethics* (Boston, MA: Beacon Press, 1985).

7 John Wesley, *Sermons on Several Occasions* (London: Epworth Press, 1975), p. vii.

8 See John Stuart Mill, *On Liberty*, edited by E. Rapaport (Indianapolis, IN: Hackett, 1978) and Jürgen Habermas, *Postmetaphysical Thinking: Philosophical Essays*, translated by W. M. Hohengarten (Cambridge, MA: MIT Press, 1992).

9 It is important to note that I am speaking in the chapter about distinctly political claims. It is another thing to ask how matters of religious faith are validated. It would be odd to demand that Christian convictions about Christ as savior be validated only and exclusively by appeal to public debate! And this is the case because questions of validation are related to those about the meaning of a claim, say that Jesus is the Christ, wherein some meaning claims are always specific to a community and its life. I cannot explore the question of the validation of faith claims.

10 Unlike the liberal irony that Richard Rorty advocates, the position here is more fully humanistic, in the sense that the admission of fallibility is crucial to the process of self and communal cultivation, to "culture," in a narrow sense, or education. Rorty's claims about irony are not linked to a claim about our continual need to learn; they are a way of avoiding strong beliefs that could lead to conflict. On the humanist argument, see chapter 10.

11 For a rejection of the demand to meet public criteria, see Stanley Hauerwas, *Christian Existence Today: Essays on Church, World, and Living In Between* (Durham, NC: Labyrinth Press, 1988). For an account of this demand for validity, see Franklin I. Gamwell, *The Meaning of Religious Freedom: Modern Politics and the Democratic Resolution* (Albany: State University of New York Press, 1995).

12 The classical statement is given by Thomas Aquinas in *Summa Theologiae*, Ia qq. 75–87. Other examples could be easily found, however.

13 Donald W. Shriver, Jr., *An Ethic for Enemies: Forgiveness in Politics* (Oxford: Oxford University Press, 1995). On the problem of the enemy and reconciliation, see also *Politik der Versöhnung*, edited by Gerhard Beestermöller und Hans-Richard Reuter (Stuttgart: W. Kohlhammer, 2002).

14 There is of course the popular saying, attributed to Gandhi, that "an eye for an eye leaves us all blind." To be sure, that is a human possibility, but on my understanding the *lex talionis* originally was meant to stop the cycle of revenge before it destroyed everyone.

15 See *Martin Luther: Selections from His Writings*, edited with introduction by John Dillenberger (Garden City, NY: Anchor Books, 1961) and also Dietz Lange, *Ethik in evangelisher Perspektive* (Göttingen: Vanderhoeck and Ruprecht, 1992).

16 One can trace some of this ambiguity with respect to theological responses to fascism in Germany. On this see Jack Forstman, *Christian Faith in Dark Times: Theological Conflicts in the Shadow of Hitler* (Louisville, KY: Westminster/John Knox Press, 1992).

17 The literature on "Just War" is of course massive. For representative works see Paul Ramsey, *The Just War: Force and Political Responsibility* (New York: Charles Scribner's Sons, 1968); US Catholic Bishops, *The Challenge of Peace: God's Promise and Our Response* (Washington, DC: US Catholic Conference, 1983); Jean Bethke Elshtain, *Women and War* (New York: Basic Books, 1987); and especially Richard B. Miller, *Interpretations of Conflict: Ethics, Pacificism, and the Just-War Tradition* (Chicago, IL: University of Chicago Press, 1991).

18 I owe this citation to Jean Bethke Elshtain, as well as many conversations about matters moral and political. See her *Real Politics: At The Center of Everyday Life* (Baltimore, MD: Johns Hopkins University Press, 1997).

19 See Ramsey, *The Just War* and also *The Essential Paul Ramsey: A Collection*, edited by William Werpehowski and Stephen D. Crocco (New Haven, CT: Yale University Press, 1994).

20 See Hans-Dieter Betz, *Sermon on the Mount* (Minneapolis, MN: Fortress Press, 1995).

21 For a helpful consideration of this point within various religious traditions, see Darrell J. Fasching and Dell Dechant, *Comparative Religious Ethics: A Narrative Approach* (Oxford: Blackwell, 2001).

22 Iris Murdoch, *Metaphysics as a Guide to Morals* (London: Penguin Press/Allen Lane, 1992), pp. 364–5.

23 For the claim that principles of justice are just political and not metaphysical, see John Rawls, *Political Liberalism* (New York: Columbia University Press, 1993).

24 See *The Kairos Document, Challenge to the Church: A Theologiccal Comment on the Political Crisis in South Africa*, foreword by John W. deGruchy (Grand Rapids, MI: Eerdmans, 1986).

PART III

Imagination and Conscience

CHAPTER 7

Sacred Texts and the Social Imaginary

The previous parts of this book ranged through a wide array of topics besetting people and ethical reflection in the time of many worlds. Most generally, the chapters of Part I explored the place of responsibility within the spread of global dynamics, the reality of moral and cultural diversity, and the saturation of human desires by commercial images in ways that foster not just human creativity but also greed. In many respects, those chapters explore something about the political, cultural, moral, and economic "worlds" that help to make up the current situation. In terms of moral theory, we examined the source and scope of value. Part II of the book shifted attention to consider most broadly the "time" of many worlds. The tactic was to show how beliefs about time are part and parcel of a moral outlook and even bear on how people believe they should relate to others, even their enemies. In the face of the reality of conflict and legacies of hatred and suffering, we tried to isolate within those inquiries beliefs about neighbor love, toleration, and political forgiveness as responses to the travail of social existence. Again, in terms of moral theory, our main concern was with norms for responsible action. Parts I and II made the connection between creation and new creation within a Christian and also broadly naturalistic and humanistic ethics.

Throughout those chapters the theme of imagination and its relation to moral responsibility was by no means lacking. Yet that theme did not receive explicit attention. In Part III the focus is on imagination and conscience within the responsible life. Many of the themes explored before will return: various pictures of the world, claims about human transcendence, how we can and must respond to cycles of violence, and the demand for theological humanism. But these themes are now explored with more attention to the wild and confusing role that imagination and conscience play in our lives. To begin with, we turn to the place of scripture and the imagination within the Christian tradition and also Western culture and even global dynamics. This is important, since scripture is basic to the Christian moral vision and to the formation of conscience.

Scripture and the Imaginary

The world is electrified by the imagination. Images scurry around the planet thanks to the global media system.[1] There is the birth of new religions with new myths. Displaced peoples weave together highly textured identities by imaginatively mixing old practices with novel meanings. Theologians "reimagine" God in light of distinctive legacies of belief, experience, and community. We see repeated again and again the images of horrific events: an airliner exploding into the side of the World Trade Center; bombs dropped in wartime; starving children in a land ravaged by drought and war. As Arjun Appadurai observes, "people throughout the world see their lives through the prisms of the possible lives offered by mass media in all their forms. That is, fantasy is now a social practice; it enters, in a host of ways, into the fabrication of social lives for many people in many societies."[2] The global media system circulates an infinity of images of possible worlds and lives. This fact poses with new force an enduring moral challenge: given the explosion of the global imaginary, persons and communities must assess the images, symbols, and narratives that saturate consciousness and promote ideas about how to live. The work of ethics, in part, is to test and challenge the images that claim to disclose reality to us.

Mindful of this challenge, theologians and philosophers nowadays simply have to consider the meaning and truth of religious symbols, narratives, and beliefs as these circulate within and through the global media and culture. Of course, symbols and narratives have always played a role in cultural existence. Peasants in "Palestine" listened to Jesus portray the reign of God as a mustard seed and thus imagined a new world far from their poverty and hurt, and the ruthless justice of Rome (Matthew 13:31–2). They imagined the triumph of one power structure (God's reign) over another (Imperial Rome).[3] Within the *Pax Romana* life was defined by status and role; within the reign of God it might be possible to overcome the difference of Jew and Gentile, male and female, slave and free (Galatians 3:18). The imagination was in many ways limited by political power and recalcitrant dimensions of existence. Not so today. The media circulate a vast array of images, including religious ones, that overturn social and political boundaries by saturating human desires and fueling perceptions and possibilities for life.

Amid cultural flows, the Bible has become an inexhaustible text of possible lives. The Bible goads the unrelenting work of interpreting the meaning and purpose of life and the world. One can even specify the place of scripture in the work of culture more boldly. The Bible provides for the West a space in history. Burton Mack writes:

> A vague collection of the biblical story seems to be in everyone's mind, a story that begins at the creation of the world with Adam and Eve in the garden, that courses through the Bible and then the history of Western civilization to flow into the fulfillment of its promise in America with a culmination in the future consequence for all the people of the world.[4]

Mack's reading of the Bible as underwriting the American dream is extravagant, especially in a postcolonial age that witnesses liberating and destructive readings of these texts in diverse cultures. One must not overestimate the force of the Bible on Western and other societies. Granting that cautionary note, it is still true that in societies shaped by Judaism and Christianity the biblical texts are basic to a worldview. Remove these texts from cultural memory, and the shape of present Western societies would be decisively changed. That removal might, of course, be the real social experiment currently underway in the West. There is certainly a banishment of religious sources in ethical reflection. But in times of national tragedy and suffering one sees how the "removal" simply cannot work.

This chapter provides a parallel discussion to the account of globalization found in chapters 1 and 2. The difference is that in this chapter we are interested not so much in social and cultural dynamics, as with the ways in which lives are "textured," rendered meaningful, with respect to the work of the imaginary. We do so attentive to sacred texts (for example, the Bible) that are increasingly globalized through the media. The argument moves between two poles of reflection: (1) a textual pole concerned with how scripture is pictured; (2) a normative pole of inquiry with respect to the moral life. In the next section we can isolate widely shared concerns vis-à-vis the place of imagination in the moral life. Following that, the poles of reflection are brought together in relation to dominant strands of contemporary ethics – what I call narrative and encounter ethics. These ethical outlooks risk reducing scripture to one form, to "narrative" or "encounter," consistent with a particular normative outlook. Their insight is to insist that an "image" of scripture must display the most basic feature of the moral life.

The problem of "form" is too little explored in contemporary ethics, although I have already engaged modern ethical formalism in chapter 4. David Tracy reminds us that the strategy of seeking one "form" to assert the continuity of reason and reality is the essential trait of "modern" thought. Modern scientific rationality, for instance, was taken as the sole valid form of thought insofar as it sought to demonstrate a continuity of mind and reality through the laws of nature. Other forms of thought, say in the human sciences, were discredited as ways of attaining truth. The modern rationality continuum is no longer obvious, even within the sciences. Relatedly, James M. Gustafson rightly rejects one dominant "biblical ethic" and insists on acknowledging the varieties of moral discourse in scripture (e.g., prophetic, narrative, ethical).[5] Attending to a variety of uses as well as avoiding a reduction in "form" is basic to pluralistic accounts of scripture. This book proposes a pluralistic, post-critical position as well. The concern is not only with the Bible as a classic, as Tracy puts it, and its multiple uses in ethics, as Gustafson stresses. Granting those claims, we must focus in our time on human beings as travelers between "worlds," real and imaginary, who face the demand to live truthfully and responsibly. The argument presented here pictures the Bible embedded in pre-textual social and historical conditions (e.g., ancient patriarchal, economic, social systems; say, the Temple State) and yet (partially) free from those conditions when read in light of the demands of present life. This image of scripture is consistent with the explicative or mimetic hermeneutic developed throughout this book (cf. introduction).

The closest historical analogy for the picture of scripture outlined in the following pages is, surprisingly enough, ancient conceptions of allegory. Recall that for allegory any "text" has multiple levels of meaning (literal, moral, spiritual) that the reader traverses and in doing so forms her or his own soul. There was no need to reduce the text to one conceptual or linguistic form (narrative; command), but, rather, to envision it as interlocking meanings. Reading the text was a journey through dimensions of meaning in order to educate the soul; it was a movement through linguistic "worlds." The problem with allegory, as Protestant reformers like Luther and Calvin correctly noted, was that the text was supposed to point (figuratively) to great truths, and, therefore, the hermeneutic provided little check on the free play of interpretation aimed at reaching those truths. In practice the allegorical method too easily escaped the control of the rule of faith. But this is just the point in the time of many worlds. The Bible is also part of the explosion of the social imaginary around the planet! The imaginary is a free play of images in which persons and communities fashion their world and lives. Texts, images, symbols, narratives swept up into the global cultural flow, are beyond the control of any community's rule of faith or canon. The problems of allegory are as important for theological ethics as its attempt to provide an education of the "soul."[6]

Obviously, we cannot adopt classic allegorical theory without revision. Classical allegory entailed a metaphysical claim about reality. As John Herman Randall, Jr. once noted, for the ancients:

> The world was a great allegory, whose essential secret was its meaning, not its operation or its causes; it was a hierarchical order, extending from the lowest to highest, from stones and trees through man to the choirs upon choirs of angels,

> just as society ranged from the serf through lord and king to pope; and it was inspired throughout by the desire to fulfill its divine purpose.[7]

We do not live in any clear way in a many-storied universe where everything is (ontologically) symbolic of another level of reality. It is also hard to imagine a clearcut rationality continuum where mind is connected to "reality" through graded symbolic forms. The increasing reflexivity of our lives and our worlds means that every act of understanding is known and observed as partial, betraying some perspective, and those never capturing the "whole" of reality. And given this, our lives are more a matter of moving between "worlds" in a global scene than moving up and down in a hierarchical universe. Again, we live in the time of many worlds rather than in a single high-rise cosmos.

In light of our situation, my proposal is to construe scripture as a media space. A "media space" – whether enacted in texts or television or cinema – is a means of communication through the creation of an imaginary environment of possible lives. This environment or imagined world has complex connections to other worlds of human interaction. The act of interpretation is to move between worlds, real and imagined. The movement between linguistically and imaginatively donated worlds and responsibility for life is in part mediated through conscience. Conscience, as a term for the basic mode of moral being, is educated by navigating complex media spaces – like scripture. When we reach that insight, it should be clear that the argument has moved between poles of reflection (account of text; a normative outlook) on a journey from shared moral concerns, through a comparison of kinds of ethics (narrative; encounter), to scripture and conscience. In this way, the chapter enacts a movement between "worlds" aimed at an education of the soul, the formation of moral conscience needed for the life of responsibility.

We turn now to underlying issues in the debate about the use of scripture in ethics.

Consensus in Concerns

Work on the Bible and Christian ethics has focused on some very broad and related questions.[8] Specifically, scholarship has centered on the authority of scripture and also its application in moral judgments. With respect to *authority*, theologians have been led into debates about the nature and status of moral knowledge. Does scripture – or any putative sacred text – supply true moral knowledge unavailable to common reflection? Does scripture confirm, invigorate, or, perhaps, deepen, natural moral knowledge? Is moral reason tradition-constituted? Can we isolate a basic structure to moral reason? How does scripture, or any appeal to "revelation," relate to valid sanctions for moral norms? Problems also surround the *application* of scriptural claims to the moral life. These center on the logic of moral reasoning, the nature of judgments, and the applicability of norms from one situation to another; that is, generalizability in casuistic thinking. For instance, how do Jesus's teachings relate to contemporary genetics?

When post-critical thinkers turn to the topic of the Bible and ethics they address issues ranging from epistemology to theory of judgment and even to the validity of a biblical ethics. What is not often noted is that a picture of scripture (e.g., a deposit of truths; a story of redemption) is intrinsically bound to some normative moral/religious outlook. This observation is important for the rest of the present argument, since, as we will see, different "images" of scripture are actually trying to address similar challenges. Clarity about shared concerns can serve as a guide through the thicket of images of scripture in contemporary theological ethics.

First, most current thinkers insist on the need to move beyond modern accounts of the self. The modern agenda was to secure the rationality continuum, the connection of mind and reality, through the immediate certainty of self-awareness. Descartes' maxim, "I think, therefore I am" correctly asserts a principle of identity basic to human subjectivity enacted in thinking (if I am not I in my act of thinking, then who am I?), but it wrongly assumes that we come to ourselves directly in the immediacy of thinking. And it also contends that somehow in the connection between the thinking and being "I" (I am both thinker and thing thought), all other cognitive claims can be secured. After Freud, Nietzsche, and many others, it is hard to imagine a simple transparency of the self to itself. The route to self-understanding is never simply inward; it always involves relating to and understanding what is other than self (other persons, a history of which we are part, beliefs about the world, etc.). Insisting on the entanglement of self and other within understanding means that the moral problem is not, as it was for thinkers like Descartes, Kant, and especially Fichte, how to get from the ego that secures the rationality continuum to the other in a way consistent with self-determination. We necessarily exist with others in some moral space and thus must make judgments about how to orient our lives responsibly. This seems basic to the Christian and Jewish and Islamic moral outlooks. Joseph Sittler states that the human "is not only constituted in, by, and for organic relation to God who made him, but also for organic relation to other persons."[9]

Contemporary (Western) moral theory has apparently rejected the modern idealistic account of immediate self-relation, the Cartesian legacy. Many believe that in order to escape modern subjectivism we must forgo all claims about "self-consciousness" as a hopelessly opaque idea. Recall from earlier chapters Seyla Benhabib's remark that in postmodern thought "the paradigm of language has replaced the [modern] paradigm of consciousness."[10] The triumph of language has meant that narrative, tradition, and discourse – not the consciousness of persons – are the focus of moral consideration. We will see this shift later in both narrative and encounter ethics. Granting the importance of language to consciousness, I intend to hold fast to the importance of self-understanding in ethics and so to a form of reflexive thinking.[11] The distinctly moral shape of conscious human existence is called conscience.

Second, most types of current ethics are trying to find a way beyond the kinds of systemic violence that scar the twentieth century and the beginnings of the twenty-first. Sometimes the roots of violence are located in religious beliefs – the equation, for instance, of one God = one Ruler = one People = violence to what is other, different. That equation is, of course, a particular view of theistic belief and the problem of evil. More often, the challenge of violence is linked to the point about the "modern" self. The "I" can only relate to its world and others as "not-I" (Fichte), or through some abstract idea of humanity (Kant), or one must connect mind and body via the pineal gland, as Descartes quaintly put it. Sartre, in *No Exit*, drew the conclusion to this legacy of thought: "Hell is other people." The move beyond the connection between self-immediacy and violence – and thus damnation of the other – is the enterprise of much postmodern ethics.

These points about identity and violence provide a shared point of reference for exploring kinds of current ethics. At this juncture in our argument we must connect those concerns with an idea of the imagination. This will help to identify differences among options in ethics. Mark Johnson has stated matters well:

> We human beings are imaginative creatures, from our most mundane, automatic acts of perception all the way up to our most abstract conceptualization and reasoning. Consequently, our moral understanding depends in large measure on various structures of imagination such as images, image schema, metaphors, narratives and so forth.[12]

Moral rationality is never devoid of image schema. These schema are not the furniture of the individual mind; they arise from the linguistic and practical resources of communities and traditions. The moral imagination is a perception and construal of what is humanly important. It can be enlivened or deadened. All contemporary ethics grant this point. Where thinkers differ is the extent to which an image schema must pay a debt to non-linguistic reality. Narrative ethics, we will see, insists that the semantic power or intentionality of the Bible is to swallow the world of lived experience and saturate it with new meaning. Narrative ethics is the most recent form of the moral practice of "inscription." Encounter ethics, conversely, insists on an "other," God or other people, never reducible to our cognitive and evaluative schema. In the

Christian context this has come to focus on the *kerygma*. Interestingly, each of these positions tries to reclaim the rationality continuum from a specific point of view. The challenge, I believe, is to seek an image scheme that enables us to apprehend concrete others and the realities of life not reducible to, but factored through, the labors of the imagination and understanding. Can scripture play that role?

We now have before us some of the complexity of the poles of reflection in thinking about scripture and ethics: how to picture scripture mindful of the place of image schema in moral understanding and the concern to overcome a modernist vision of moral identity and its (real or possible) connection to violence to others. We can bring these points together by examining post-critical accounts of scripture in current theological ethics.

Narrative and Character

Narrative ethics holds that the moral life centers on the formation of personal and communal character, and, further, character is formed by the stories adopted. In terms that I explored in detail in chapter 5, narrative ethics seeks to "inscribe" life within the world of the biblical texts. Somehow the biblical text functions to absorb or enfold real life within itself. This kind of ethics rightly insists on an undeniable feature of the moral life: the task of human existence is to give form to one's life. As Iris Murdoch once noted, "I can only choose within the world that I can see, in the moral sense of 'see' which implies that clear vision is a result of moral imagination and moral effort."[13] What gives moral substance is the specific view of life one seeks to embody in existence. How ought we to form our lives? Narrative ethics has rejected two possible answers to this question.

First, advocates of narrative ethics reject any attempt to specify moral norms from the workings of pure practical reason. The problem with so-called Enlightenment ethics, especially Kantianism, is that it tries to generate universal moral norms from self-relation in thinking and willing. But we are social animals, and as such moral norms are rooted in traditions and not the immediacy of reason. Second, proponents of narrative ethics jettison an assumption of traditional virtue theory. Classical Western ethics explored human nature to specify the kinds of lives we ought to live. Plato and Aristotle thought we naturally seek happiness (*eudaimonia*); Augustine insisted that we seek after God; the Stoics spoke of the *logos* and moral choice (*proairesis*) as a distinctly human good. Ancient thinkers examined the real to generate ideas of possible lives. Ethics presented a theory of human nature and not simply an account of moral formation through tradition.

In spite of a love for Aristotle, moral naturalism has been rejected in narrative ethics. The reasons for this rejection are beyond the scope of this inquiry, but the main one is that "nature," for moderns, is purposeless, without goal or good.[14] Insofar as that rejection is accomplished, where does one look to develop ideas of morally possible lives? One turns to narratives that constitute a vision of reality for the reading community. The paradigm of language, to repeat Benhabib's words, has replaced consciousness (Kant) and nature as well (classical ethics). This shift means, for Stanley Hauerwas, James McClendon, and John Howard Yoder, a politicization of the text. The church as a cultural/political reality reads scripture to envision possible lives beyond the violence of the world.[15] The activity basic to character formation is the performative practice of "reading" in communion with other Christians.[16] The insight in this position is that we develop character by appropriating what is other than ourselves; specifically, the vision of human life presented in scripture. Yet the "biblical world," in honesty, is an abstraction created by encoding within Christian doctrine quite diverse strata of texts from divergent historical contexts, social life-worlds, and ideologics. To speak of *the* Bible or *the* Christian story as a seamless whole is a doctrinal and not a textual claim.[17] That is why I developed the idea of inscription, in order to explain how identities can be formed through such encoding of life. Realizing that claims about *the* Bible are doctrinal and not textual is why thinkers like Hauerwas insist that the Bible is the "church's book." The faith and doctrines of the church determine the meaning and coherence of scripture; the vision of life presented by the text is to form and test the lives of Christians. Narrative is the reduction of these diverse texts to one linguistic form.

Narrative ethics, despite claims to be in continuity with classical virtue theory, presents an image of scripture nicely tailored to a media age of cultural flows. The moral life is not grounded in reason or reality. It is about how we (whoever this "we" happens to be) fashion concrete moral existence in the light of the multiplicity of possible lives mediated to us through culturally or ecclesially constructed and interpreted image, story, metaphor, and narrative. For most (but not all) narrative ethicists, the central possibility for human life presented in scripture is peaceableness. The church is to be a community that lives out a story of peace not available to the "world."[18] Narrative ethics responds to the problem of self-formation and the social imaginary. It does so around a moral norm (peaceableness) necessary to keep radically diverse communities and belief systems from a fall into violence.

Any adequate ethics for our time must take seriously the question of character formation simply because of the challenge global cultural flows present to coherent lives. Oddly, narrative ethics does not grasp how the idea of "narrative world" as a unitary form might warrant violence by inscribing the other into the community's vision. Those outside the church are defined as what is not-church – call it the "world," or, worse yet, the Enlightenment! Christian narrative ethics continues the idealist, Fichtean dyad of "I and not-I," but at the level of image schema (church and not-church). The ethics risks a loss of reality within the narrative world; it risks the contemporary nightfall of value in reality. That was the point made earlier in chapter 5 about the moral practice of inscription. For many narrative thinkers, the inscription of life within the church's book sets Christians, as supposedly peaceable people, against the "world," the arena of violence.

Encounter and Command

Narrative ethics can easily slide into a postmodern version of modern moral idealism or a moral dualism. What is real are the "ideas," the narratives or image schema, we use to see the world. An ethics of encounter is a challenge to all forms of thought that focus on acts of imagination and meaning-making by self, culture, or the "church." Versions of "encounter ethics" are found in twentieth-century thinkers like Karl Barth, Abraham Heschel, Rudolf Bultmann, and Martin Buber, as well as recent exponents, such as Emmanuel Lévinas.[19] Especially among Christian theologians, this type of ethics focuses on the *kerygma*, that is, the proclamation of Christ encountering the individual with the demand and possibility of obedience. As Bultmann insisted, the event of this encounter, the moment of "crisis," is the living heart of the moral life, not general moral laws or virtues or a story-formed community. The basic feature of the moral life is that we are addressed by something or someone that makes an unquestionable claim for recognition. According to Lévinas, the Other utters a primal command: "Do not Murder Me."[20] If I begin to approach life from the perspective of, say, the search for happiness, the demands of social justice, or even the church as a peaceable community, I will never escape the ambit of the personal or communal ego. Ethics in that case is caught in a kind of moral solipsism. This entrapment of the other within our projects is what Lévinas calls "totality;" it is the murder of the other. Karl Barth called it sin: the attempt to define the good outside of what God commands. The command of God shatters the totalizing drive of cultural production. The command undoes all our practices of inscribing life in a textual matrix.

For encounter ethics, there is no morally valid perspective outside of the command of the other. Barth insisted that the Christian does not even reason about the command of God; one hears the command and immediately obeys or disobeys. Bultmann stressed that it is in response to the "crisis" of faith that one comes to be, one exists, as a Christian. In the moral event, one is commanded by the word of God, the Thou, the face of the Other. The command does not issue forth from nature or reason. In this respect, advocates of encounter ethics join the paradigm shift to language, or word-event. In that event, the reality of the other and my own moral being are given. Yet in distinction from narrative ethics, the basic moral act is not moral formation. It is obedience. The moral "ought" is the key to self and reality. Put in Lévinas's terms, ethics, not ontology, is philosophically basic.

Lévinas, Barth, Heschel, Bultmann, and others would not deny that communities generate moral laws from the immanent structures of reason, tradition, or nature. They are claiming that insofar as distinctly "moral" action concerns how one responds to the other – a person or the Other who is God – then a valid moral command must instantiate the responsive dynamic of the moral relation. Moral commands "supervene" on non-moral relations, as philosophers might put it. The command of God, Barth would contend, does not destroy the natural spheres of life, nor natural moral knowledge, even as it is not reducible to them. The command allows for a redescription of normal relations in order to understand them in distinctly moral terms.[21]

What does this account of the moral life mean for the image and use of scripture? According to Lévinas, language, and thus the medium of any narrative world, is not prior to my encounter with the Other. Language is created in the event of encounter. In a similar way, Barth insists that scripture witnesses to the command of God who is Jesus Christ. This command is linked to, but not bound by, the biblical texts. The Bible, preaching, and theology become the Word of God if and only if God freely chooses to speak in and through them. This is what enabled Barth to use biblical criticism while insisting on the Word. The text is a witness to what is required of us.

An ethics of encounter is a powerful counter-voice within post-critical hermeneutics to the celebration of the imaginary. By insisting on the "reality" of the command of the Other, this outlook focuses the moral life on an either/or: either I am obedient to the command of God, or I am in sin; either I respond to the face of the Other, or I enact murder. And that is the problem. While encounter ethics insists on the intersubjective character of moral identity, and thus escapes solipsism, it still understands, as did modern idealists, the moral "ought" in terms of an *undoubtable immediacy* that founds subjectivity, the immediacy of the command of God or the face of the Other. As Heschel pointedly remarked: "I am commanded – therefore I am." By insisting on the *immediacy of the ought* at the birth of moral subjectivity, this ethics reduces the complexity of existence and risks undercutting the demand critically to assess all claims upon us. As Lévinas puts it, the self is under a demand of infinite responsibility to the other. This has led some thinkers, especially feminist theologians, rightly to note that an unquestioned claim of the other can enact violence to self.

Conscience and Media Space

We have come some distance in our inquiry. Noting the dissemination of images within cultural flows and shared concerns in current thought, we have seen how in narrative ethics the connection between subjectivity and violence is broken if and only if Christian life is shaped by the church through the story of Jesus. Yet, in its account of scripture, the actual world of human joy and travail is oddly engulfed by the intentionality of the narrative world. The ethics of encounter holds fast to the claim of the living God and persons on the self. This outlook breaks the connection between subjectivity and violence by attending to the event of encounter. But it makes this point in a way that seems to disallow critical assessment of the validity of that demand in any concrete situation. While enacting the postmodern shift to the paradigm of language, ironically, encounter and narrative ethics continue aspects of the Cartesian legacy, either in the immediacy of the "ought" or in a dualistic view of identity construction (church/not-church).

A pluralistic approach to scripture and ethics requires examining the poles of reflection noted before, namely a construal of text and an account of the moral outlook infusing that construal. I propose that we picture scripture as a media space, rooted in but also in its intentionality (partially) free from pre-textual social and historical conditions. Relatedly, the moral life involves moving between and rightly orienting life within situations or worlds, real and imaginary. The most radical claim is that scripture as media space articulates in textual form the shape, intentionality, and task of conscience. This argument can be made by moving from formal features of media space and conscience to a more substantive account of each. In doing so we draw from yet move beyond narrative and encounter ethics, inscription and *kerygma*, in the direction of Christian philosophy.

Formal features

A media space is a complex, but structured, flow of images that shapes perception by imaginatively configuring an intelligible world of possibilities and limits. A media space can take various – even interwoven – forms: written texts, oral presentation, cinema, and the like. Scripture as a media space presents a bewildering multidimensional vision of reality (e.g., heaven and earth; eschaton and present; demonic powers and political forces) within which historical/fictive characters live and act. This implies an anthropological fact: human life is always situated somewhere, in some socio-historical and value-laden context, in which persons must orient their lives with and for others.

The "moral space" of human existence is never simply given nor one-dimensional; it is always configured in some imaginative way in beliefs, values, image schema, practices, and so on. It is culturally saturated with meaning. The space of human existence is thus a "world." The concrete situation of life and the culturally shaped nature of any human space means that forms of cultural saturation, including scripture, are open to assessment, appropriation, and transformation with respect to the perplexity of living.

What does scripture "intend" and how ought we to dwell in that vision of the world? As we have seen, positions in theological ethics differ about the intentionality of scripture. Does the text intend to swallow or inscribe the world of lived experience, saturating it with a distinctively new vision? Does the text witness to what is other and yet encounters and commands the reader? Picturing scripture as a media space means insisting on an important reflexive relation between "text" and interpreter. The interpretive community participates in the enactment of meanings even as this shapes the lives of that community. What texts "mean," and hence their semantic intentionality, is intimately related to the world of the interpreters; meaning is, as Hans-Georg Gadamer famously put it, a fusion of horizons.[22] How first-century Roman Christians read scripture is related to but decidedly different than late twentieth-century Korean Christians! That difference, so a pluralist account goes, is not something to bemoan; it bespeaks the richness but also the ambiguity of meanings. Beyond the austere demands of encounter ethics and the clean storyline of narrative, scripture as a media space is more chaotic and participatory.

Scripture as a media space entails, then, a distinctive claim about the semantic power or intentionality of a "text." Any text, as Paul Ricoeur notes, presents a world in front of itself in which can be found one's innermost possibility.[23] Reading helps donate possibilities and thereby discloses our freedom to live in various ways: we can adopt, modify, or negate the kind of life presented by a text. On Ricoeur's account, semantic power is uniquely related to the temporal, especially futural, dynamic of human existence: as beings on the way to wholeness, creatures who hope, we are always projecting possible courses of action and ways of life. But the intentionality of scripture, we have argued, is not only to be defined in terms of the opening of future possibilities. The idea of media space is also meant to signify the presentation of a "world" in which persons and communities must orient their lives. The intentionality of scripture – or any media, imaginative space – is not only temporal but also spatial and thus contextual. Stated otherwise, the intentionality of a text is to explicate motivating reasons and the structure of lived experience, thereby giving direction to life. The task of interpretation is to grasp and articulate, to explicate, the complexity of the text as a space of reasons and to show how, in the event of understanding, a person's or community's life is thereby formed to see, evaluate, and live in specific ways. The event of understanding is the movement between and bridging of the textual world of reasons and otherwise inarticulate structures of life in such a manner as to enact the meanings of actions and relations.[24]

This account of the semantic power of a media space moves us another step into the density of our being as conscience. Part of the enduring challenge of anyone's life is rooted in the all too human capacity to imagine and to confuse real and fictive worlds in directing conduct and shaping character. One can imaginatively enter the world of, say, the prophet Micah, the latest movie, or a lover's heart. Fanatics throughout the ages have imaginatively entered the world of St. John's revelation, often to destructive ends. Scripture, no less than advanced media cultures, circulates textually a host of lives that saturate moral sensibilities. Possibilities for life presented in scripture range from the Song of Songs to the letter of James, from God's command to Abraham to sacrifice his son, to the gospel vision of love. Which orientations ought we to embody in our lives? How should we responsibly inhabit and traverse the worlds that are the environments for our existence?

Precisely as imaginative, fanciful creatures who move with dread and delight between "worlds," we can never – within this life – be utterly at one with ourselves. Descartes' dream of absolute, immediate identity ("I" am "I") to secure the rationality continuum misses the tragedy and task of life, that is, our incompleteness and struggle for integrity with ourselves, others, the world, and God. The intentionality of the moral life pictured through conscience is "integrity" and not rock-hard self-relatedness. Integrity, as known from Part I of this book, is about right orientation within complex relations, as well as the proper coherence of a life. The deep epistemic and moral question is the relation between media "worlds," actual life in all its complexity, and the moral intentionality of integrity.

Dimensions and rules

Thus far there has been outlined an image of scripture as media space and also conscience in terms of their most formal features (imaginative space; existential orientations) and intentionalities (world; integrity). Our next step is more fine grained. With a little reflection, we can see that a media space, and especially scripture, has dimensions and constitutive rules. First, a media space, despite what some narrative theorists insist, is not easily emploted as having a "beginning, middle and end;" it is not a unified whole rooted in the fact that one can picture time as a process or flowing stream. Unless submitted to doctrine, scripture – with sayings, parables, proverbs, visions, narratives, etc. –

exceeds reduction to narrative form. The Bible is the home or site of many discursive forms, as Gustafson noted. And this means, as seen in other chapters of this book, that manifold perceptions of time and our place within a timely reality are complex. The future depicted in (say) Mark 13 (see chapter 4) is reflexively interwoven in tensive ways with the multiplicity of time sequences in the creation story (cf. chapters 1–2). Picturing scripture as a media space allows us to apprehend the reflexive interaction among "books" and how those interactions constitute a new world of meaning, a new space of reasons.

While this is so about the complex structure of scripture as a media space, narrative ethics is right that one constitutive rule of any "text" is *followability*: it must (whether narratively or not) make sense and be sense-making. Followability also means that the lives of specific characters in the text offer moral examples; they can be "followed" or imitated. Indeed, the call of Jesus to "follow me" may instigate a novel form of reason.[25] The rule of followability requires that one attend not only to possible lives but also to the actual characters and operative ideas presented in the various strata, forms, and *Sitze im Leben* of biblical texts. Thanks to cultural flows, these lives (consider Moses in Disney's movie *The Prince of Egypt*) saturate moral sensibilities and spark the social imaginary on a global scale. The duplicity of Judas no less than the faithfulness of Sarah or the leadership of Moses sharpens and refines moral sensibilities. By insisting on the actual lives presented in the texts, we are avoiding a reduction of those individuals to the intricate and often tacit logic of canon. The rule of followability demands attention to the lives of characters (e.g., Moses), ideas (e.g., justice), and beliefs (e.g., apocalypses), as these move in and through the complex intersection of layers of scripture and then out to the global media. In this way, "Judas," to take an example, has saturated the Western moral imagination with beliefs about betrayal.

For Christians and Jews, scripture articulates a "sacred" media space. The biblical texts present lives in relation to and contention with the living God. This allows us to identify a second constitutive rule aside from that of followability. Sacred, media space is constituted by a decidedly theocentric vision of reality, something encounter ethics surely has right. God is pictured in radically diverse ways: creator and destroyer, lover and lord, redeemer and judge. The polysemic ways of naming God need to be considered in terms of their moral meanings.[26] By various strategies – ranging from covenantal fidelity to discipleship, from conquest to resurrection – the plethora of images sets human life within the domain of highly differentiated divine activity. This enables us to isolate two things: (1) a constitutive rule of *theocentricity*, that is, scripture as media space sets human life amid God's complex workings; and (2) the dimensionality of this "space" is conceivable in terms of foreground and horizon. In the *foreground* are the actual lives of characters (Judas no less than

Sarah; Job and Satan; Christ and Peter) that can be morally followed and engaged; the *horizon* is a claim about the theocentric shape of reality presented in namings of God and God's activity (e.g., creation, judgment, heaven and earth, eschatological kingdom, liberation, covenant, etc.).

Some of the contours of scripture as media space, specifically its multidimensionality and two constitutive rules, have now been isolated. How is one to articulate the relation of foreground to horizon or, put otherwise, the rule of followability to theocentricity? 1 John 4:20 gives, intertextually, a third constitutive rule of scripture as a media space: "Those who say, 'I love God,' and hate their brothers or sisters, are liars; for those who do not love a brother or sister whom they have seen, cannot love God whom they have not seen." This presents a religious–moral rule – built on the double love command (see chapter 6) – beyond the demands of intelligibility (followability) and sacredness (theocentricity). Let us call it the rule of *iconicity*, that is, relations to actual others ought to be "images" or "icons" for apprehending the divine. Under this rule, the complex relation between the claims of responsibility and engaging the text is such that we come to understand rightly the horizon of the moral life as divine goodness only via the extent of relations among concrete, actual individuals. The many ways of knowing God are tested by responsiveness to others. Scripture is a sacred but also a profoundly moral space.

We have now returned to a basic problem facing ethics. As noted, one challenge of global times is that persons and communities must assess the images, symbols, and narratives that work via the social imaginary to saturate consciousness and form existence and moral character. By isolating some of the dimensions and constitutive rules of scriptural "space" we have conceptual tools to decode the social imaginary. What is the horizon of that "space"? How do persons fare within it? Does it have, beyond the maximization of power, any moral rule? Do the media enhance or impede perception of the depth of goodness, God's very being, in and through moral relations? By way of such questions what is examined in theological ethics is not simply the "depth" of culture, nor the "culture" of Christian community, but the working of scriptural images within the moral imagination of cultures. The aim is to check vicious "images" that saturate experience and legitimate violence. One seeks to transform the rules and dimensions of the social imaginary via scriptural space in order to respect and enhance the integrity of life before God. We have already done so in chapter 5 in terms of an early Christian text, the *Didache*, and the same kind of reading will be undertaken later around the story of Cain and Abel (chapter 9).

Now the question becomes: what is the account of the moral life consistent with this task of theological ethics and picture of scripture? To answer this question we must shift to the second pole of reflection and a richer account of conscience.

Presenting conscience

Picturing scripture as media space is also meant to articulate the shape, intentionality, and task of Christian conscience. That is, conscience "appears" indirectly through the figuration of the text in all of its complexity. We come to see that what it means to be moral creatures is to dwell in a theocentric reality that is marked by a certain intelligibility and also the struggle to live responsibly. Laboring to understand and assess the flow of images of possible and actual lives that runs through scripture also helps to form (or deform) our capacity to respond to others and be responsible for self. Conscience is a way to speak of this "capacity" and its formation. But in order to see this, we have to escape the idealist captivity of "conscience" as the self's moral immediacy to itself. Conscience is not simply authentic human being calling to itself; it is not an inner-psychic tribunal where the self stands nakedly before a divine judge; it is not the sovereign voice of truth.[27] Rather, conscience is the inwardness of our whole being as creatures with the power to move between, examine, and respond rightly to others and complex situations called moral spaces or worlds. For the Christian, conscience is always challenged to traverse responsibly biblical spaces and lived reality. This is consistent with the multidimensional vision of reality seen in scripture as a media space and the social imaginary.

The idea of conscience enables one to draw upon insights of narrative and encounter ethics, but within a pluralist conception of scripture. It parallels the image of scripture as media space that, we have seen, draws together ideas of "encounter" (theocentricity; iconicity) and "narrative" (followability). Like advocates of encounter ethics, conscience manifests a form of *moral realism*. The point of every kind of moral realism is that there is an "outside" to our acts of meaning-making, our "narratives." This "outside" is represented biblically in terms of the divine and the claims of the neighbor (hence rules of theocentricity and iconicity and not just followability). The norm of moral perception cannot be one's own image schema, but what we are trying to see – the reality and worth of actual others. In fact, as it was argued in chapter 4, a Christian sees reality through Christ, lives in Christ. Perception is "christomorphic." The most basic delivery of conscience is the sense of responsibility, i.e., the sense that we ought to respect and enhance the integrity of life. However, we must assess the claims of others with respect to possible lives. Not all commands are valid; not every summons ought to be heeded. Attention to the place of image schema in the moral life – and so the social imaginary – means that only those demands are valid that open real possibilities for the integrity of life. On this point narrative ethics is right. Becoming responsible persons and communities is a more arduous task than simply being encountered with the claim of the Other. One must speak of moral formation, even spiritual discipline, in ways often missing in the ethics of encounter.

The moral life is in good measure about the claim of others (human and non-human) on self and the right formation of character and perception. Engaging scripture and media flows in light of the demand to respect and enhance the integrity of life is part of the practice of forming and sharpening conscience. But this means – and here is the point of this chapter – that the use of scripture in ethics is finally and ultimately bound to the question of how the sense of responsibility – the claim of conscience – can be tutored so to apprehend rightly the dignity and worth of the integrity of life. Undertaking that education is the work of the Christian life. It is the act of living in the new creation. And in this way the frightful connection between identity and violence that scars human history can and must be broken.

Conclusion

What ethical reflection now faces in the time of many worlds is the fact of how deeply moral sensibility is saturated by the whirl and consumption of images. The moral paradox of our lives as creatures endowed with imagination is that we must create image schema needed to apprehend the world and yet struggle to exceed these schema. In order to escape the seduction of the giant mall that is global cultural flows, the Christian conscience must use and break, create and shatter, the very cultural and scriptural images used to "see" the world in order better to understand, respect, and enhance the integrity of life before God. The complexity and ambiguity of scripture as a trove of possible and actual lives and its impact on the social imaginary is a school in which Christian conscience is forged and formed. The use of scripture in ethics is not simply to form Christian community, nor witness to God's claim on our lives, although it includes those facts. Much more, one interprets scripture in order to navigate worlds in truth and responsibility.

Perhaps the way best to use scripture in life is not to allow it or any other image schema to become an idol (see chapter 3). Is this not the freedom of conscience in an age of global cultural flows? The conscientious life is neither as direct as adopting biblical narratives nor as immediate as responding to the other. Yet it might well be for all of that a life worth living.

NOTES

1 See Günter Thomas, *Medien, Ritual, Religion: Zur religiösen Funktion des Fernsehens* (Frankfurt am Main: Suhrkamp, 1998).

2 Arjun Appadurai, *Modernity at Large: Cultural Dimensions of Globalization* (Minneapolis: University of Minnesota Press, 1996), pp. 53–4.

3 See N. T. Wright, "Paul's Gospel and Caesar's Empire" in *Reflections: Center of Theological Inquiry* 2 (spring 1999): 42–65.

4 Burton Mack, *Who Wrote the New Testament: The Making of the Christian Myth* (New York: HarperCollins, 1995), p. 3. Also see *Power, Powerlessness, and the Divine: New Inquiries in Bible and Theology*, edited by Cinthia Rigby (Atlanta, GA: Scholar's Press, 1998), pp. 103–24. In this essay I use "Bible" and "scripture" as synonymous terms; in other contexts a distinction would need to be drawn.

5 See David Tracy, *Plurality and Ambiguity: Hermeneutics, Religion, Hope* (New York: Harper and Row, 1986) and James M. Gustafson, *Varieties of Moral Discourse* (Grand Rapids, MI: Calvin College and Seminary, 1988).

6 For a classical discussion, see Thomas Aquinas, *Summa Theologiae* I, q. 1, aa. 9–10 and also Augustine, *On Christian Doctrine*. For the roots of allegory, see Werner Jaeger, *Early Christianity and Greek Paideia* (Oxford: Oxford University Press, 1961).

7 John Herman Randall, Jr., *The Making of the Modern Mind* (New York: Columbia University Press, 1976), p. 36.

8 See, for example, William C. Spohn, *What Are They Saying about Scripture and Ethics*, revd. edn. (New York: Paulist Press, 1995); Richard B. Hays, *The Moral Vision of the New Testament: A Contemporary Introduction to New Testament Ethics* (San Francisco, CA: HarperSanFrancisco, 1996); Lisa Sowle Cahill, "The Bible and Christian Moral Practice" in *Christian Ethics: Problems and Prospects*, edited by Lisa Sowle Cahill and James Childress (Cleveland, OH: Pilgrim Press, 1996), pp. 3–17; and Allen Verhey, "Scripture and Ethics: Practices, Performances, and Prescriptions," ibid, pp. 18–45. See also James M. Gustafson, "The Place of Scripture in Christian Ethics: A Methodological Study" in *Interpretation* 24 (1970): 430–55 and "The Use of Scripture in Christian Ethics" in *Studia Theologica: Scandinavian Journal of Theology* 51: 1 (1997): 15–29; Sharon D. Welch, "Biblical Interpretation in Christian Feminist Ethics," ibid., pp. 30–42; and William Schweiker, "Iconoclasts, Builders and Dramatists: The Use of Scripture in Theological Ethics" in *Annual of the Society of Christian Ethics* (1986): 129–62. Also consider the issue on "The Bible and Christian Theology" in *The Journal of Religion* 76: 2 (1996).

9 Joseph Sittler, *The Structure of Christian Ethics*, introduction by Franklin Sherman. The Library of Theological Ethics (Louisville, KY: Westminster/John Knox Press, 1998), p. 5.

10 Seyla Benhabib, *Situating the Self: Gender, Community and Postmodernism in Contemporary Ethics* (New York: Routledge, 1992), p. 208.

11 See William Schweiker, *Power, Value and Conviction: Theological Ethics in the Postmodern Age* (Cleveland, OH: Pilgrim Press, 1998); James M. Gustafson, *Ethics from a Theocentric Perspective*, 2 vols. (Chicago, IL: University of Chicago Press, 1981, 1984); Iris Murdoch, *Metaphysics as a Guide to Morals* (London: Penguin Press/Allen Lane, 1992); Charles Taylor, *Sources of the Self: The Making of Modern Identity* (Cambridge, MA: Harvard University Press, 1990); and Maria Antonaccio, *Picturing the Human: The Moral Thought of Iris Murdoch* (Oxford: Oxford University Press, 2000).

12 Mark Johnson, *Moral Imagination* (Chicago, IL: University of Chicago Press, 1993), p. ix.

13 Iris Murdoch, *The Sovereignty of Good* (New York: Routledge and Kegan Paul, 1970), p. 37. On responses to this idea, see *Iris Murdoch and the Search for Human Goodness*, edited by Maria Antonaccio and William Schweiker (Chicago, IL: University of Chicago Press, 1996). There is massive work in feminist ethics on this point. See Martha C. Nussbaum, *Love's Knowledge: Essays on Philosophy and Literature* (New York: Oxford University Press, 1990); Elisabeth Schüssler Fiorenza, *Bread Not Stone: The Challenge of Feminist Biblical Interpretation* (Boston, MA: Beacon Press, 1984) and *But She Said: Feminist Practices of Biblical Interpretation* (Boston, MA: Beacon Press, 1992); *Feminist Perspective on Biblical Scholarship*, edited by A. Yarbro Collins (Atlanta, GA: Scholar's Press, 1985); Katie G. Cannon, *Black Womanist Ethics* (Atlanta, GA: Scholar's Press, 1988); and *Voices from the Margins: Interpreting the Bible in the Third World*, edited by R. S. Sugirtharajah (Maryknoll, NY: Orbis Books, 1991).

14 On the need to reject Aristotle's metaphysical biology, see Alasdair MacIntrye, *After Virtue: A Study in Moral Theory* (Notre Dame, IN: University of Notre Dame Press, 1981). He has recently modified that stance. See his *Dependent Rational Animals: Why Human Beings Need the Virtues* (LaSalle, IL: Open Court, 1999). For a challenge to the modern rejection of teleology, consider Franklin I. Gamwell, *The Divine Good: Modern Moral Theory and the Necessity of God* (San Francisco, CA: HarperCollins, 1990).

15 Stanley Hauerwas and William H. Willimon, *Resident Aliens* (Nashville, TN: Abingdon Press, 1989). Also see James McClendon, *Ethics: Systematic Theology* vol. 1 (Nashville, TN: Abingdon Press, 1986) and John Howard Yoder, *The Priestly Kingdom: Social Ethics as Gospel* (Notre Dame, IN: University of Notre Dame Press, 1984).

16 Stephen E. Fowl and L. Gregory Jones, *Reading in Communion: Scripture and Ethics in Christian Life* (Grand Rapids, MI: Eerdmans, 1991). See also Michael G. Cartwright, "The Practice and Performance of Scripture: Grounding Christian Ethics in a Communal Hermeneutic" in *The Annual of the Society of Christian Ethics* (1988): 31–54.

17 See George Lindbeck, *The Nature of Doctrine: Religion and Theology in a Postliberal Age* (Philadelphia, PA: Westminster Press, 1984). For a different account, see William Schweiker and Michael Welker, "A New Paradigm of Theological and Biblical Inquiry" in *Power, Powerlessness and the Divine: New Inquiry in Bible and Theology*, edited by Cynthia L. Rigby (Atlanta, GA: Scholars Press, 1997), pp. 3–20.

18 See Réne Girard, *The Scapegoat*, translated by Yvonne Freccero (Baltimore, MD: Johns Hopkins University Press, 1986); *Curing Violence*, edited by Mark I. Wallace and Theophus H. Smith (Sonoma, CA: Polebridge Press, 1994); and John Milbank, *Theology and Social Theory* (Oxford: Blackwell, 1990).

19 See Karl Barth, *Church Dogmatics*, edited by G. W. Bromiley and T. F. Torrance (Edinburgh: T. & T. Clark, 1957–70), and his famous essay "Das Problem der Ethik in der Gegenwart" in *Das Wort Gottes und die Theologie* (Munich: Ges. Vorträge, 1924): 125–55; Rudolf Bultmann, *Jesus and the World* (New York:

Scribner, 1934); Abraham J. Heschel, *Who is Man?* (Stanford, CA: Stanford University Press, 1965); Martin Buber, *I and Thou* (Edinburgh: T. & T. Clark, 1937); and Emmanuel Lévinas, *Totality and Infinity: An Essay in Exteriority*, translated by Alphonso Lingus (Pittsburgh, PA: Duquesne University Press, 1969). No doubt the most pointed form of this position is the work of the great biblical scholar Rudolf Bultmann and his kind of Christian existentialism. Yet other theologians, say, Barth's insistence on the command of God or Paul Tillich's rejection of "moralism" in the name of "theonomous ethics," aptly show how much that generation of thinkers hoped to free Christian thought from other forms of ethics. It is ironic that current virtue theorists and narrative theologians strive so ardently to make Barth one of their own! For other helpful works on this matter, see Paul Ricoeur, *Oneself as Another*, translated by Kathleen Blamey (Chicago, IL: University of Chicago Press, 1992); Dietz Lange, *Ethik in evangelischer Perspektive* (Göttingen: Vandenhoeck and Ruprecht, 1992); and James M. Gustafson, *Christ and the Moral Life* (New York: Harper and Row, 1968); and Svend Andersen, *Einfuührung in die Ethik* (Berlin: Walter de Gruyter, 2000).

20 See Emmanuel Lévinas, *Entre Nous* (Paris: Grasset, 1991).

21 See William Schweiker, "Divine Command Ethics and the Otherness of God" in *The Otherness of God*, edited by Orrin F. Summerell (Charlottesville: University of Virginia Press, 1998), pp. 246–65. Also see R. M. Adams, *The Virtue of Faith and Other Essays in Philosophical Theology* (New York: Oxford University Press, 1987) and R. J. Mouw, *The God Who Commands* (Notre Dame, IN: University of Notre Dame Press, 1990).

22 Hans-Georg Gadamer, *Truth and Method*, revised translation by Joel B. Weinsheimer and Donald G. Marshall (New York: Continuum, 1989).

23 Paul Ricoeur, *Essays on Biblical Interpretation*, edited by Lewis S. Mudge (Philadelphia, PA: Fortress Press, 1981). Also see Robert P. Scharlemann, "The Textuality of Texts" in *Meanings in Texts and Action: Questioning Paul Ricoeur*, edited by David E. Klemm and William Schweiker (Charlottesville: University of Virginia Press, 1993), pp. 13–25.

24 On this hermeneutical theory (what was called an explicative or mimetic theory in the introduction), see William Schweiker, *Mimetic Reflection: A Study in Hermeneutics, Theology and Ethics* (New York: Fordham University Press, 1990).

25 See Robert Scharlemann, *The Reason of Following: Christology and the Ecstatic I* (Chicago, IL: University of Chicago Press, 1991).

26 See Sallie McFague, *Models of God: A Theology for an Ecological, Nuclear Age* (Philadelphia, PA: Fortress Press, 1987) and David Tracy, "Literary Theory and the Return of the Forms of Naming and Thinking God in Theology" in *The Journal of Religion* 74: 3 (1994): 302–19.

27 Thomas Aquinas speaks of conscience with respect to the first precept of natural law (seek good, avoid evil) and also as a habit. See *Summa Theologiae* I/II q. 94, a. 1, ad. 2; I q. 79, a. 13. Paul Tillich and Martin Heidegger understood "conscience" as the human claim on itself. See Paul Tillich, *Morality and Beyond*, Library of Theological Ethics (Louisville, KY: Westminster/John Knox Press, 1995) and Martin Heidegger, *Being and Time*, translated by John Macquarrie and Edward Robinson (New York: Harper and Row, 1962). Still others understood

conscience with respect to a social practice. See H. Richard Niebuhr, *The Responsible Self: An Essay in Christian Moral Philosophy*, Library of Theological Ethics (Louisville, KY: Westminster/John Knox Press, 1999). Also see Anne Patrick, *Liberating Conscience: Feminist Explorations in Catholic Moral Theology* (New York: Continuum, 1997) and Kenneth E. Kirk, *Conscience and Its Problems: An Introduction to Casuistry*, Library of Theological Ethics (Louisville, KY: Westminster/John Knox Press, 1999). For a further discussion, see William Schweiker, *Responsibility and Christian Ethics* (Cambridge: Cambridge University Press, 1995).

CHAPTER 8

Comparing Religions, Comparing Lives

The theologian Bernard Meland once famously said, "we live more profoundly than we can think."[1] Our actual lives are inexhaustible sources of reflection; thought must always aim at, but never succeeds in plumbing the depths of, existence. This chapter follows Meland's lead. The previous chapter examined the entanglement between scripture and conscience. In an age of global cultural flows, religious texts must be understood with respect to the social imaginary. This raises the challenge not simply of how to grasp religious depictions of possible lives, but also how religious sources can foster conflict. Insofar as the time of many worlds is deeply marked by interactions among the religions, the purpose of this chapter, like chapter 5, is to explore how and in what ways the religions can go wrong, can foster and further violence and fanaticism. This is the work of comparative ethical thinking. The work of comparison seeks to isolate a shared moral framework among the so-called Religions of the Book (Judaism, Christianity, and Islam), in order to isolate the points of possible fanaticism, the failure of conscience, and to show the importance of these traditions for current ethics.

Of course, there are moments when we must just live and not engage in critical reflection on our moral sources. There are times when we must endure experience and not analyze it. This is true whenever unexpected violence and horror thwart life. Surely that was the case right after September 11, 2001. In the days and weeks following the attack, many lived in shock and with a sense that something had changed forever in their lives. To be sure, there was a lot of ethical reflection on these events, especially about the warrants, if any, for justified retaliation against terrorist networks or oppressive state action. But there was often little thinking about people's felt responses to common tragedy. Sometimes all we can do is to mourn. In the light of world events and the horror of human violence, one ought to approach the topic of this chapter with care.

However, it seems that now is a time for reflection on the ways we do and can compare our lives with others. This is especially true for anyone interested in a humane expression of religious conviction, that is, anyone who hopes to thwart the vicious impulses of her or his own tradition and live with convictions aimed at respecting and enhancing the integrity of life. After all, that is the claim of conscience, the basic mode of our moral being. Amid a spreading and ill-defined global war on terrorism punctuated by responses to terrorist action and other nations, as well as self-conceit on a national scale, a time also marked by jubilee and yet sorrow, we need to consider how we see our lives in relation to others. One needs to ponder how best to understand others and also how to comport life in a world where human differences too easily and too often lead to violence.

The intention of this chapter, mindful of Meland's sage words, is to explore the interaction between two kinds of comparison, one felt in the depth of experience and the other at the level of explicit ethical reflection. We return, then, to the complex connection between belief and experience, conviction and desire noted elsewhere in this book. Recall that previously we explored the saturation of human desire by cultural valuations in greed (chapter 3). Later, in chapter 9, we will undertake a similar analysis of rage and anger. The present discussion extends those claims about the infusing of emotion with cognitive weight by examining laughter about others. The reason for this focus is that laughter exposes how deeply we live by comparing ourselves with others. Comparative reflection, as the second task of this chapter, will try to think just as deeply. So let us begin with a few words on laugher as comparison felt, before launching into the work of comparative religious ethics.[2]

Comparison Felt

Moralists throughout the ages have fretted about laughter. This was not because of a striking lack of humor so often found among moral thinkers, although one could easily make a long list of the humorless. John Calvin, it is said, told one joke in his life, and it was not funny. The same is probably true of Kant and Aquinas and Heidegger and Spinoza, and, well, many others. But humor and jokes are not the point. The real issue is that laughter, however evoked, discloses the way we see and value our lives and the lives of others. In the minds of many classical thinkers, wild laughter signaled a loss of rational control over our lives, the upsurge of forces that contort our bodies and our souls. It meant a loss of tranquility of mind. "Just as the shoe is turned with the foot, and not the contrary," wrote Plutarch, "so do men's dispositions make their lives like themselves . . . Therefore let us cleanse the fountain of tranquility that is in our own selves."[3] As the great Renaissance scholar M. A.

Screech has rightly noted, "over the centuries theologian after theologian rediscovered for himself that the Jesus of Scripture is shown weeping but never laughing."[4] The paradox of Christian faith, Screech recognizes, is that it is a religion of profound joy in the resurrection and new creation, but also a religion of sorrows. "Blessed are those who mourn, for they will be comforted" (Matthew 5:4). Other thinkers, especially satirists and the Renaissance humanists, saw that laughter can heal. Sad to say, laughter is also enlisted in the causes of war.

Not surprisingly, there is a long history of debate about the origins of laughter. Mark Twain, for one, thought that humor and laughter arise from sorrow, even anger. Aristotle held that laughter was a unique property of human beings. And Rabelais, satirist and Christian humanist, knowing laughter and Aristotle's philosophy, began his *Gargantua* like this:

> 'Tis better to write of laughter than of tears,
> Since laughter is the property of Man.[5]

The question of the origin of laughter will never be settled, although I believe we need a mixture of Twain and Rabelais. For the sake of the present inquiry, what is important is not the question of the origins of laughter. What is important in this chapter is how laughter reveals at a visceral level the ways we relate to other human beings, relations ranging from scorn to pity, mockery to sympathy. Laughter discloses the shape of conscience, the moral tenor of a person's life. At least some kinds of laughter, but surely not all, are comparison felt, experienced. Sometimes when we laugh, we feel or sense a judgment about our lives in comparison to others and how they live and what they value. Some kinds of laughter express the ways in which deep desires and emotions are saturated and shaped by moral evaluations. This kind of laughter exposes the cognitive weight and force of emotions.

To get the point about laughter as comparison felt, consider a joke that circulated almost immediately after the events of 9/11. The United States should not attack Afghanistan to destroy the Taliban, so the joke went. What Americans should do is to capture Osama bin Laden, given him a sex change operation, and then force him to live as a woman under the rule of the Taliban! Many Americans laughed at this joke, because the joke reveals in the very act of laughing human commonality and also difference. It is the time of many worlds felt from the inside. This laughter disclosed the confusing requirements of religion about the sexes; it also shows us very different outlooks on gender roles, the demands of God, and the status of basic political rights. The laughter passed judgment about a religious and moral outlook seen as tyrannical and patriarchal. Human equality, a deep but admittedly hard-won belief in Western cultures, is held to be part and parcel of claims about God. Can one understand religious convictions that seem to deny equality? Laughter is a moral comparison. The felt comparison lurking in this laughter reveals unstated evaluations about religious codes, sexuality, other people, and God's will.

Laughter is a disclosure of the shape of conscience from within emotional responses. The most basic mode of our moral being is a reflexive self-understanding co-constituted by a sense of responsibility. The extent to which our moral being, conscience, is in fact true and good depends on the degree to which actions and relations to self and others are oriented by that sense. The careful examination or interpretation of laughter is one of the ways we can come to know the tenor and direction of conscience. It can reveal the fallen or distorted conscience as much as the rectitude of moral being. This is vitally important. Insofar as no one has direct, immediate, clear knowledge of themselves, then sometime, much of the time, we come to self-understanding through an act of indirection, exploring what we do, say, feel, and even laugh about. In this respect, the analysis of this chapter is meant also to provide means for the examination of conscience in the time of many worlds.

Much later in this chapter we will return to the theme of laughter as comparison felt. It will be important for clarifying a theological humanist response to religiously and morally driven violence, like the horror of September 11, 2001. At this juncture we must engage in another form of comparison, specifically some work in comparative religious ethics. In a sense, we are trying to uncover the reasons why religious conviction can turn fanatical and murderous, thereby better to defuse those impulses. We are also trying to clarify the deep roots of certain kinds of laughter as comparison felt. This is to think as deeply as we live. Of course, I am not by any stretch of the imagination an expert in Islam or Judaism. Admitting that fact, it is still the case that in the time of many worlds we must risk trying to understand others and ourselves, always mindful of our own partiality, ignorance, and blindness. Hopefully, the work of comparison can serve as a remedy to human foibles. We need next to clarify the context for comparison in terms of the current situation and features of the time of many worlds.

The Clash of Civilizations?

In all moral reflection it is important to grasp and assess how a situation is defined. Throughout this book, the present situation has been defined as the time of many worlds and in doing so we have explored many of the dimensions and processes that characterize the age. Ever since September 11 and surely with the war in Iraq, there has been a lot of talk about a clash of civilizations.[6] This description is meant to signal something about the social and moral reality in which we now live. There is some truth to it, but also much that is wrong with the idea.

The idea of a clash of civilizations is meant to stress that the forms of conflict we should now expect on the global scene are not just political and economic, but also profoundly cultural or civilizational. Throughout the modern West much conflict has been driven by political forces, ranging from civil wars and wars of liberation to colonial conquest as well as the tumultuous economic revolutions seen in the industrial revolution, the former Soviet Union, China, and elsewhere. These kinds of conflict continue, of course. There are ongoing political confrontations around the world, as well as the endless plight of the world's poor and the struggle for liberation and economic justice.[7] But nowadays there is also plenty of cultural and religiously driven violence in the world. We know this all too well. The idea of a "clash" frees our thinking from rather shop-worn patterns of analysis based on ideas about discrete political entities in a world of *Realpolitik*. It also frees us from any overly economistic accounts of the present situation, Marxist no less than capitalistic ones, which see the world in terms of the interaction and conflict between labor, market, and capital. Put differently, without denying the insights of political and economic analysis, we have to understand the global scene in new ways.

The real force of the new insight into the presence of "civilizations" on the global field is that we see human existence within diverse "spaces of reasons." As used in this book, a space of reasons designates some context (real or imagined) that provides motivation and meaning for action. Cultures are spaces of reasons that provide motivations for actions in complex ways: persons' lives are situated in diverse social subsystems (economics, law, politics, etc.) that operate with ends, values, rules, and norms; cultural media, driven by the social imagination, saturate human desires and motivate behavior; there are widespread values and convictions that shape the identities of those in a culture, a surrounding "ethos." But there are many kinds of spaces of reasons. For instance, myths (Cain and Abel; the Titans) are spaces of reasons when they shape human life. Economic and other social systems are spaces of reasons as well. We know better now than in the past that the "world" is simply a name for the conglomerate of diverse, conflicting but also interacting spaces of reasons.[8] The time of many worlds, our age, is one in which human beings are motivated to live and act and relate in and through reflexively interacting spaces of reasons. The religions motivate human behavior because they are complex means of making sense of life. As spaces of reasons, the religions must interact with other ways human beings are motivated to act, to make sense of their lives – political, economic, and the like.

So it is true that what moves people to live in certain ways are matters of belief and value bound to their identity as people. These beliefs and values saturate human desires through the media of the social imaginary. This gives rise to various imagined worlds that are "the multiple worlds that are constituted by the historically situated imaginations of persons and groups spread around the globe."[9] But these "worlds," it has been argued throughout this book, are themselves spaces of reasons. Who can doubt this after watching terrorists fly jetliners into buildings in the name of their faith and their hatred of "Western values?" Yet even that horrific action shows that all human behavior is moved by a variety of reasons. Presumably, many reasons motivated the terrorists' action: beliefs about cultures and histories of conflict, technological beliefs, economic ones, and so on. When we turn shortly to explore the moral framework of the monotheistic religions, the aim will be to pinpoint where and why fanaticism, moral madness, is found in these religions. At this juncture, we must admit that the idea of a clash of civilizations has some merit to it.

However, the idea is not really adequate. First, as theorists of globalization say, there is a "compression of the world" that brings with it an awareness of global interdependence as well as increasing conflict. The idea of a "clash" of civilizations misses something found in forms of interdependence, namely, *global reflexivity*, that is not just about conflict. Recall from Part I of this book that by global reflexivity we mean the ways in which cultures or civilizations act back upon themselves with respect to information coming from other cultures or civilizations. Reflexivity is a term for entities that can observe themselves. It is rooted in the wondrous human capacity to be aware of oneself in the midst of acting and to be able to make adjustments, to learn, in that very process.[10] Human rights doctrine is a good example of how the religions are adjusting in various ways to ideals and values moving within global reflexivity. In the "war on terrorism" think how quickly every nation involved had to respond to charges of the denial of human rights to women. That is reflected, as noted above, even at the level of popular jokes circulating in a culture. The reflexive dynamic is present now in terms of how cultures and traditions, themselves internally complex, adjust to others and to widespread human concerns, like human rights.[11]

Reflexivity can be violent, of course. One way to react to information coming from another culture is to try to destroy that culture because of the fear that one's own identity will be changed through interaction. But reflexivity can also be seen as part of the ongoing, complex way in which cultures do define and understand themselves as spaces of reasons. This is the second point about why the description of our situation as the clash of civilizations is not ultimately helpful. It assumes that cultures or "civilizations" are more or less bloc-like entities, homogeneous, rather than internally complex and contested spaces of reasons.[12] The idea of a clash of civilizations seems to suggest that the only way in which these cultures can and will respond to the infusion of information from other cultures is through conflict. That account fails to see that we have some choices to make, that it might be possible to work for more peaceful and exciting forms of reflexivity.

The current world situation is difficult to describe. Ideas like the clash of civilizations and global reflexivity aid in trying to understand what is going on. If we value life, we must work in this context to bend the reflexive interactions among cultures towards non-destructive forms. Insofar as religions are major players defining the world as a space of motivating reasons, then in order to avoid ongoing systemic conflict we need to foster reflexive interactions among religions. I have even hinted that laughter reveals diverse ways of living reflexively within a space of reasons. And we might imagine that some kinds of laughter support clashes among peoples rather than the peaceful interaction of civilizations. At least that is what will be argued. On the way to that conclusion, we need to engage in some careful ethical reflection. Comparative ethics must play a role in responding to our situation.

A Shared Moral Framework

We start with a paradox. We must refer to various religions, like Christianity, Islam, and Judaism, and yet one must always keep in mind that the very idea of religion is contested as a way to organize talking about these sociocultural or civilizational realities. Furthermore, each of these religions is itself wildly complex and internally contested. In a sense, it is doubly wrong to speak of (say) Judaism – wrong first because it is not at all evident that modern ideas of religion make sense of that community, and wrong secondly because there is not one thing that *is* Judaism, a kind of essential Judaism. That being said, we must think about the interaction of these complex civilizational forces, these spaces of reasons, as they interact internally and with each other on the global field. And so, with all due caution, I am concerned to isolate a broad shared moral framework found among the various versions of these religions.[13]

In this light, it is very important to realize that the Islamic, Christian, and Jewish traditions share a lot in common. They share some of the same textual lineage; they are Religions of the Book, as Muslims first put it.[14] As religions, they are monotheistic: there is one God and not a pantheon of deities. To be sure, there are massive differences among these religions on just these points. Jews and Muslims worry about Christian talk of the Trinity and Christ. Christian trinitarian faith sounds an awfully lot like a pantheon of deities or the denial, in some radical claims about God's incarnation, of any deity. Christians too often imagine that Muslims obey Allah just out of fear and the hope of eternal reward, even as they often think Jews stress God's demands over God's mercy. Further, the Religions of the Book are not religions of the *same* book. They have different canons. And these diverse canons have spawned a diverse range of interpretive strategies and practices, ranging from commentary to allegory, as well as hermeneutical methods unique to particular expressions of each tradition. After all, Christians speak about "theology" while Muslims engage in *sharia* reasoning and Jews engage in diverse patterns of rabbinical interpretation. Finally, there is the dismal history of conflict between these traditions, a story of hatred, blood, and clashing civilizations. Granting these differences, there are still some commonalities that come to light when we see these traditions together rather than setting them against one another.[15] It is a shared moral framework that we need to explore. This framework is a deep, profound, but also ambiguous space of reasons for life.

First, these traditions are versions of what theorists call *moral realism.* Muslims, Jews, and Christians do not believe that standards for good and evil, right and wrong, are simply and solely human inventions. Despite what modern Western intellectuals argue – from David Hume to Friedrich Nietzsche, from Sigmund Freud to Michel Foucault – and despite what cultural relativists claim, these traditions hold that moral standards are rooted in the nature of things, specifically in the will of the divine. To be sure, there has been a shift among some people, even within these religions, from a naive realism – where the specific revelation or ideas in the mind somehow are at one with "reality" – to something like what is called in this book *hermeneutical realism.* In that form of realism one must interpret complex and wild imaginative forms in order to understand the world in which we live and even the reality and will of the divine. But the intention of the interpretive act is to discover some fundamental truths. This means that for Christians, Muslims, and Jews the point of our lives – if we are to be good people – is to live in *conformity* with that moral order and in doing so our lives will be fulfilled. That is why Muslims speak of submission to Allah; it is why Jews seek to imitate God's way; it is why Christians focus on discipleship to Christ. By conformity to the will of God, human life is right and rich. This is a radical claim in our present situation. For members of these traditions, justice, for instance, is not a matter of political expedience or cultural preference; it is about living in conformity with what is most real, most true. This point about realism and the moral passion it ignites is misunderstood by contemporary Western policy makers, social critics, and cultural commentators.

The moral realism of these traditions brings us to a second point. How does one know the will of Allah or the purposes of God? Questions about the sources and character of moral knowledge, or debates in moral epistemology, are very complex. There are differences within and between these traditions as well as some commonality. The commonality is that each tradition, by and large, insists that there are two interacting sources of moral knowledge: (1) the decisive revelation of God's will, and (2) the disciplined use of human reason in moral matters. Each tradition has some conception of natural moral knowledge, say in ideas about *Taqwa*, the covenant with Noah, or conscience as the law written on the heart (cf. Romans 2). The traditions differ from each other in terms of what is the decisive revelation of God. While Muslims see Jews and Christians as People of the Book, nevertheless, it is the Qur'an, the example of Muhammad, and Sharia, that is decisive. While Jews recognize kinship with Christians and Muslims, it is nevertheless Torah – written, oral, and eternal – that is decisive for knowing the will of God. While Christians acknowledge a kinship with these other monotheistic religions, the decisive revelation for knowing the will of the One God is Jesus as the Christ.

On exactly this point about moral knowledge we also uncover differences *within* each of these traditions that enable us to pinpoint matters of great import for ethics. As I understand it, within each tradition there are long and difficult struggles about the degree to which human reason can validly grasp moral truth and rightly address moral problems. There are those in each tradition who argue that human reason is so distorted or so feeble or so impotent that we cannot make valid moral judgments about how to live rightly. Within Christianity one finds this outlook in thinkers ranging from Tertullian in the ancient church, who famously said "I believe because it is absurd," to some of the medieval nominalists, to theologians who insisted that any use of human reason outside of obedience to divine revelation is sin. Among Muslims there was the conflict between traditionalists and the *Mu'tazila*, who held that if God is to judge action and reward the just then human beings must be free and not determined. Consistent with that conviction, they also affirmed that since ethical norms have objective meaning, these norms could be grasped by reason – independent of revelation. This school died out and was not deemed acceptable, thereby giving way to the traditionalists, who focused on revelation as the ultimate source for the definition of good and evil. Analogous developments can be found in Judaism.

From these claims about the poverty of the human mind flow strands of piety, mysticism, and authoritarianism. The Muslim thinker and Sufi mystic al-Ghazzali traces out in his *Alchemy of Happiness* the very limits of human thought and the importance of the Sufi life. Christian mystics, looking to the dark night of the soul, charted a relation to God through the negation of what we can say and think about God. The Kabbalistic masters in Judaism focused on Torah and also the limits of thought in faith.[16] Of course, strands of "mysticism" are exceedingly complex and there are many "mystical" forms of thought and practice in each of these "religions." The point is simply that some Muslims and Christians and Jews hold fast to a mystical vision of the religious life.

An admission of the limits and even corruption of the human mind can take forms other than the mystical journey. An authoritarian mindset insists that one must utterly submit all thinking to those who can authoritatively interpret the decisive revelation of God's will.[17] Those outside of the religious community, as we saw in chapter 5, lacking this revelation and authoritative teaching, are left in darkness, bereft of moral wisdom. They are infidels or sinners or dwell in the way of death. Within Islam there is no official class of clergy endowed with the exclusive ability to explain the text to other Muslims. In principle, every Muslim can interpret the text, so long as he or she has the knowledge to do so. Thus, the power of imams and mullahs arises in a specific, authoritarian political milieu or from the fact that others, for whatever reasons, do not have the knowledge needed to engage in legal reasoning. As we have recently seen, that political milieu is readily present. Some imams and mullahs have claimed exclusive power to deliver *fatwa*, legal opinions, and to interpret text and tradition. Within strands of ultraorthodox Judaism, so it seems, certain rabbis or rabbinic councils must make determinations about the legality of moral decisions. Orthodox Roman Catholicism requires submission to the teachings of the church. Ultraconservative elements within the Roman Catholic Church resist even those changes that the magisterium with the pope enacted at Vatican II in order to make Christian faith understandable to the world. This is because the "world" is fallen and bereft of any knowledge of God's will and way. Fundamentalist Protestants attack free human inquiry and demand complete submission to a literal reading of the Bible. These kinds of "religion" are too easily the backbone of fanatical movements around the world and within each of these traditions. They rest upon a claim about the impotence and sinfulness of natural reason.

It is vitally important to realize that there are other options in each of these traditions beyond the mystical and the authoritarian. These other positions insist that while human reason is fallible and too often distorted, we can and must and may think about how best to lead our lives, we must interpret our sacred texts and traditions, and we must bear the burden of responsibility. Those outside of the community might have moral insight that even the faithful need (think of Plato, Socrates, and Aristotle in the ancient world.) This is why there have been Muslim philosophers and also Jewish and Christian philosophers: Christians like Clement of Alexandria, Augustine, Thomas Aquinas, Erasmus, Schleiermacher, Tillich, and many others; Jews like Maimonides, Martin Buber, Emmanuel Lévinas, and many others; Muslims from Averroës and Avicenna to modernists like Fazlur Rahman and many others.[18] This "non-authoritarian" strand in each tradition makes the further claim – sometimes explicitly, most of the time implicitly – that when one interprets tradition, one must interpret in the direction of what is most humane, most conducive to a way of acting and relating that respects and enhances the integrity of life.[19] Thus Lévinas insists that the trace of God is found in an encounter of responsibility for the other. Islamic and Christian thinkers from the so-called Third World speak on behalf of the poor and the marginalized. This strand in each tradition is measured; it seeks a reasoned faith, not the authoritarian imposition of belief.

Thus far it has been argued that the monotheistic traditions (1) endorse some form of moral realism and (2) work with complex theories of moral knowledge. From beliefs about the sources of moral knowledge (reason and revelation) flow the possibility of extreme authoritarianism and also the possibility of a capacious account of moral conscience and its search for what is good and right. How moral knowledge is defined has profound implications for the way the lives of those outside the community are seen and how they are to be treated.

The third and final point to make is about the texture or domain of morals. Many modern Western people think morality is primarily about "do's" and "don'ts," especially about sex. Much modern ethics has trimmed down the arena of moral responsibility solely to public demands for justice. Jews, Muslims, and Christians have resources for a much more complex picture. Morality in these religions has different dimensions. One dimension is about a range of goods necessary for human life to endure and to flourish: goods like sexuality, family, economic production, and social and political life, and goods of culture, say music or the arts. These "values" necessary for the survival and flourishing of human beings are rooted in God's will.[20] This is why each tradition has concern for the poor, the outcast, and the destitute. It is why these traditions have profound commitments to education and social policy. It is also why, in certain expressions of each tradition (say, Calvinism in Christianity, but also in Islam and Judaism), there is the need to establish a political order permeated with the religious vision – a theocracy. Only in this way will the real goods of human life and the moral order of reality exist in harmony. The point is that these religious work with a multidimensional theory of value. We have developed in this book just that kind of value theory through the discourse of creation and the integrity of life.

There is a second domain of morality. It is about obligations that bear on how we live within spheres of value: obligations like truth-telling, fidelity, respect for property, prohibitions of murder, and the like. These obligations are intimately linked to the sphere of goods, but distinct from them. For example, everyone needs some measure of economic well-being to survive. Economic behavior is about certain basic goods. But the duty or obligation that one ought to be honest in one's economic life is another matter! Obligations aim to protect and promote some domain of goods, but their meaning and validity are not reducible to those goods. This is why each of these traditions, as versions of moral realism, holds that duties and obligations are not just matters of social convention; they are rooted in the divine will. Living by those obligations is to respect and enhance the domain of basic goods important for human and non-human life to endure and flourish. In terms of the argument of this book, we have specified the imperative of responsibility along the lines of the double love command and the Golden Rule just to make this point. What one is called to respect and enhance is the integrity of life before God. This requires neighbor love and moral reciprocity.

In addition to this picture of the extent of moral values and the importance of moral obligations, Jews and Christians and Muslims add a third dimension to morality. By living out one's moral obligations, by conforming to the will of God, there is a distinct kind of good, a human excellence, not definable just in terms of the sphere of goods or sets of obligation. One becomes a *righteous person*, a person of what we have called moral integrity. Each of the traditions has long histories of saints, righteous people, and martyrs who are models of how one can and may and must live the faithful life. Oddly enough, this kind of human excellence, this profound realization of human goodness, is not something one can directly seek. One cannot, for instance, decide to be a saint! Rather, a saint is someone whose total life is dedicated not to their own self-realization but to serving the cause of goodness.

If we have some grasp of the complexity of each tradition's picture of the domain of morality (goods, obligations, human excellence), then we can note a tension that introduces profound moral ambiguity into each of these religions. It opens the possibility of moral madness. If one believes that human reason is unable to grasp the moral order of life, unable to discern in some degree what is good and right, then the purpose of life is simply adherence to divinely sanctioned obligations interpreted by those in power. One cannot question those dictates, since any question betrays fallen human reason. One should be willing to sacrifice basic human goods that seem obvious to ordinary human beings precisely because one must simply obey a command of those in authority in order to be "faithful." What is more, unquestioned obedience is believed to be the pathway to moral excellence, a saintly life, even in the act of martyrdom.

This is what makes the fanatic's mind almost unintelligible to others. The fanatic cannot acknowledge that others have a valid grasp of those goods that moral obligations, even obligations commanded by God, are to respect and enhance. Given that, the fanatic is willing to sacrifice the whole range of natural, basic human goods – even to the point of killing innocent people – out of obedience to a supreme moral demand. What is supreme is obedience to an overriding obligation, even to the destruction of obvious natural goods and in the hopes of reclaiming these goods as reward for obedience. This logic is found in *each* and *every* religion on this planet. Moral madness is tragically found everywhere.

Conversely, if one believes – as a faithful Christian or Muslim or Jew – that all human beings do have some capacity to apprehend the tenure and task of the moral life, then obedience to a divinely revealed moral code is meant to serve human flourishing and the integrity of life. If one does claim a wide notion of human reason, then the purpose of life is to respect and enhance the domain of human goods. That too is to live in conformity with God's will. Whether we call it so or not, it will be a life of theological humanism. One will acknowledge the folly of life and yet insist that the purpose of human existence is to live and act by our best insights and the deepest wisdom of our traditions so that life might flourish. And the theological humanist will insist on freedom of conscience as a sacred right of each and every human being, the demand that authority alone does not determine what is good and true.

How a community or an individual person understands the sources and validity of moral reason and how they construe the multiple dimensions of value has profound impact on what living a faithful life means. This explains why morally driven fanaticism and also a humane outlook are found within each tradition and its moral realism. We see the profound ambiguity of the religions. This also shows why the labor of making reflexive interactions among civilizations is a pressing demand.

Laughter and Conscience

We have tried to isolate within the great monotheistic traditions a shared framework of moral conviction and also the points at which each tradition can, at least in principle, become fanatical and so breed moral madness. We have isolated points where the reflexive interaction of a community and its surrounding social context can decay into a clash – a violent clash – of civilizations. This vulnerability to distortion and violence, the failure of conscience, is revealed also in kinds of laughter. Different kinds of laughter are different ways the spaces of reasons that make up the world are felt and experienced. We should imagine that moral madness is marked by its own kind of laughter, even as a humane outlook on life comes to expression in its own distinctive ways.

For the Christian theological humanist, laughter is rooted in the folly of the Gospel as itself wiser than this world (cf. 1 Corinthians 1:18–30). As Erasmus in his classic *In Praise of Folly* puts it:

> All mortals are fools, even the pious, Christ too, though he is the wisdom of the Father, was made something of a fool himself in order to help the folly of mankind, when he assumed the nature of man and was seen in man's form; just as he was made sin so that he could redeem sinners.[21]

Humane laughter does not scorn human foibles. It is a kind of reflexivity that understands the common lot of human existence even as it works to further life. Yet kinds of laughter confirm the contrast found in our comparative reflection between authoritarian and fanatical kinds of life and those seeking humane goods.

Fanatics are not known for their subtle sense of humor. What laughter there is among them is a form of derision of others. Jonathan Glover has noted the scornful laughter of Nazi SS guards and torturers in other places loosed on their victims. That kind of laughter is meant to dehumanize others, to rob them of dignity.

> The cold joke mocks the victims. It is an added cruelty and it is also a display of power: we can put you through hell merely for our mild amusement. It adds emphasis to the difference between "us" and "them": we the interrogators are a group who share a joke at the expense of you the victims. It is also a display of hardness: we are so little troubled by feelings of sympathy that we can laugh at your torment.[22]

As M. A. Screech notes in his study of laughter in the Christian tradition, "Laughter is one of the ways in which crowds, thoughtless, cruel or wicked, may react to the sight of suffering."[23] We should recall, for example, those who scoffed at Jesus when he died or the soldiers who mocked him as king.

Scornful, cruel laughter is profoundly unreflexive; it is meant to distance one's own self-understanding from any involvement with the lives of others. As Glover rightly notes, this kind of laughter seeks to draw strict moral boundaries between them and us in such a way that "them" can never be "us" and therefore we are free to treat "them" with impunity, with gas chambers and terrorist attacks and unrelenting bombing with minimal "collateral damage." This kind of laughter bellows forth from people dancing with glee when they learn innocent people of all races and creeds were incinerated in the World Trade Center. Do those in the Way of Life laugh at those in the Way of Death?[24] Laughter may be the "property of Man," as Rabelais believed, but that can merely be a way to note that we are brutish and violent creatures. Laughter is comparison felt in mocking and scorn aimed at dehumanizing others. This kind of laughter is testimony to the fallen conscience, the reality of human sin. And in this way, inhumane laughter is also a wretched cry for redemption, for new creation, and for deliverance from the distortion and hatred that infest the human heart.

There is the possibility of another kind of laughter. It is found in traditions, as in the image of Sarah laughing when she learns that she will bear a child in her old age. This laughter draws an encompassing moral boundary, including everyone in the limits and folly that beset our lives. It is the expansiveness of the right conscience. Such laughter is not without its scorn, but what it scorns is the stupidity and horrors of life in the name of our higher natures, the insistence on human dignity. We could call this "good" laughter. It is the ability to laugh at oneself and to mock violence and stupidity born of genuine sympathy for others and our shared human plight. Mark Twain once said, "It is a noble thing to be a good man. But it is a far nobler thing to lead others to goodness, and much easier." We laugh at Twain's remark because we feel the democracy of hypocrisy. I am better at telling others how to live than living rightly myself. That is true of all of us. We need to denounce hypocrisy, but also to ennoble our humanity. Good laughter is sympathy with folly aimed at making us more humane. It can also be an act of resistance against dehumanizing forces while preserving human dignity amid oppression and violence. In this way, good laughter is part of the transformation of conscience, our moral being.

Good laughter is absent in the lives of those motivated by fanatical reasons for action. One also suspects that this kind of laughter is especially hard for Americans and others at this time, especially with respect to war and terrorists. In the heat of war, when the moral weight seems on one's side, sympathy and an honest look at one's own bloated and inflated national pride will hardly do. Consider again the joke that circulated after September 11, 2001: the joke about how Americans should capture Osama bin Laden, give him a sex change operation, and then free him to live under Taliban rule. It is funny and pointed. But it can easily slide off the edge. Our laughter can easily fail to co-implicate us in the denial of freedom and self-determination to women. The joke scorns bin Laden and the Taliban, but, if we are not careful, we forget the plight of women and especially women of color in this and other "free" nations.

It is hard to laugh at oneself. It is hard to laugh with righteous scorn at human fault and still abort the hatred that so easily arises in us when we confront violence and stupidity. But if we are to increase our interactions with other people and approach our traditions with humane purpose, good laughter is needed. Good laughter is how we preserve spheres of value, basic goods, by insisting, despite human folly, on the furthest reach of conscience. Good laughter strikes at the roots of fanaticism because it preserves reason and insists on shared humanity. Good laughter is one way to foster the global reflexivity that enhances rather than destroys diverse cultural resources. It makes us see the commonalities that bind our lives into a common destiny, a commonality of folly and insight, sorrow and joy, stupidity and awesome creativity in the human adventure. Good laughter is how we can live in our traditions and resist their fanatical possibilities.

Now let us be clear. Judgments must be made. In terms of the ethics of war, any nation is justified to use force in order to restrain those who indiscriminately kill innocent non-combatants. While the theological humanist has a profound bias against the use of force, there is, as argued in chapter 6, the possibility, at least in principle, of justifiable war aimed at restorative justice. The point now is not about the possibility of the use of lethal force. It is, rather, that the justice of one's cause and the justice of the conduct of conflict are diminished and maybe lost if one loses the ability to laugh at shared human folly. The justice of one's cause is lost if one resists evil, but demonizes its human agents.

What then is the response of a theological humanist to a world of violence and hatred? In all actions and relations we are to respect and enhance the integrity of life before God. This imperative of responsibility is not only for those who live in our nation, or share our "religion," or advocate our values. One is to respond to and with all of life. In situations of grave suffering and loss, the human penchant is to constrict moral boundaries, to draw lines between "us" and "them" in an attitude of fear and defensiveness. The theological humanist must labor against that constriction and always seek to include others within the scope of moral concern. And one does so, in fact, through careful reflection, built on convictions about the folly but also the resources of human thinking. One does so as well, I have suggested, in simple acts of good laughter as part of the labor of conscience. This does not mean that terror should not be resisted, that the innocent should not be defended. Quite the contrary. It does mean that responsible existence requires that our actions, even actions of resistance and protection, aim to respect and enhance, not demean or destroy, the lives of all involved. And that simply is thc task of the moral life in a world weeping in pain and marked by hatred and violence. Good laughter is a way to live in global reflexivity, resisting the forces driving us towards a clash of civilizations. One can only hope and labor daily to bend the machineries of politics towards more humane purposes.

Being Religious Humanly

Thankfully, there have always been people within the religious traditions who labor for a humane life and seek to redress human woe. They have sought to think as profoundly as we live, so that our living might be less violent and all the more creative. These persons have staked their lives on the fragile resources of moral reason, good laughter, and the insights of their traditions. We have called them Islamic and Jewish and Christian humanists. One might call them something else. But whatever they are called, the responsibility of serious religious people in our time is to join their ranks. For we must labor to make the ambiguity of our traditions – an ambiguity that lives in our own hearts and minds – into a resource for life rather than a force of fanatical destruction. We need to expand the boundaries of moral concern in order to live responsibly in the time of many worlds.

NOTES

1 Portions of this chapter have appeared elsewhere. It was originally given, in a different form, for the series "9/11: Causes and Consequences: Beyond the Clash of Civilizations" at the University of Chicago, November 2001. That lecture then appeared in *Sightings* in a three part series in October 2001. Other parts of the chapter were given at University of Chicago Alumni Dinners in New York City, Los Angeles, and San Francisco. Those remarks were called "Comparing Religions – Comparing Lives: Laughter and Ethics After 9/11." I was fortunate to speak at those events with my colleague Wendy Doniger. Not only have I benefited from her massive knowledge of the history of religions, but also from her own wise and human insight.

2 The work in comparative ethics is extensive. For representative texts see *Ethics in the World Religions*, edited by Joseph Runzo and Nancy M. Martin (Oxford: Oneworld, 2001); *Our Religions*, edited by Arvind Sharma (San Francisco, CA: HarperSanFrancisco, 1993); and especially *A Companion to Religious Ethics*, edited by William Schweiker (Oxford: Blackwell, 2004).

3 Plutarch, "On the Tranquility of Mind" in *Plutarch Moralia* vol. 4, translated by W. C. Helmbold, Loeb Classical Library (Cambridge, MA: Harvard University Press, 1939), 466D4, p. 179.

4 M. A. Screech, *Laughter at the Foot of the Cross* (Boulder, CO: Westview Press, 1999), p. 7.

5 François Rabelais, *Gargantua and Pantagruel*, translated by J. M. Cohen (New York: Penguin Classics, 1955). Also see Aristotle's *On the Parts of Animals* (X, 29) and also Plato's *Philebus*.

6 The idea of a clash of civilizations is from Samuel P. Huntington, "The Clash of Civilizations" in *Foreign Affairs* 72: 3 (summer 1993): 22–49. Also see Benjamin R. Barber, *Jihad vs. McWorld* (New York: Time Books, 1995). For a different approach to the issue, see *God and Globalization*, 4 vols., edited by Max L. Stackhouse, et al. (Harrisburg, PA: Trinity Press International, 2000–2). For a competing account within social theory of how to understand the present situation, see *Culture, Globalization and the World-System: Contemporary Conditions for the Representation of Identity*, edited by Anthony D. King (Minneapolis: University of Minnesota Press, 1997).

7 I have explored some of these forms of conflict elsewhere in this book. We examined not only beliefs about the origin of the world and social order in violence (chapter 1) but also problems of greed in a global context (chapter 3), as well as political conflict and the need for restorative justice (chapter 6).

8 We should note here that this is one of the reasons that the idea of "world" is systematic and complex in Christian thought. "World" can mean the arena of sin opposed to God. It can mean that for which Christ died. Christians even pray for "world without end." The analogical use of the idea of "world" to speak of these diverse and interlocking realities expresses the insight that "world" is best seen as a conglomerate of interacting and conflicting spaces of reasons. On this point see William Schweiker, "Responsibility and the World of Mammon: Theology,

Justice, and Transnational Corporations" in Stackhouse, et al., *God and Globalization*, vol. 1, pp. 105–39.

9 Arjun Appadurai, *Modernity at Large: Cultural Dimensions of Globalization* (Minneapolis: University of Minnesota Press, 1996), p. 33.

10 On this see John Tomlinson, *Globalization and Culture* (Chicago, IL: University of Chicago Press, 1999).

11 Cultural reflexivity is actually an old phenomenon. Religions and cultures have been interacting and adjusting to each other for a very long time, so that their own identities are constituted by these reflexive interactions. This is especially true of Christianity and Islam, given their history of mission, conquest, and empire. One also sees it in the so-called Middle Ages in Europe when Jewish, Islamic, and Christian thinkers and jurists were reading and responding to each other's work. It was found earlier in economic interactions through trade.

12 For an account of the internally complex and contested nature of any culture and the importance of this for theology, see Kathryn Tanner, *Theories of Culture: A New Agenda for Theology* (Minneapolis: Fortress Press, 1997).

13 The debate about "religion" and the comparison of religions is of course ongoing and never ending. For some wildly different approaches, see Ninian Smart, *Worldviews: Cross-Cultural Explorations in Human Belief* (New York: Scribner's Sons, 1983); Jonathan Z. Smith, *Imagining Religion: From Babylon to Jonestown* (Chicago, IL: University of Chicago Press, 1982); *Critical Terms for Religious Studies*, edited by Mark C. Taylor (Chicago, IL: University of Chicago Press, 1998); Donald Wiebe, *Beyond Legitimation: Essays on the Problem of Religious Knowledge* (New York: St. Martin's Press, 1994); Wilfred Cantwell Smith, *The Meaning and End of Religion* (New York: Macmillan, 1962); and Theo Sundermeier, *Was ist Religion? Religionswissenschaft in theologischen Kontext. Ein Studienbuck* (Gütersloh: Chr. Kaiser/Gütersloh Verlaghaus, 1999).

14 One finds this designation, as well as claims about the relation between the religions, in Sura 5 (The Table) in the Qur'an. See *The Koran Interpreted*, translated by Arthur J. Arberry (New York: Macmillan, 1955).

15 For the account of comparative moral reflection, see William Schweiker, *Responsibility and Christian Ethics* (Cambridge: Cambridge University Press, 1995) and *Power, Value and Conviction: Theological Ethics in the Postmodern Age* (Cleveland, OH: Pilgrim Press, 1998), esp. ch. 6.

16 For a fine account of these matters, see Bernard McGinn's magisterial *The Presence of God: A History of Western Christian Mysticism*, 5 vols. (New York: Crossroad, 1988).

17 Interestingly enough, there are current moral philosophers who make this argument about submission to authority in order to attain the capacity for valid moral reasoning. One this see Alasdair MacIntyre, *Three Rival Versions of Moral Enquiry: Encyclopedia, Genealogy, and Tradition* (Notre Dame, IN: University of Notre Dame Press, 1990). I have been helped in the formulations made in this chapter by remarks made by Azizah al-Hibri and Louis A. Shapiro in response to my *Sightings* articles noted above.

18 For an overview see Ninian Smart, *World Philosophies* (New York: Routledge, 1999).

19 St. Augustine is a good example. He argues in his *De Doctrina Christiana*, the virtual blueprint for the Western medieval university, that when in doubt scripture is always about *caritas*, love.

20 There is considerable discussion presently among theologians and philosophers about the range and kinds of premoral goods and their place within a comprehensive moral theory. For helpful discussions of the issues surrounding goods and norms, see Martha C. Nussbaum, *Woman and Human Development: The Capabilities Approach* (Cambridge: Cambridge University Press, 2000); Don Browning, *A Fundamental Practical Theology: Descriptive and Strategic Proposals* (Minneapolis, MN: Fortress Press, 1996); John Finnis, *Fundamentals of Ethics* (Washington, DC: Georgetown University Press, 1983); Robin W. Lovin, *Christian Ethics: An Essential Guide* (Nashville, TN: Abingdon Press, 2000); and William Schweiker, *Responsibility and Christian Ethics*.

21 Erasmus, *In Praise of Folly*, translated by Betty Rice with introduction by A. H. T. Levi (New York: Penguin Books, 1971), p. 199.

22 Jonathan Glover, *Humanity: A Moral History of the Twentieth Century* (New Haven, CT: Yale University Press, 2000), p. 37

23 Screech, *Laughter at the Foot of the Cross*, p. 17.

24 On this one should read Books 20 and 22 of Augustine's *City of God*!

CHAPTER 9

On Moral Madness

The Rage of Conviction

The scenes are engraved on collective memory. A man bursts into an office building releasing a flurry of bullets upon screaming workers. Surrounded by blood and carnage, he turns the gun on himself. The confusion, remorse, anger, and pain endured by the family and friends of the victims of wanton violence last a lifetime. Explanations are sought. He was abused as a child. He was a disgruntled worker. He was delusional. The same faulting explanations follow the trail of gang violence and ethnic–religious conflict. A nation watches in horror and disbelief as a commercial airliner filled with mothers and children and office workers and young men dives into the World Trade Center, evaporating in a ball of fire. Minutes later there is another explosion. In other parts of the world, children are tied to the front of trucks in ongoing conflict. Fundamentalist zealots within all the religions kill those seen as evil, unredeemable. Fundamentalist Christians in the USA bomb abortion clinics in the name of the sanctity of life. Muslim extremists carry out crimes of terror around the world. Ultraorthodox Jews want to turn Israel into an intolerant theocratic state. Militaristic Hindus engage in acts of hatred. Examples of violence abound within each and every tradition, each and every culture.

In our age, ethnic groups, individuals, and even whole societies are led to acts of cruelty and destruction by the logic of their convictions. Moral creeds too easily provoke the violation of life. Sadly, the usual explanations for these violent acts and movements never seem adequate. And so we flounder on basic questions. How can a slight from a superior lead a man into an office building armed with the thirst for blood in order to avenge his tarnished self-esteem? How can religious convictions about love fail to stop rape and murder? How is it that submission to the living God can lead to gross acts of violence against innocent people? Can we make sense of profound convictions about goodness turned towards destruction?

In order to understand and change contemporary life, one is forced to consider the connections between moral beliefs and the forces of destruction people unleash upon each other and their own societies. One must examine conscience. As argued throughout this book, it is necessary for those who hold a humane outlook to work against the violent potential of their own traditions. At stake are matters of human dignity, respect for life, and the truth of moral convictions. This chapter builds on the work of the last one by turning from laughter to moral madness. It tries to uncover at the level of felt experience the point at which convictions about what is good and holy turn hateful. The argument will be that the imaginative connection between certain moral convictions and the deep and abiding human need to expel psychic and physical energies can lead to distinctive forms of cruelty seen around the globe. We can call this phenomenon *moral madness*. It is the moral imagination gone wrong in a triumph over the good conscience. Let us start to clarify this idea by looking at the connection sometimes drawn between morality and violence.

The Moral Logic of Cruelty

There are parallels among cultures on matters of morally backed cruelty. This suggests that there are limits to moral diversity written into the fabric of cultural life and also human energies. If this is the case, then the forces of destruction and dehumanization fueled by moral beliefs must be examined in their depth and breadth without being blunted too easily by appeals to moral diversity or relativism. The cry of many cultural theorists about the relativity of morals blinds us to the moral mechanisms implicit in human violence.[1] It leads to a situation in which contemporary Western societies seem unable to speak cogently about evil. At best one hears that such violence is senseless. But the claim that acts of cruelty are senseless, and hence meaningless, is neither correct nor satisfying. This is why the usual explanations of social violence, gang rage, or ethnic–religious conflict seem so hollow. If we are going to face forces of violence motivated by deep moral impulses, then we need the means to think and speak about genuine evil as well as its logic and meaning.

Insisting on the moral depth of cultural life and violence is not to make the erroneous, and nihilistic, assertion that morality itself is the problem. We cannot overcome forms of violence by trying somehow to live beyond morality, to imagine that human life is or can ever transpire beyond distinctions of good and bad, right and wrong.[2] To live as a human being is to inhabit a moral space of life, a space of reasons, which endows existence with meaning and purpose. It is to engage in the ongoing task of culture-creation and thus to order values by which we orient our lives. The cruelty endemic to social existence is bound to the human problem of meaning and value in life. Clarity about what we ought to believe and how we ought to live with respect to convictions about good and evil, right and wrong, justice and injustice aid future life in a dangerous world. The wholesale rejection of the moral dimension of culture by positivist social scientists, cultural relativists, and some philosophers, merely aids and furthers destructive impulses.

While not rejecting morality for some vision of life "beyond good and evil," there is a subtle and more persuasive version of the idea that moral ideas themselves are the root problem. This is the claim made by some theorists that high ideals, beliefs about moral perfection, are the fuel of human cruelty.[3] We can call this the "anti-perfectionist theory" of social conflict. These thinkers contend that high ideals demand that all persons adopt them, and, failing that fact, warrant the use of force to compel moral conformity. The very idea of a universal morality or a determinate human good is therefore dangerous. For these theorists, two things are needed in order to counter morally backed cruelty. First, we need a minimal public morality to guide human interactions, one based mainly on sympathy and revulsion over cruelty. Linked to that minimal public morality is, second, a moral attitude, a way of holding one's own most cherished beliefs. As Richard Rorty puts it, we must become liberal ironists. We must hold our beliefs but always in an ironic manner, willing to revise them in order to preserve the minimal public standards necessary to avoid social conflict. While we can undertake all manner of personal self-formation, we cannot and ought not impose those beliefs about human goodness on others in pluralistic societies. Beliefs about the human good, what kinds of persons we should strive to be, and the ultimate sanction of morality ought not to occupy our attention. Since every war is waged in the name of ideals, the task of today is to deflate our ideals and the claims they make upon us. Ironic detachment about values is the heart of this response to social violence fueled by moral conviction.

This contemporary argument seems appealing even though it makes morality the root of our problems. All around us we see examples of violent conflict ignited by high ideals. The difficulties of the anti-perfectionist theory are obvious. The assumption that human conduct can be changed by altering how we think about moral ideals fails to grasp the simple fact that human conduct also finds its roots deep within life, in passions, affections, and human vitality. Only an account that can address the cognitive and the affective dimensions of human behavior is sufficient to counter the forms of violence irrupting in contemporary societies. The plea of ironic detachment is as hollow as the usual explanations of violence. These arguments condemn us to silence about the real threats to human dignity and innocent life that rage within contemporary cultures.

Against critics who see late-modern Western cultures as a happy cacophony of moral beliefs, or those conservatives who fear we are trapped within the death grip of moral decay, the logic of destruction and violence in these cultures bespeaks deep convictions about moral righteousness. The problem is that these convictions run wild. One task of ethics is to test convictions about moral goodness and to provide direction for conduct based upon clarity of moral belief. Moral reflection must confront, challenge, and transform the viciousness of a community's moral outlook or individual's conscience. Surprisingly, the means to test moral convictions and to direct human life are found in inherited religious traditions. Demonstrating that contention requires reclaiming the radical insights of biblical beliefs about righteousness from within a biblical story that manifests all the features of moral madness.

As done before (for example, in chapter 3 on greed or chapter 8 on laughter), we aim to offer a rough and ready phenomenology of moral experience. Yet this is done in hermeneutical fashion by exploring the story of Cain's murder of his brother Abel. This text manifests all the features of moral madness, as well as suggesting ways to overcome it. The story shows us how human evil irrupts within the goodness of creation. Yet, importantly, the text also hints at the moral meaning of new creation. By engaging this story we can continue a post-critical, explicative reading of texts, moving between "worlds," in order to articulate the space of life and the structure of lived experience. That is to say, we continue the kind of hermeneutic outlined in chapter 7 on sacred texts and the social imaginary, and, in fact, developed throughout this book. Biblical understandings of the moral life, if rightly grasped, short-circuit, rather than augment, the dynamics of moral violence. These beliefs can function like a computer virus that infects a civilization and rewrites its code of how human conflict is conducted and finally ended. Conversely, the film *Natural Born Killers*, as we will see later, shows the weakness of popular beliefs about violence, its causes and its end. The film reflects the poverty of modern moral thinking rooted in the banishment of religious and symbolic resources in ethics. To offer a way out of cycles of morally driven violence is more complex than our culture imagines. So, we turn now to an initial description of moral madness.

On Moral Madness

After being expelled from the Garden of Eden (Genesis 3), Adam and Eve, armed with the knowledge of good and evil, establish themselves in the land. The man "knows" his wife; she bears a son. The modesty of language hardly conceals the fact that sexual intercourse happens outside of paradise even though God had decreed this joy in creation. Human life is born in pain, and not in paradise. The passion for sexual union generates life, but also division between persons. Cain is the first-born. His name means "spear." He is a tiller of the ground, a farmer, whose labors, like other ancient Near Eastern peoples, signify the growth of established communities and agrarian civilization. Man and woman "know" each other again. The younger son, Abel, is born; he is a keeper of sheep. The name calls to mind the Hebrew *hebel*, meaning "breath," "futility," and thus foreshadows the terror to come. Culturally, Abel is a nomad, wandering through the country caring for his sheep. Futility and Spear, Abel and Cain, are the fruits of human passion outside of Paradise. The union of man and woman breeds human difference of occupation, culture, and ways of life that under the pressure of proximity are ripe for conflict.

The background of the story is the relation between and conflicts among nomadic and agrarian cultures.[4] These denote different ways of life, and hence contrasting values and beliefs about human goodness. An agrarian way of life is based on the trials and expectations worked by dependence on the forces of the seasons and the earth. Human existence is interwoven with the fragility of nature upon which it depends and against which it struggles to forge a viable and sustainable life. Adaptability and perseverance are central values when one is a tiller of the ground. Nomadic life severs human community from a set locale and requires the skills of travel and journey. The nomad must also adapt to new situations, but those situations are not as predictable as the flow of seasons. The sheepherder must fend off the attacks of predators; predation and blood is the constant fact of nomadic life.

Within this context of divergent cultural values, the text introduces the demands of cult, that is, the demand to offer gifts and sacrifices to the deity in order to fortify cultural values. We learn little about the reasons for the sacrifice or the actual working of the cultic act. There also seems to be no hint whatsoever of rivalry between the brothers for the deity's favor. Each brother simply offers God from the bounty of his labor: grain from the earth; sheep from the flock. Here the difference in ways of life, and hence what is valued and sought through human labor, is so deep that it is manifest in distinctive acts of reverence and worship. Cain offers the fruit of the earth; Abel completes the act of predation in a blood sacrifice to God. The unique connection between religious conviction and cultural form, between cult and culture, is presented rather starkly in the text. Every culture brings forth its own form of worship and thereby secures its most basic values in the sacred. In the biblical text, the differences between cultures are so profound that there is more than one altar. Now the divisions born of the passion of Adam and Eve are redoubled. Cultural activity, the tilling of the ground and the domestication of beasts, manifests a division in the depth of human gratitude and reverence.

Two altars and two sacrifices increase the divisions that permeate human existence.

God does not honor Cain's sacrifice. The text does not give a reason for this judgment. It is clearly not due to a fault of ritual, or, conversely, some failure of devotion or attitude on Cain's part. The only clue seems to be that a *sacrifice of blood* is more acceptable to God.[5] The giving of the life-force, which biblical authors thought resided in blood, is, unexplainably, honored by the deity, while the bounty of the earth accords no favor. Does this anchor the fact of predation in the sacred? Conversely, does God's honoring of blood stop the cycle of bloodletting through cult? We are not told, although this will be debated throughout the Bible by sages, lawgivers, prophets, and even the messiah. In any event, the text does shift the question of what is acceptable from human intention to the free and seemingly inscrutable will of God. In the context of the narrative this means that the divisions of human labor and cultural forms are judged by a power not definable within the logic of human expectations. Accordingly, there opens within the text yet another division. It is a division between the deep human need for acceptance and worth expressed in the cultic act of worship and the inscrutable will of God judging that worth. This division is also born of blood, just as the narrative recounts Cain and Abel entering the world in passion and blood. God accepts the sacrifice of blood and that acceptance creates division.

Now the murder. Cain calls to his brother to meet him in the fields. Cain "rose up" against Abel and brutally killed him. The "spear" vents itself on human "breath," returning Abel's life to the soil from which it came. Abel's blood, his life force, cries out from the ground for protection or vindication. Cain is questioned by God, the God who – much as he accepted the blood sacrifice of Abel – recognizes the screams of the life force from the ground. The deity again acknowledges blood. Yet this time, blood is recognized in order to judge the act of predation unacceptable. Cain's act of predation crossed a moral boundary: this act of taking life is not killing or sacrifice, it is murder. "Where is Abel your brother?" God's question places Cain's action in an explicitly moral context revolving around the bonds of familial care and regard. Cain denies that he is his brother's keeper. His denial has sparked centuries of reflection on the duties of love and family. And later in this chapter we will see here the opening from within the biblical imagination for the Golden Rule as a response to the problem of violence to the other. At this juncture what is of more interest to us is the fact that the text compresses several things into its brief depiction of fratricide. It is vitally important to isolate these factors basic to moral madness. We miss the profundity of the text if we make it the occasion to determine what family members owe each other.

While we do not know how Cain learned of God's lack of regard for his offering, the text in two short verses discloses crucial dimensions of moral madness. Cain is angry about God's action. The anger shows itself physically; it is etched into Cain's body. God asks why Cain is angry and why his countenance has fallen. This is important. Cain construes the rejection of his cultic offering as in fact a rejection of the *totality of his person and life*. This is depicted in the narrative through the bodily inscription of Cain's anger; his whole being, body and soul, are now involved. Of course, Cain is not utterly rejected. God only rejected his sacrifice. This is the first element of moral madness. It is what I will call the *logic of totality*. Cain inflates the divine rejection and applies it to the totality of his life. This is a profound failure of conscience as the labor of moral being.

It is important to grasp that this "inflation," the logic of totality, rests upon a basic dynamic of moral action: respect is given or withdrawn from persons. By "respect" we mean simply the *recognition* that a person is part of the moral community, and, accordingly, must be *regarded* as bearing worth. The force of Cain's anger is that the divine rejection of his sacrifice places him beyond the bounds of the moral community, in that there is no recognition of or regard for his worth. In so doing, a basic principle of rightness *seems* violated. Of course, Cain makes the faulty inference from part to whole; he is trapped in the logic of totality. Under this logic, Cain believes he has suffered an injustice that ought to be made right. The logic of totality, in other words, provides the warrant for vindication of human worth *in the name of justice*. One dimension of moral madness as a failure of conscience is strictly cognitive: it has to do with how we think about actions of giving and withdrawing respect. The problem is not, as liberal theorists like Rorty have held, ideas about moral perfection or goodness. The cognitive problem centers on the faulty widening of the claims about rightness such that a specific, determinate judgment about an aspect of life or conduct (God's rejection of Cain's sacrifice) is taken as an affront to the *whole* of a person's or community's life. The error in his moral reflection is such that it places human dignity, his own dignity, at the center of dispute rather than some other aspect of life.[6]

The text conjoins this logic of totality with a claim about human motives. God warns Cain to do well and he will be accepted. And if Cain does not do well, "sin is crouching at the door; its desire is for you, but you must master it." Sin is depicted as a predator that waits for its prey. This is, seemingly, an intensification of the "Satan" figure (Genesis 3) associated with the temptation and sin of Adam and Eve. For Adam and Eve, the personification of sin merely tempted them to disobey the divine; now, outside of Eden, the personified evil is a predator seeking to destroy its prey. In this way, the logic of the movement from the "fall" of Adam and Eve to the murder of Abel is one of intensification of evil's power and also the increasing vulnerability of human beings to that power. Surprisingly, the picture of "sin" as a beast awaiting its prey folds the discourse about blood and predation seen throughout the story (birth; Abel's labor; blood sacrifice; the murder) back on itself at the level of human motives. So the seemingly primitive depiction of sin as a beast ought not to fool us. Moral madness is driven not only by a logic of totality in which a perception or conviction about moral rightness is wrongly extended beyond it proper domain. Moral madness is, second, expressed in *images of possession.* It is as if some external force (the beast) captures and consumes the agent, distorting conscience and driving one's actions. In this respect, moral madness has the very opposite structure we found in chapter 3 to characterize greed. Whereas greed is marked by a desire to be absorbed, inscribed, into a culture's scale of values, moral madness besets the individual as an external force driving them to action.

We might infer that the image of a beast waiting to consume one is simple psychological projection; the moral imagination, we might say, fills out human experiences pictorially in ideas of beasts, serpents, demons, or furies. And that is surely the case. But the point is that these depictions articulate something important about distinctive forms of human existence: the experience of being overtaken, possessed, by some force internalizing itself in one's behavior. This is why, surprisingly enough, love can be a form of moral madness.[7] Love, the ancients knew, can possess the soul and drive a person to wrongful actions. It can be a divine or demonic madness. The insight is found in Greek antiquity in the figure of Dionysus, for example in Euripides' *Bacchae*, where the god possesses women worshipers, driving them into an orgy of violence. This figure of thought about moral madness has influenced a long line of thinkers from late antiquity, through the work of Friedrich Nietzsche, to contemporary theorists.[8] What is missing in this line of thought, despite its similarities to the argument developed here, is that there is no mechanism for ending the violence as there is in the biblical story of Cain and Abel. Moral madness must just exhaust itself, a troubling thought that we see continued in Dionysian films like *Natural Born Killers.*

Not only does moral madness have a cognitive dimension where erroneous judgments about worth are falsely inflated and applied to a person or group, but there is also an affective, conative, or motivational dimension to it. It is the inability to grasp the connection between the cognitive and conative dimensions of moral madness that renders forms of cruelty opaque to contemporary persons. In fact, when these dimensions are joined in a single person or a community, wrath is released under the banner of righteousness. It is hardly surprising that in the very next verse after God's rejection of the sacrifice, Cain calls to his brother to join him in the field. Moral madness will vent itself on innocent life.

The biblical text does not attempt to explain the cause of Cain's faulty judgment, nor does it explore the origin of the predatory force of sin that consumes him. We do know, of course, that Adam and Eve left the Garden of Eden with the knowledge of good and evil, but also with no assurance that their knowledge was without error. There is a mythological background to the tenuous and fallible character of human moral knowledge. We also know from the story of Eden that negative motivating forces are personified in the image of the serpent trying to influence human life. In this sense, the explanation of the origin of Cain's action in its cognitive and conative aspects is interwoven with the dawning on earth of distinctly human life. But the claim of the biblical stories seems to be that the origin of human fault and evil can at best be symbolically depicted and not rationally explained.[9]

Insofar as the biblical text does not attempt to *explain* the origin of Cain's cognitive error and affective possession, but rather simply *depicts* them, what else can we glean from the text about the phenomenon of moral madness? Some other features immediately stand out. In response to the screams of Abel's blood, Cain is "cursed from the ground, which has opened its mouth to receive [his] brother's blood." The very soil upon which Cain depends for his life, the space of all agrarian values, now turns against him. The earth is depicted as a predator opening its mouth for Abel's blood, and, accordingly, will no longer sustain Cain in his farming labor. Moral madness turns against itself. It is destructive of the ostensible cause of injustice (Abel) driven by powerful and uncontrollable forces (sin). This madness ends in the destruction of those in its grip. Cain is ripped from his culture and livelihood; he is forced to wander like a nomad. His punishment is to become what he despised, a theme repeated over and over in other myths, stories, and dramas. It is to experience God's judgment internalized in the tortured and bound conscience. Importantly, this theme is lost in contemporary Western cultures. We live in a time when the agents of violence are depicted as escaping this kind of (internalized) punishment. And in these cultures, people have tried mightily to banish any sense that one can and ought to be judged by conscience. The loss of moral conscience and the fantastic danger it poses will concern us below.

Cain sees that his action has subjected him to the ways of predation. "Whoever finds me will slay me!" The effect of moral madness is not only to destroy its perpetrators. It also undercuts the very demand for justice which, under the logic of totality, drove the violence. Because of this, the effect of moral madness is to reduce human life to a condition of conflict between the strong and the weak. What began as a demand for moral vindication, ends by instituting the triumph of brute power in human life. The only answer to this horrible conclusion offered by the biblical text, an answer lacking in the modern world, is that the divine will demand, surprisingly, vengeance on *Cain's behalf.* This is of course the final irony of the text. It is a clue about how to avoid the terror of moral madness. While Cain's offering was rejected, Cain himself remains under divine protection, even as God executed justice for the murder of Abel. God does not in fact withdraw respect from Cain; the deity is not trapped by the logic of totality. The divine justice institutes the possibility of future life; it does not destroy that fragile possibility. This is stated more forcefully later in the scriptures when Jesus insists that God lets the rain fall on the just and the unjust alike (Matthew 5:43–8). Without this kind of creative, divine justice (a creation event, as it was called before), the effects of moral madness are self-destruction and the breakdown of the very order of values to which the perpetrator of the violence appealed in action. That breakdown signals the victory of power over all. The divine actions show us, again, that from within the created order are signs of the new creation, a revolution of heart and mind.

The complexity of the biblical story of Cain and Abel is that in a few short verses we have disclosed central features of the human phenomenon we are calling moral madness. The logic of totality and the externalization of motive, images of possession, are features of moral madness the effects of which threaten self-destruction and the breakdown of cultural values needed to sustain a way of life. We will see these features played out and given different expressions in a moment. Our claim is that moral madness is not senseless; it is characterized by some rationality about values and justice within cultural life. Nevertheless, it is a genuine madness because it leads to derangement of life and self-destruction. The kinds of violence that manifest moral madness are the anti-type, the inverted image, of viable personal and cultural life. Moral madness manifests the depths of human moral being turned against itself and others. If the biblical text is right, this kind of madness is always crouching at the door waiting to consume us. Cultural activity always confronts forces of destruction waiting to consume the life and vitality of human existence. Only a realistic assessment of this fact might help us to master these forces operative in the human heart and in the dynamics of culture.

An Interlude

What is the warrant for the claims just made about moral madness as a permanent possibility in cultural life? In order to make some headway in answering that question, and also to clarify how to think about the forms of moral madness, we can turn from the biblical text to contemporary debates about culture. And we might imagine that these issues are interrelated. Only if we have a subtle enough means to detect the forms of moral madness in cultural artifacts and current life can we ever hope to make good on the larger claim about it being a feature of cultural existence. Put more simply, how are we to interpret cultural forms and activities from an ethical perspective? The reason to pause in order to answer this methodological question is to be clear about the course of the chapter's inquiry. We do not want confusion on this point to keep us from concern with the complexity of types of morally backed violence.

Questions about interpretation are deep and much debated by contemporary cultural critics. Among post-critical approaches part of the debate has to do with the *character* of the artifacts we are exploring. Is there some substratum of human life that comes to expression in cultural forms, say in art, literature, music, or cinema? If that is the case, then we can decode those forms in order to isolate and analyze the dynamics of life they represent. This is sometimes called a romantic hermeneutic or theory of interpretation. Cultural forms (works of art, music, architecture) on this account express the genius of the artist or the distinctive form of life of a community. They do not create or define a way of life; they express vital impulses and the creativity of the artist or the culture.[10] So we should look to the biblical as an expression of that impulse. Conversely, there are critics who argue that cultural forms do not express any substratum of life, either the mind of the artist or myriad social forces. This is sometimes called a postliberal theory of interpretation because it does not rest on individual genius, as romantic hermeneutics seems to do. Postliberal theorists contend that cultural artifacts constitute a meaning system with its own set of rules and ideas, which provide a culture with an identity. Personal life requires learning those cultural rules of meaning and gaining cultural literacy. This hermeneutic, or theory of interpretation, does not try to dig through works of art, music, or social activities like sport or cinema in order to uncover some expressive impulse. The interpreter analyzes cultural actions to see how they work and how they are learned.[11] We should interpret the Cain and Abel story in terms of how it is used in Christian or Jewish communities.

The difficulties in these positions seem obvious. Romantic hermeneutics rests upon the too easy assumption that human beings are down deep really just the same. Postliberal thought for its part risks missing the substantial similarities between cultures. The task is to grasp similarities and differences in the moral outlooks and cultural activities of persons. We can do so, I believe, by keeping our focus on the relation between culture and the moral imagination. Human beings continually face the great task of civilization, of world-making, and any culture, as we saw before, is a space of meanings and values that define and guide human life. The moral imagination is how that space of meanings and values (i.e., culture) is formed and apprehended by people for the purpose of deciding how to live personally and communally. Explicative or mimetic hermeneutics, as we have called it, is the interpretation of these meanings and values found in cultures in order to understand others and ourselves. This act of understanding does not mean that we become those whom we study; it does not entail reducing other cultural creations and moral lives to our own categories of meaning.

The point, as one theorist put it, is to grasp "how it is that other people's creations can be so utterly their own and so deeply part of us."[12] This is decidedly the case with moral madness. The forms of cultural meaning-making found in the wild and wily course of Western civilization have sought to understand and curtail moral madness. These have impressed themselves upon us more deeply than we imagine; they provide a framework of understanding. One task of this book has been to reclaim those frameworks from cultural forgetfulness so that we might use them today and also critically revise them when needed. Sadly, the forms of moral madness have also impressed themselves in cultural life. This is why we see the numbing repetition of types of violence throughout history and also the boring reiteration of claims and excuses on the part of the agents of destruction, their paltry appeals to justification. This hermeneutic aims to understand these matters; it hopes to apprehend the meaning of other people's cultures as well as the moral significance of our own lives.

If this is right, the debate between romantic and postliberal theorists is misplaced, at least in terms of trying to understand the complex connections between violence and justice. The brief account of the Cain and Abel story shows why this is the case. On the one hand, moral madness rests upon a set of moral beliefs held by a culture, beliefs, as we have seen, about what is valuable (agrarian; nomadic) and also rules pertaining to the just treatment of persons. We might imagine that these beliefs are communicated through a myriad of cultural activities found in a society. Cult itself, as we saw, is an activity which reaffirms the values held by a society, in this case agrarian civilization (Cain) and nomadic existence (Abel). There is a logic to these processes we must try to understand. A key element of that logic with respect to moral madness is the *logic of totality* that falsely widens the scope of moral judgments. This logic and the ideas used to convey it have impressed themselves on subsequent life. On this score postliberal hermeneutics seems right. The story of Cain and Abel is not only the creation of ancient Near Eastern cultures, although it is that too. This story is also deeply part of us and the practices of our religious communities.

On the other hand, we have also seen that at least in ancient societies there was a perception that human conduct, especially violent, destructive behavior, is often motivated by forces objective to the self but which well-up within the self. These forces seem to be antecedent to the cultural activities that specify and affirm social values. This is the real insight of romantic hermeneutics. The springs of human action strike deep into passions and vitalities. This depth is such that it comes to expression in bodily form (Cain's fallen countenance), in behavior, and also in cultural forms. Part of the oddity of this ancient text is precisely the objectification of motive force, depicting it as a beast crouching at the door. These depictions seem naive to the modern mind set. That is an assumption our inquiry challenges. Maybe we need to think less literally about these ancient texts; perhaps we need to try to grasp the moral meaning of these depictions in order to understand the real depth and power of moral madness. At this level of hermeneutics one needs an open mind, a willingness to think that we do not know it all, and thus might learn something about human existence by engaging other people's creations. In any case, it is clearly possible to interpret cultural activities by seeking to uncover the human vitalities that drive them.

The cognitive and conative dimensions of moral madness require that we sidestep the debate between romantic and postliberal theories of interpretation. What is important, again, is to examine cultural creations as spaces of meaning and value, as moral spaces, realizing that other people's worlds are different than our own even while they might also be part of us. But this opens another question. It is also deep and much disputed. This is a debate not in hermeneutics but in moral theory about the *status* of moral beliefs and values. Are moral beliefs and values simply human responses to conditions of life, or, conversely, do they attempt to be faithful to something beyond human responses?

Some theorists – let us call them anti-realists – believe that human beings create value in order to endow life with sense and significance. Moral interpretation aims at how persons and societies create value because values strike no deeper than human responses to the problems of life.[13] The status of moral values, then, is that they are cultural products just like other social inventions, say law or economics. On this theory, the Cain and Abel story is a cultural artifact that aims at creating and sustaining a set of values about the worth of human life endorsed by "God." Other theorists disagree. They claim that moral value is rooted in reality, and, further, that moral thinking is not simply about how best to cope with matters of human conduct, but about trying to get it right. Moral values have ontological status; they strike into the way things are.[14] From this perspective, the Cain and Abel story articulates something true about human life as such, perhaps the truth of the sanctity of life that backs all duties we have to others and to ourselves. Moral realists, as we call them in chapter 8, insist that moral ideas and values can be true or false. What is more, moral statements are about what is the case, independent of our ideas and beliefs about what is the case. The story of Cain and Abel, accordingly, can be tested for its truth in terms other than the story itself and how it has been used in the moral lives of cultures informed by the biblical religions.

Debates over realism and anti-realism divide moral theologians and philosophers. It would be nice to be able to offer a simple way through the thicket of this debate about the *status* of values, just as it would be nice to call a truce to the hermeneutical debate between romantic and postliberal theorists over the *character* of cultural creations. That is not going to happen.

Besides, it is actually not needed for the purposes of the present inquiry. There is another way to think about these matters. In this alternate approach to interpretation and ethics, the basic claim is that people create values in order to discover something true about the nature of their existence. Cultural meanings and values are obviously human inventions, but the creativity of the moral imagination is always limited by features of existence for the purpose of living truthfully in the world. The stark contrast between realism and anti-realism in ethics can blind us to this simple fact. Cultural creations do have a realistic purpose, but they are always human inventions. Furthermore, the purpose of grasping truthfully the human condition is realized expressively, like romantics hold, but also, as postliberals see, regulatively by endowing social actions with meaning. We have to understand human meanings and values from the perspective of their felt significance, but also in terms of their social function. Again, the overwrought difference between postliberal and romantic hermeneutical theories, as well as realism and anti-realism, is unhelpful. We need to be more generous in trying to understand meanings and values.[15]

Only a complex understanding of the character and status of cultural artifacts and moral values lets us see other people's and our own creations as central to self-understanding while requiring that we also test understandings against the world in which we find ourselves. In other words, the view of interpretation offered here insists that meanings and value are corrigible, they can be changed, since they are about something more than cultural regulation or self-expression. We cannot merely peer through cultural forms and activities to see reality. What we want to understand is the moral world of other people and ourselves. Specifically, we want in this chapter to grasp the moral dynamics of cruelty within cultural creation. If this is the purpose, then we must adopt a hermeneutically realistic form of moral interpretation. The truth of this approach can only be judged by whether or not as a pathway of interpretation it fulfills its purpose. We must seek to understand moral madness without getting caught in the endless debates about how we ought to interpret culture.

The Madness Trap

One might imagine that these issues of interpretation could lead to questions about the nature of knowledge, the limits to understanding other people, and debates about moral relativism. Hopefully, the above comments, along with the rest of this book, signal awareness of these issues and also judgments made about them. But the concern now is with moral madness. On that score we have begun to set out some basic ideas. Let us return to a theme noted above but quickly dropped. It will help to confirm the very possibility of moving between cultures and times as we try to understand and also undercut forms of human violence. Recall that we noted a striking – even dangerous – difference between the ancient, biblical texts and contemporary high-modern societies in terms of the texture of moral consciousness and how the cycle of destruction driven by moral madness is stopped. As the next step of reflection we need to clarify that difference. A leap from the Cain and Abel story to Oliver Stone's film *Natural Born Killers* (1994) will make the point.

The plot of Stone's film is quite simple. A young man, Mickey, and his girlfriend, Mallory, go on a killing spree. They kill Mallory's abusive father and mother, and then proceed to carry out brutal, random acts of violence, leaving a trail of witnesses to tell the story. The movie follows their spree and portrays the public's odd and horrific fascination with mass murders.[16] Mickey and Mallory become media celebrities; they attract and also repel the popular imagination. Their love for each other is praised even as their violence is eroticized. At last, they are captured and imprisoned. Yet their mere presence in the prison is dangerous; it seems to incite the inmates to violence. In this explosive situation, Mickey grants a self-seeking television pundit an interview. This is permitted by the prison warden on the hopes of esteem and profit. In the turn of events, Mickey manages to incite a prison riot; amid the blood and carnage Mickey and Mallory escape, dragging the pundit with them. The interviewer joins in the violence, feeling that finally he is alive, possessed, we might say, by the beast of violence. The movie ends with Mickey and Mallory executing this man and then fleeing. The parting shots of the movie depict Mickey and Mallory with children happily driving across country in their camping trailer. The violence has exhausted itself and its agents calmly return to "ordinary" life as loving parents.

The movie is repulsive. It graphically depicts extreme acts of gratuitous violence. It portrays a culture gripped by a sickening love of violence and death because it lacks genuine vitality. The film also reveals elements of moral madness noted before, as well as the crucial difference between the ancient and the contemporary Western, high-modern world. What do I mean?

At a crucial point in the plot Mickey is being interviewed. Pressed about his violence and the death of over fifty innocent people, Mickey answers the questions put to him in a way that manifests the dynamics of moral madness. The mass murderer speaks of the *demon*, an external force, he is born with that takes possession of him. He is a "natural born killer." Predation is natural; man is a beast like other beasts waiting to devour his victims. Any attempt to deny this, Mickey insists, is delusional; it is to live a lie. Here the externalization of violent motive in the demon is radically naturalized. Whereas "sin" was crouching at the door waiting for Cain, it raged against nature and was within the ability of Cain to resist. For Mickey, the demon simply is the natural and any attempt to deny it through self-control or moral rigor is fated to fail. This line of thinking seeks to undercut the possibility of any moral judgment about mass murder. It casts life into a beastly condition in which strength and weakness are the only determination.[17] An image of possession dominates the plot.

Not surprisingly, Mickey is also trapped in the *logic of totality*. In response to questions about the innocence of his victims, Mickey retorts that *no one is innocent*. He glares at the interviewer, supposedly convicting the man of sin. From the fact that some persons are guilty of wrong, Mickey inflates the judgment to include *all human beings*. He articulates a secularized and distorted version of the Christian doctrine of original sin. Mickey believes that in virtue of being alive one is guilty. This is the moral justification for mass murder, in his demented mind. All are guilty. Justice must be done. The murderer is an agent of justice. So compelling is this line of reasoning within the prison culture that a riot breaks out following these words. The agents of justice need not be right or pure, and, further, wrath is rightly rained on anyone because all are guilty. With the riot we see the joining of the logic of totality and the affective dimensions of moral violence. We see the venting of moral madness. In this sense, *Natural Born Killers* reduplicates in contemporary terms the very same dynamic of moral violence seen in the Cain and Abel story.

However, there are differences between the stories. These should give us pause. The differences show us why we must be very concerned to understand and defuse the logic of moral madness. In the Cain and Abel story, the cycle of violence is broken by divine justice. This justice, while it punishes the evildoer, does not vent itself with wholesale violence. In fact, the worth of Cain is reaffirmed even as moral boundaries are established. The divine wrath, unlike moral madness, opens the possibility for future life. The biblical thought world provides a language and set of images for the moral imagination to use in aborting its own most pernicious logic. Wrath can never simply run its course; there are limits to human violence in the name of justice rooted in divine action. *Natural Born Killers* presents a different and less complex vision. In its vision, violence is simply supposed to exhaust itself. For some inexplicable reason Mickey and Mallory stop killing and begin to raise a family. Presumably, everyone still remains guilty and the demands of justice retain their claim to enforcement. But the agents of death no longer vindicate justice with blood.

In Stone's film human life is portrayed as suspended over an irrational abyss of violence without purpose or necessary end. The earth itself opens its mouth to consume the human project. History is just a slaughtering block. Human time marks itself in blood and the madness ends – temporarily to be sure – for no reason, no purpose. This is the implication of the Dionysian vision, noted above. It is found in this contemporary film. Is our society bereft of any sacred structure that might curtail and limit violence? If that is so, then the fact of predation seems the basic social reality. The fact of predation is the basic truth of history. Whirl is let loose on the earth, as we saw earlier in this book.[18]

The prospect that we are developing a culture in which *exhaustion* is the only answer to the fact of moral violence should terrify us. Do the horrific and diabolical forms of violence that destroy thousands of lives in a few moments by using commercial jetliners as bombs have no end or answer than exhaustion? Do military actions aimed to bolster political legitimation have no measure but economic exhaustion? Yet the moral poverty of Stone's film does not stop in its inability to imagine an answer other than exhaustion. I noted before that Cain was condemned to become what he despised; this was manifest in a form of consciousness aware of life flung into the teeth of predation. "Whoever sees me will slay me!" This form of moral consciousness, true conscience, is missing in *Natural Born Killers*. The film ends with Mickey and Mallory living as normal parents. Life can supposedly return to patterns set on insuring the future, on having children, without remorse or the scars of violence. We are to believe, somehow, that Mickey and Mallory can love their child without any threat of renewed violence even though, in Mickey's own words, *everyone* is guilty. Why not murder the children? Mickey testifies to the loss of the form of consciousness, the pangs of conscience, we have seen in Cain.

Two options are possible here. One is that Mickey represents a form of human life which is simply empty. We might imagine that this kind of person is so lacking in critical self-reflection and so utterly narcissistic that he cannot experience a shift in consciousness wrought by interaction with others. He is incapable of remorse or love. This does not seem to be the case with Mickey. We are forced to the second option in understanding this character, an option briefly mentioned amid the interview in the prison. At a crucial juncture in the interview Mickey insists that he is beyond the form of life of others. He is a new form of life, a kind of Nietzschean *Übermensch* living beyond cultural beliefs about good and evil. Mickey enacts the most violent version of inner-worldly self-transcendence advocated by Nietzschean thinkers, as we will explore in the next chapter. He vents wrath on injustice unconstrained by remorse or guilt as somehow a testimony to his higher, purer form of existence. Mickey is utterly self-determining in his moral existence; he creates value and defines justice. He is Zeus-like. His inscrutable will decides who is deemed worthy of respect and life. The path beyond moral madness rests not simply in the exhaustion of wrathful energies, in a catharsis of violence. Freedom from moral violence is possible only when the agents of violence – and this must be seen as humanity it self – evolve to a mode of existence beyond good and evil and simply decide in a supreme act of will to forgo violence. In this respect *Natural Born*

Killers portrays morality itself as the problem. The answer to moral mad ness is the emergence of a new form of human life, the *Übermensch*, beyond good and evil.

Stone's film returns us to elements of moral madness isolated above. It also graphically presents the basic differences between the ancient, biblical thought world and high modern cultures. These differences center on the logic of totality, the naturalization of objectified motives, and how the spread of violence is to be stopped. By exploring the Cain and Abel narrative along with *Natural Born Killers* much of the terrain captured by the idea of moral madness has been covered. We have begun to acquire a language to think critically about moral violence by drawing comparative insights from products of difficult cultures. Of course, a host of questions remains to be answered. How is it that a story arising out of ancient Near Eastern cultures finds analogues in a late twentieth-century movie about mass murderers? Is it the case that other people's creations have impressed themselves deeply in our own self-understanding? Then again, how do we account for the radical difference between the works about moral madness? Is it enough to blame modern unrelenting violence on the loss of God and a sacred structure of society? Do other social powers and ideas about life grip our moral imaginations? How are we to make judgments about the truth of these various accounts of moral madness and the ways we might escape such forms of human violence?

These are the questions we must all ponder. We cannot hope to address them all in this chapter or even this book. Granting that limitation, there is a final step in the inquiry of this chapter. We need to glean insights from the rich complexity of the biblical story into the possibilities for escaping a future of violence. We hope to isolate within religious texts, texts that can and sometimes do lead to violence, a way beyond the narrative logic of the text. One reads the text at cross-purposes with itself and thereby, surprisingly, uncovers its real moral possibility (cf. chapter 5).

Violence and the Principle of Morality

Within the story of Cain and Abel is found a vital key to what can and may and must thwart moral madness and the cycles of violence it drives. This is found in the fact that God does not withhold respect from Cain. Even as God executes justice for the murder of Abel by banishing Cain, the deity does not deny protection to him. Further, we should realize that what initially exposes Cain's guilt is his denial of reciprocal responsibility for his brother. Upon being questioned, Cain retorts: "Am I my brother's keeper?" Yet in his response to God's act of banishment, Cain, though he violated and denied the dignity of his own brother, fears that the dignity of his life will be violated, that he will be killed by whomever he meets. Again, the divine insures that Cain's life will not be wantonly violated. In various ways, the divine stops the cycle of violence born of moral madness. But the text also presents in and through the dialogue between God and Cain a claim about *reciprocal responsibility*. This claim becomes formulated much later as the Golden Rule: "do unto others as you would have done unto you." I want to finish our inquiry exploring this "rule" as a response to moral madness, as one way to specify further the meaning of the imperative that we are to *respect and enhance the integrity of life before God*. The discussion here compliments the earlier interpretation of the double love command. The concern now is to formulate the norm for the formation of conscience.

For many Jews and Christians, the Golden Rule is the supreme moral principle. In the Jewish tradition, as noted previously, it was given in negative form by Hillel: "Do not do unto others what you would not want done to you." In the New Testament, the rule is announced by Jesus, although there are differences between Matthew's positive statement of it and Luke's negative formulation (cf. Matthew 7:12; Luke 6:31). Yet in each gospel the rule is located in what is presented as the epitome of Jesus's teaching, namely, the Sermon on the Mount and the Sermon on the Plain. The widespread use of the rule as well as its positive and negative formulation implies an interpretive principle. As Paul Ricoeur has noted, one must explore the Golden Rule set "in the perspective delimited by the symbolic order underlying the Jewish and Christian Scripture."[19] In doing so, one sees that the rule formulates with respect to actions a connection to creation. Recall Hans Dieter Betz's insight noted before in this book: "How do you love your neighbor? Look at creation: this is the way God loves the neighbor. God provides the bounty of life even to the enemy, to the rebellious and ungrateful humans."[20] In Pauline terms, God loves us "while we were yet sinners" (Romans 5:8) and because of this obligation to others does not rest on their moral worth, an insight missed in *Natural Born Killers* and virtually all forms of Nietzschean/Dionysian morals.

As the Golden Rule has been understood in the context of Western religious thought, it has three special features.[21] First, the Golden Rule focuses on the intersubjective nature of human action. This means that the point of the rule is not simply obedience to an imperative. What comes first is relations among persons. Furthermore, it is not simply "humanity" (the idea, say in Kantian ethics, of rational freedom) in persons that is the focus of moral concern. The different and unique character of individuals is what morally matters. This is seen in the biblical story of Cain and Abel, not only through the density of their names (Spear, Futility) and vocations (agrarian, herder), but also in God's mark of mercy on Cain. Second, it is important to see that the Golden Rule, whether in Hillel's negative formulation or Jesus's positive statement, centers on wants, aversions, and desires. In so doing, the rule locates morality within the scope of basic human goods, things we value and fear to forsake at the level of passions and desires. Goods implied in our actions must be protected and promoted. Unjustified violence against these goods is immoral, evil.

There is a range of basic goods in human life: natural goods of sensibility and experience (sexuality, pleasure, play, etc.), social goods (friendship, family, political or communal involvement, etc.), and also reflective goods, like self-understanding and cultural activity.[22] These forms of basic goods – natural, social, reflexive – are the background to the Golden Rule. They were clearly violated in Cain's murder of Abel, but affirmed in God's act of merciful justice. What we want for ourselves is to integrate or bring into some coherence the diversity of these goods so that our lives are rich and deep. We ought to expect that other people aim at some integration of their lives as well, even if (as is usually the case) they do so in ways that differ from us. The Golden Rule insists on this point: we should treat others as we ourselves wish to be treated, namely, to be able to draw together a range of goods we desire into some integral life. Unlike some kinds of current ethics, then, the Golden Rule specifies a vision of the field of morality in which a range of human goods are to be respected and enhanced under a norm aimed at intersubjective relations as well as a host of motives for acting, like desire and fear. It articulates the complex view of morality that we found in chapter 8 to be basic to the great monotheistic religions.

A third trait of the Golden Rule brings us to the problem of moral madness. By focusing on human interaction as well as presuming basic goods, the rule, in Paul Ricoeur's words, "emphasizes the fundamental asymmetry between what someone *does* and what *is done* to another." The other "is potentially the victim of my action as much as its adversary."[23] The Golden Rule, centered on interaction, presupposes not only intersubjectivity and basic goods, but also the power to act and the potential exercise of power over others. The Golden Rule aims to thwart the tyranny of power on and over others; in this way it formulates as a maxim for action the very insight of the Cain and Abel story. At issue is what someone does and what is done to another, an actor and a patient. The other person is potentially beloved, victim, or adversary. The moral life is the demand and possibility that in actions and relations people are to use the power at their disposal to respect and enhance the integrity of life.

However, we must note a challenge to the Golden Rule as an adequate formulation of the domain of moral norms. As theorists have often noted, the rule rests on a suppressed premise, namely the good will.[24] It should read: do unto others as *ought* to be done to you. The evil will can endorse ill to itself and thereby legitimate violence under the requirement of universalizability. The horror of this possibility is seen, for example, in Adolf Eichmann, the Nazi, adamant in the face of war crimes that he followed the categorical imperative. It is seen, at least by implication, in *Natural Born Killers*: Mickey would have to agree that he too is guilty and thus rightly, justly executed. An "evil will," the fallen conscience, can use the most glorious moral principle to horrific ends. Is there any way in which the biblical story of moral madness we have been exploring can address this challenge?

Creation and Moral Regeneration

Within the biblical imagination, the Golden Rule formulates as a moral imperative the insight of stories like Cain and Abel about how to stop the cycle of violence driven by moral madness. If the Golden Rule or something very much like it forms the core of moral duties, then moral madness is rejected on principle. Yet we have now reached a rather sobering point: the Golden Rule or any other moral imperative is only felt and binding on the person who desires to live rightly. The evil will is impervious to moral claims. Does this mean that in the final analysis the profound insights of the Golden Rule are for naught, since they seem to rely on precisely what they are meant to guide, namely, that a person or community desire to live the responsible life? Stated differently, how are we to think about moral transformation or regeneration in the face of moral madness? We seem to have reached the connecting point between morality and religion, responsibility and grace. One returns to the connection between creation and new creation, explored in previous chapters.

It is important to recall that the Cain and Abel story is part of the complex cosmogonic myth of Genesis. This means that the face-to-face interaction of agent and patient, Cain and his brother in this case, governed by the Golden Rule, is set mythically within the creation account. Human existence is situated within a space defined by the divine. God creates, is sovereign, and yet recognizes, if we follow the Genesis account, the goodness of what is other than God (cf. Genesis 1:31). A sense of relation to God can, but need not, engender a love of being. The creature makes no valid demand on the divine for the right to exist or for ultimate redemption. These are gifts. In terms of the moral life, the redemptive character of creation comes pointedly to expression in the love of enemies. God loves the neighbor by providing the bounty of life even to the enemy and thereby seeks conversion. That is God's action toward Cain. Yet how does this idea of creation focused on God's action help to answer the question we are now pursuing, namely, the problem of motive to abide by the Golden Rule, the conversion of the will? How do the symbolics of creation disclose a power working for regeneration, a transformation of conscience and so the new creation?

The idea of regeneration, new creation, appears in the Cain and Abel story in God's mark on Cain.[25] That is, it appears indirectly in a symbol of God's action. This mark shows recognition and care for Cain under a distinct sign that designates God's willingness to defend even the sinner's life. In this respect, Cain's whole existence appears in the sign. Bearing this mark, Cain is able to participate anew in the ongoing work of "creation," that is, bring into existence a highly differentiated space of life, a world. Cain "goes away from the presence of the Lord" and settles east of Eden. But in that space he and his wife bear children and his kin form a civilization. Regeneration is a new birth, the revitalization of the self as the *imago Dei*, in and through the transformation of heart and mind, the will. Unlike a Nietzschean *Übermensch*, the renewed self is not a brute overcoming of "man"; it is the revitalization of the human project, to participate in creation. Morally speaking, one is enabled and empowered to dwell responsibly with and for others, to enact the Golden Rule in one's actions and the double love command in one's relations. The presupposition of the moral life is that human existence has worth and evokes care and respect even in its brokenness and radical finitude. Without that conviction, all is reduced to the workings of the all-too-human will to power. The open-ended, active, and even hopeful structure of existence, as well as the coherence of the symbolic order of scripture, can (and I think must) be read via creation/new creation if we are to articulate a response to the reality of moral madness.

The most decisive point of the complex symbolics of creation/new creation is that divine goodness is not an act of brute power, but a non-coercive acknowledgment and enhancement of the integrity of life. The regeneration of the will, the conversion of conscience, operates at the level of the imagination through a new picture of reality saturated with value. It works at the level of sensibilities in response to God's continued care for all of life, even Cain. Regeneration issues forth in the possibility of a new beginning to the human project, rather than being trapped in cycles of destruction. It is a creation event. When the imagination is gripped by a vision of justice not trapped in the logic of totality and human sensibilities infused with a sense of life's fragility, then life can begin anew.

The theological meaning of regeneration centers on the reality of faith. Reconciling faith is the trust in this regenerative power of God that ignites a way of life. The moral meaning of faith is that reality itself, its intelligibility and purposes, transpires before goodness, the living God, beyond the will-to-power. The claim of conscience is testimony to this divine goodness as an injunction to responsible existence. It is the mark of our being. As thinkers down the ages have known, our brokenness, vice, and even violence are not so deep or so thorough as to efface that testimony. From the divine goodness arises the moral adventure of human life. In that goodness one hopes and labors. Beyond consent to a destiny of unending cycles of violence driven by moral madness is a realistic and responsible love of life. And this love of life can permeate human time, countering the chronicle of blood, the slaughtering block of history.

NOTES

1 For discussion of the problem, see Charles T. Mathewes, *Evil and the Augustinian Tradition* (Cambridge: Cambridge University Press, 2001).
2 One should consider places like Dachau and the ideology of the Nazi SS to live beyond good and evil. For a rejection of that option in ethics, see Ekkehard Martens, *Zwischen Gut und Böse: Elementare Fragen angewandter Philosophie* (Stuttgart: Philipp Reclam, 1997).
3 See Richard Rorty, *Contingency, Irony, and Solidarity* (Cambridge: Cambridge University Press, 1989) and Judith N. Shklar, *Ordinary Vices* (Cambridge, MA: Harvard University Press, 1984).
4 See Gerhard von Rad, *Genesis: A Commentary*, translated by John H. Marks (London: SCM Press, 1961).
5 On this theme see Friedrich Nietzsche, *The Birth of Tragedy and the Genealogy of Morals*, translated by Francis Gilffing (New York: Doubleday Anchor, 1956) and René Girard, *Violence and the Sacred*, translated by Patrick Gregory (Baltimore, MD: Johns Hopkins University Press, 1977). Also see *Opfer: Theologische und kulturelle Kontexte*, edited by Bernard Janowski and Michael Welker (Frankfurt: Suhrkamp, 2000) and *Curing Violence*, edited by Mark I. Wallace and Theophus H. Smith (Sonoma, CA: Polebridge Press, 1994).
6 For an interesting discussion of the place of self-esteem and dignity in these matters, see Jeffrie G. Murphy and Jean Hampton, *Forgiveness and Mercy*, Cambridge Studies in Philosophy and Law (Cambridge: Cambridge University Press, 1988).
7 It was of course Plato and St. Augustine who, I judge, explored these complex dynamics of love most profoundly in the ancient world. See Plato's *Symposium* and also *Phaedrus* as well as Augustine's *City of God.*
8 For a discussion of the Dionysian model for explaining religious violence and other models as well, see Jonathan Z. Smith, *Imagining Religion: From Babylon to Jonestown* (Chicago, IL: University of Chicago Press, 1982).
9 See Paul Ricoeur, *The Symbolism of Evil*, translated by Emerson Buchanan (New York: Harper and Row, 1967).
10 For a discussion of hermeneutical positions, see William Schweiker, *Mimetic Reflections: A Study in Hermeneutic, Theology, and Ethics* (New York: Fordham University Press, 1990). The most important exponent of a "romantic hermeneutic" within theology was F. D. E. Schleiermacher. See his *Hermeneutics: The Handwritten Manuscripts*, edited by Heinz Kimerle, translated by James Duke and Jack Forstman (Missoula, MT: Scholars Press, 1977). Also see E. D. Hirsch, Jr., *Validity in Interpretation* (New Haven, CT: Yale University Press, 1967).

11 For examples see George Lindbeck, *The Nature of Doctrine: Religion and Theology in a Postliberal Age* (Philadelphia, PA: Westminster Press, 1984) and Kathryn Tanner, *Theories of Culture: A New Agenda for Theology* (Minneapolis, MN: Fortress Press, 1997).

12 Clifford Geertz, *Local Knowledge: Further Essays in Interpretive Anthropology* (New York: Basic Books, 1983), p. 54.

13 See Irving Singer, *Meaning in Life: The Creation of Value* (New York: Free Press, 1992).

14 See Robin W. Lovin, *Reinhold Niebuhr and Christian Realism* (Cambridge: Cambridge University Press, 1995).

15 For "hermeneutical realism" see William Schweiker, *Responsibility and Christian Ethics* (Cambridge: Cambridge University Press, 1995). Also see Charles Taylor, *Philosophy and the Human Sciences: Philosophical Papers 2* (Cambridge: Cambridge University Press, 1985).

16 The connection between attraction and repulsion in encounter with the sublime has been explored as defining religion itself. On this see Rudolf Otto, *The Idea of the Holy*, translated by John H. Harvey (New York: Oxford University Press, 1936).

17 I should note here that I am completely aware of the ambiguity, and lack of moral imagination, in these claims about the "beast" found both in the biblical text and Stone's film. That is to say, there seems to be the need to demonize animals as the inverse image of the human. For an excellent account of this problem and what it means for ethics, see Mary Midgley, *Beast and Man: The Roots of Human Nature* (Brighton: Harvester Press, 1979).

18 Recall that we met similar arguments in chapter 1 through exploring the myth of Zeus and Chronos and its resonance with much modern political theory, like that of Thomas Hobbes.

19 Paul Ricoeur, "Ethical and Theological Considerations on the Golden Rule," in *Figuring the Sacred: Religion, Narrative and Imagination*, translated by David Pellauer and edited by Mark I. Wallace (Minneapolis, MN: Fortress Press, 1995), p. 293.

20 Hans Dieter Betz and William Schweiker, "Concerning Mountains and Morals: A Conversation about the Sermon on the Mount" in *Criterion* 36: 2 (1997): 23. On this topic one must see Hans Dieter Betz, *The Sermon on the Mount* (Minneapolis, MN: Fortress Press, 1995).

21 I have developed some aspects of this argument in another context. See William Schweiker, "Starry Heavens and Moral Worth: Hope and Responsibility in the Structure of Theological Ethics," in *Paul Ricoeur and Contemporary Moral Thought*, edited by John Wall, William Schweiker, and W. David Hall (New York: Routledge, 2002). In each of these discussions I have been informed by the work of Paul Ricoeur and also my colleague Hans Dieter Betz.

22 This list is obviously not meant to be exhaustive. My point is that the various forms of basic goods fall into types (natural, social, reflective) that often, tragically, compete in our lives and thereby require discriminating decisions. Despite

the real and importance differences between cultures and human beings on this planet, there seem to be types of goods that we ought to respect and enhance. These goods are important for integrated, rather than chaotic, lives. That is why they claim our responsibility. Of course, someone might freely choose to give up some basic good, say, forgo family and sexual relations out of devotion to God. But that does not mean denying a basic good; it is simply a decision about how to shape a life. On the idea of basic goods, see chapter 8.

23 Ricoeur, "Ethical and Theological Considerations on the Golden Rule," p. 294.

24 See, for example, Alan Gewirth, *Reason and Morality* (Chicago, IL: University of Chicago Press, 1978).

25 I realize that this "mark" has in the history of Western Christianity often been interpreted in negative and racist ways. Part of the force of my interpretation is precisely to cut off that form of moral madness where people of color, especially Africans, are somehow marked as murderers.

Postscript

CHAPTER 10

Presenting Theological Humanism

One feature of much Western philosophical and religious ethics has been the belief that what is morally good and right is bound to the flourishing of human persons and human communities.[1] Despite the radical differences among moral systems and communities, human well-being was always in some way intrinsic to a conception of the highest good and ideas about moral obligation and social justice. As Immanuel Kant, the philosopher of the Enlightenment, put it, humanity is an end in itself and this insight is the foundation for a universal categorical imperative. Christian communions made a similar claim. Hardly seen as a humanistic manifesto, the Westminster Shorter Catechism (1647) nevertheless insisted "man's chief end is to glorify God and enjoy him forever." God is the highest good; God is the end of human flourishing. Much earlier, Thomas Aquinas argued that the highest human good is to know God in and through God's own being, a perfection of love that is also the perfection of human being. Even today, thinkers such as the Jewish philosopher Emmanuel Lévinas have championed a "humanism of the other man." In this respect, most Western ethics, religious and otherwise, have had a decidedly humanist flavor, even if conceptions of the human and of the human good differ. What Kant or Protestant divines or Thomas or Lévinas meant by the human good differs in substance and grounding. Yet human well-being seems intrinsic to what is morally good and right.[2]

The twentieth century was in many ways an attack on humanity. The century was a weary chronicle of wars, gas chambers, killing fields, and rape camps.[3] Ironically enough, many philosophers and social theorists joined the attack on humanity. In the nineteenth century, Nietzsche bluntly stated, "The world is beautiful, but has a disease called Man." Twentieth-century thinkers were more ambiguous in their criticism of "man," if no less strident. Martin Heidegger puzzled over the ontological meaning of human action in his "Letter on Humanism," seemingly more worried about the fate of Being than the blood of innocent people. Michel Foucault and other poststructuralist thinkers announced the end of man. And more recently Peter Singer in the name of non-human animals and logical rigor has advocated "unsanctifying human life."[4] These anti-humanist critiques center on conceptions of the human and also the distinctive value Western religious and cultural traditions assign to human beings.

The attack on humanity was not the only story of the twentieth century. At the same time there were responses to intolerable horror in the name of shared human dignity and vulnerability. These responses took various shapes. We witnessed movements of social justice and liberation in Martin Luther King, Jr. and the civil rights movement, Gandhi in India, the struggle in South Africa, and the current worldwide women's movement. Theologians and religious thinkers sought to preserve human dignity not against but within the wider reaches of life. It is also important to see that anti-humanism was never lacking "moral passion." Even Nietzsche, let us remember, sought to overcome man in the name of a higher type of human being.[5] There is often a passion for the dignity of all life that drives the attack on humanism. It is important, then, to gain some clarity about the question of humanism in ethics if we are to meet the massive challenges of our day.

The purpose of this chapter is probative and constructive. We want to probe the question of humanism as it is taking shape in the present situation. In other times and places how one should see and appraise the worth of human existence took different forms. But the question of how one is rightly to value and properly esteem human beings is presently being debated against the backdrop of the massive extension of human power in the modern age and so the problem of overhumanization. The constructive task of the chapter builds on probing other forms of thought. It presents theological humanism as a stance in ethics.[6] In this way, the chapter completes the argument of this book. Along the lines of inquiry charted in Part III, we are concerned in what follows with how the moral life is imagined and what this means for responsible existence. Even more specifically, the argument here is to advance a vision of human freedom needed to live beyond the sad fact of moral madness. The following pages also complete the book in that they bring to articulation the stance in ethics that has guided each chapter. A case for theological humanism is offered with respect to larger debates about human worth in the face of global endangerments to life.

We turn first to explore in some detail the form the question of humanism is taking in contemporary ethics. In doing so, we can isolate a range of responses to it that will occupy our attention through the remainder of this chapter. The dialectical and hermeneutical method of argumentation is part and parcel of the constructive task of presenting theological humanism.

The Question of Humanism

The question of humanism takes one to the heart of many widespread (even global) moral and political debates, some of which have been explored in this book. What is meant by the "moral good" and what is its relation to human flourishing? How does one understand human freedom and what is its dignity? Can we speak of the "human" when we are more and more mindful of the wild cultural diversity that permeates this world? Does it makes sense to speak of the "human" when new developments in technology and biology move us towards total genetic control and the possibility of forms of cyborg existence? Are social systems best understood with reference to human action or must we explore social processes on their own terms? What is the relation, morally speaking, between human well-being and the moral status of non-human animals? What is one to make of claims that we are now living amid the end of nature and thus the triumph of human power?

These and a host of other questions obviously deserve attention. One can explore these questions microscopically by giving detailed attention to some specific concrete issue, say, issues in biotechnology. But it is also possible to address the topic telescopically, that is, to attempt to grasp the widest array of issues posed by the question of humanism in our postmodern, global times. When we turn a telescope on the current situation what can we regard as the basic question humanism poses for ethics?

Presently, diverse thinkers and cultural movements are responses to a widespread challenge that is especially pressing in our time. This challenge arises out of the fantastic extension of human capacity to respond to, shape, and even create reality. The challenge has two interlocking elements. First, how, if at all, can we limit the relentless drive of technological power to enfold all life within its kingdom and thereby subdue any "outside" to the human project. We have called this enfolding of life, overhumanization. Many people find the enfolding of life suffocating; they long for an "outside," for some transcendence. They live with a sense of nausea about the violence, vulgarity, and wanton destructiveness of human powers, including the religions. These people long for some way to face the intolerable facts of existence armed with a realistic and yet vibrant gratitude for the gift of life. The question is, how do we avoid the human as a disease on earth? Second, in the light of the obvious threat that unbridled human power poses to all life on this planet, how are we, if at all, to provide a sustained vision adequate to orient human life? In a complex and culturally diverse global situation can we even speak of a "we" in any morally relevant way? Seen with a telescope, the central challenge facing ethics, then, is how to fashion in a global context a form of thought and way of life that respects and enhances the integrity of human existence within but not against other forms of life. Stated bluntly, must one reject any claim to the distinctive worth of human beings in order to counter the many endangerments to other forms of life? This is the specific form the question of humanism is taking in our time.

This challenge is well known, often noted, and deeply felt. The difficulty is how to go about addressing it. We can isolate a range of positions that must be examined in greater detail throughout the remainder of this chapter. None of these positions, much less theological humanism, entails a wholesale rejection of human powers creatively to shape and transform reality. Yet each of these positions is mindful that when power is measured only by its continual increase, then difficulties arise for the sustaining of human and non-human forms of life. By the idea of overhumanization, we do not mean a celebration of human creativity or technological power, but, rather, an ideology and social condition in which maximizing power becomes a good in itself. Against this possibility, one kind of position we can isolate is found among *humanists* of various stripes. Most forms of contemporary humanism are avowedly anthropocentric and secular in focus. They delimit all value to human, mundane ends. The good is thereby circumscribed within intra-human purposes and flourishing, even if they hope to curtail the drive of over humanization. On this account, one worries about other non-human forms of life as crucial for human well-being. The focus in those kinds of ethics is on what Tzvetan Todorov has called "lateral transcendence" and, in a similar way, Martha Nussbaum dubs "inner-worldly transcendence." We can speak of these neo-humanist positions as *inner-worldly humanism*.[7]

The other set of positions we must explore moves reflection beyond the agency of actual human beings in order to look at trans-human or suprapersonal realities as the operative powers in history. There is the negation of all human inner-worldly transcendence in order to focus on the reality and power of trans-human dynamics, like social systems or the fate of being, as Heidegger might put it. Humanism is false on this account not only because it focuses on the worth of actual human beings, but also because it tries to explain the working of complex systems simply with reference to the lives and actions of human individual agents. This twofold claim is a defining feature of contemporary forms of *anti-humanism*, with its roots in Nietzschean insights.

A theological humanist is obviously concerned with human well-being. But as we will see, she or he also insists on a wider, more complex reach of value than inner-worldly humanists. This wider realm of value is understood in relation to the divine or sacred as the *source* and *scope* of goodness. As seen in Part I of this book, there is a profound connection between the realms of being and the domain of value such that the worth of any specific being is not simply a matter of human power and appraisals. In other words, one uses the language of a tradition, one does "theology," in order to articulate how the moral space of life is saturated with worth not reducible to human power and what that means for the conduct of life. This position remains humanistic. Against kinds of anti-humanism, a theological humanist joins other forms of humanism to argue that individuals possessing the freedom of self-development and the capacities to form communities have distinctive moral status. It is precisely because of these powers for action that persons bear worth not subsumable to supra-human realities (social systems, nature, the state).[8] This is why we have insisted throughout on the idea of conscience as the best way to conceptualize the distinctive mode of moral being. The failing of too much anti-humanist thought is its hope that somehow trans-human realities devoid of moral purpose or moral meaning will nevertheless save us.

The intuitive appeal of theological humanism rests on the insight that supra-human realities and intra-human ends do not and cannot exhaust the realm of value or the meaning of human life. There is something about the reality of freedom within the wider compass of life that exceeds mundane ends and resists supra-human forces. Human beings strive for what exceeds a reduction of life to the mundane – we do not live by bread alone – and yet, as known from concentration camps to battles against racism, people unceasingly resist the submersion of their lives into supra-human realities impervious to individual existence. For the theological humanist, the good of freedom, that is, the worth and dignity of our capacity to shape, respond to, and create reality, is thereby bound to ideas about human transcendence. That connection is crucial if we are to take responsibility for the integrity of life against its endangerments, if we are, in other words, to combat overhumanization in the time of many worlds.

We turn next to basic themes in traditional humanism and the revisions that contemporary inner-worldly humanists have made in their tradition. Anti-humanist arguments will be unfolded along the way and their specific account of human transcendence.

Humanism: Its Forms and Critics

What does one mean by "humanism"? It is, of course, notoriously difficult to define. Typically, one traces its lineage back to the Renaissance and the origins of the study of the "humanities" as well as charts the differences between secular, naturalistic, and religious humanists. However, more could be said about the roots of humanism. It reaches at least as far back as Socrates, who brought philosophy down to earth. On some accounts it goes back further, to the Hebrew scriptures and Christ's claim that the Sabbath was made for man, not man for the Sabbath. Whatever the history, all humanists share the desire to respect and enhance the integrity of human existence. This desire entails an affirmation of autonomy, an insistence on distinctly human goods, and also some version of moral universality, namely, that all human beings – not just me or my kin – are due respect and esteem. Tzvetan Todorov has noted that humanists hold "freedom exists and that it is precious, but at the same time they appreciate the benefit of shared values, life with others, and a self that is held responsible for its actions."[9]

Beyond concern for freedom, shared life, and responsible action, there is a deeper claim about human existence important to humanistic thinkers. As Laszlo Versényi put it in his study of Socratic humanism,

> Metaphorically speaking, [man] is only a symbol, a fragment, something fundamentally incomplete and unwhole which, aware of its incompleteness, is moved toward self-completion, strives for what would make it into that which it by nature must be in order to fulfill itself ... [Man] is a movement, a transcendence, a "thing in between" (*metaxu*).[10]

Human beings love and hate, weep and laugh. We are fallible creatures duped by our own illusions and yet also truth-seeking beings. That being the case, if one's life is to be anything more than fancy and sorrow, then one must undertake a process of self-surpassing aimed at wholeness or integrity. One does so with the awareness that, tragically or comically, integrity is never fully attainable in time. Yet one does so also with some dim awareness that to be human is to move between realms, between worlds, in an ongoing struggle for wholeness.

Granting broad lines of agreement among humanists on these ideals, debates among thinkers begin. A religious thinker will insist that what defines the integrity of human existence and thus the distinctive good of human life is a unique capacity on the part of human beings for a free, responsive relationship to God. The transcendence that we are is already and always in part a movement towards and in response to the divine. The heart is restless until it rests in God, as Augustine famously put it. Hermann Deuser has shown in his study of the Decalogue that, theologically considered, the first command articulates the fact that to be human is to have some "god," some orienting good. The ethical and theological question then is what good can and ought we to trust.[11] Conversely, a non-religious humanist denies this claim and argues, in the words of Todorov, that humanism "marks out the space in which the agents of these [human] acts evolve: the space of all human beings, and of them alone."[12] The debate among humanists is over the scope of value, the extent of the moral space of life, conjoined to an affirmation of the preciousness of freedom. The debate at root is about the nature and reach of human transcendence. As we will see later, this is bound to the problem of overhumanization and its endangerment to all forms of life.

Humanists have long understood that human freedom is historically, socially, and culturally situated or embodied in the world. Yet it is important to grasp that within the history of humanistic writing the connection between freedom and the struggle for integrity has been expressed through contrasting imaginative, metaphoric schemes. These metaphors provide insight into different ideas of human transcendence. Freedom as the capacity of transcendence has been imagined differently with profound impact for a moral outlook. Consider three metaphors that are dominant in, though not exhaustive of, classical humanism: the theatre, the garden, and the school.[13] They are ways of picturing transcendence. We must examine these metaphors of freedom in which human transcendence appears amid the struggle for wholeness and moral integrity.

There are two good reasons for proceeding in this way. First, there is a hermeneutical reason for undertaking this kind of reflection on metaphors of freedom. While we cannot explore these metaphors in extensive detail, a rough and ready typology of these accounts of the place of freedom in the world will isolate salient features of humanism, as well as current inner-worldly humanism and strands in contemporary anti-humanism.[14] Contemporary neo-humanists have revised traditional humanistic claims about freedom in the direction of responsibility for the other, for the "you." The moral achievement of life is not just about the self and its fulfillment. What matters is the well-being of the "other." While this is an important development within humanism, the question of freedom and transcendence is still at issue. And so, second, we engage these metaphors in order to advance a dialectical argument for theological humanism.

The human as fable and play

"All the world's a stage," Shakespeare wrote. The idea that the space of human existence is a stage and that human beings are actors is widespread among humanistic thinkers.[15] Juan Luis Vives, the Renaissance Spanish author, wrote in his *Fabula de homine* that "man himself is a fable and a play." The distinctiveness of a human being is the power to transform herself or himself, to appear under various "masks" and even be the archmime of the gods. "Verily, man, peering oft through the mask which hides him, almost ready to burst forth and reveal himself distinctly in many things, is divine and Jupiter-like."[16] Indebted to Pico della Mirandola and Cicero, Vives locates human dignity in the power that free action has to define human existence. Humans have complete moral power to fashion and construct their lives unencumbered by natural or supernatural limits. And what is more, the extension of this power shows that human being is revealed precisely in those things and realities shaped by human power. Works of culture and society are the prism for the disclosure of the Jupiter-like power that is human nature.

One can easily see a forerunner to radical existentialism in this account of human freedom. Existence precedes essence, as Jean-Paul Sartre would put it much later.[17] This conception of radical freedom is the principle object of criticism in one strand of current anti-humanism. The idea of unencumbered freedom implies an effacement of other realms of being, as well as a reduction of other forms of life solely to instrumental purposes for human beings. The project of radical freedom backs overhumanization as the enfolding, enframing, and encoding of all existence within the kingdom of human power. Not surprisingly, many twentieth-century anti-humanists challenged the idea of human power to shape all realms of being. Martin Heidegger in his response to Sartre argued that "humanism" too easily reduced all of being to a "standing reserve" for human purposes. Heidegger saw in humanism the roots of the modern technological domination of being.[18] Humanism must be rejected because the idea of the human as archmime, the image of Jupiter, isolates human existence from the rest of life and warrants the domination of realms of being.

Many thinkers have followed Heidegger's criticism. Some ecological philosophers see the drive to domination rooted in ideas about radical freedom and in the biblical tradition's sanction of human sovereignty over nature due to the unique dignity of the human being as the *imago Dei*, the mime of God who dominates the world.[19] While insisting on human dignity and responsibility, there are also theologians, like James M. Gustafson, who rightly argue against the anthropocentrism of much Western ethics. And there are others who reimagine human life embedded in the wider web of life, as the feminist Sallie McFague does.[20] Interestingly enough, it is precisely on this point that theological humanism strikes a different, if related, path to theocentrists and ecological holists. The world as theatre is not a claim about the human power of self-invention, a staging of the masks under which human being appears, but, as even John Calvin could put it, the arena of God's glory. As argued elsewhere in this book, the theatre of the world has its ontological and axiological reference to divine and not only human creativity. Only in this way does human transcendence protect the integrity of other forms of life. For the theological humanist, this fact about the moral space of life does not thereby diminish the distinctiveness of human capacities for action nor deny the moral vocation of human beings. At issue theologically is how to understand freedom, not as the power of self-creation, but as a distinctive way of being in a world saturated with value and in response to others. This will later require a theological account of human existence.

The self in the garden

The metaphors of the garden and the school are also prevalent in humanistic discourse about freedom in the world. The accent in these metaphors is not on self-invention but rather cultivation or moral formation.

> "I also know," said Candide, "that we must cultivate our own garden."
> "You're right," said Pangloss, "for when man was placed in the garden of Eden, he was placed there *ut operaretur eum* – that he might work – which proves that man was not born to rest . . ."
> "That is well put," replied Candide, "but we must cultivate our own garden."[21]

Like Vives, Voltaire retrieves a longstanding image of human life in the world in order to complete the story of Candide.

The image of life in the garden is found in the Book of Genesis and the commentaries it has spawned, and also among the ancient Epicureans and later in Montaigne. The aim of life on this account should be moral cultivation. One must have an honest, if not always appreciative, awareness of the limits that life places on human existence. Within those limits, the human task is to cultivate a character befitting one's own judgments and one's relations with others. Valuing friendship and sociality, the garden image has nonetheless given rise to the praise of solitude. As Montaigne would put it, "As much as I can, I employ myself entirely upon myself." And, again, in the *Essays*: "You have quite enough to do at home, don't go away."[22] In other words, true freedom is self-labor removed from the tangle of cares that too easily and too often preoccupy us with matters of penultimate importance.

It is in this light that we can understand other criticisms of classical humanism. These have found two expressions. In one form, the idea that the purpose of life is to "cultivate self" has fallen to the critique of totality famously made by Lévinas. His point, recall from previous discussions, is that any system of thought that begins with the "I" enfolds the "other" into "totality," into the same.[23] Totality expresses what I have called overhumanization, the project of enfolding, enframing, and encoding of the other in the realm of the self. Despite this criticism, Lévinas remains a kind of neo-humanist. The second line of critique of the image of the garden has taken a decidedly anti-humanist form. This position challenges the idea that we have natural propensities that can be cultivated to their perfection. The very notion of perfection requires some conception of distinctive human nature that is hard to sustain in light of what we know of other species.[24] Unlike humanists such as Vives and Pico, who see human dignity in the unique power of the individual to define self, some anti-humanists deny any difference between the human and the non-human. They do so by speaking of the "post-human," cyborg existence, or the "end of nature."[25] Religious and philosophical claims to the uniqueness of human nature have made "man" a disease on earth.

Contemporary inner-worldly humanists have responded to these anti-humanist criticisms as well. Their response is linked to my point about the need to reconceive the meaning and status of freedom within the humanistic project. Thinkers as diverse as Todorov and also Paul Ricoeur have argued that the "I" is not an origin, as Descartes would have it, but an end, a goal to be valued and achieved. To be a human being is to be an incomplete project. Yet the goal of action is not only one's own life, but other actual persons as well. To be human is to be on the way to an identity bound to others.[26] A theological humanist will make a similar but different response. The self is not the origin of value, but likewise the domain of value exceeds even the human as end, as goal. In brief, Todorov's claim must finally be rejected as too limited when he writes that the "human being takes the place of the divine. But not just any human being, only one who is embodied in individuals other than myself."[27] "Lateral transcendence" is finally inadequate for rethinking the place of freedom in the world. Later, we will see why this is the case and how it relates to the demand to respond rightly to the integrity of life.

Discipline and the school

Let us consider one last metaphor of human freedom found among classical humanists. It is the image of the school. Not only have humanists always been interested in education, but also, more importantly, they often thought that life itself is a school of virtue. Erasmus and Calvin, surely at some theological odds, could nevertheless speak of the philosophy and the school of Christ. Self-cultivation is not simply a matter of autonomous judgments aimed at cultivating one's own garden, as Montaigne believed. It is also a form of learning and habituation, *paideia*, through patterns of discipline. Philosophy is a way of life, as Pierre Hadot might put it. The formation of life is through practices.[28]

The idea is that freedom is not the power of self-creation appearing through various masks human beings choose to wear; nor is it the ability to cultivate the self. Discipline and practice are the means of self-overcoming on the way to the integration of life in community and tradition. The image of the school articulates the place of freedom in the moral space of life in a way decidedly different than the theatre. Formation is not invention. Yet the metaphor of the school also stresses the social character of human existence rather than the solitude of the garden. One finds hints of this strand of thought in some contemporary virtue theorists, like Alasdair MacIntrye, and also communitarian, narrative theologians.[29]

Around the image of the school one also confronts contemporary anti-humanist rhetoric. Anti-humanists like Michael Foucault, while profoundly interested in self-fashioning, would see the metaphor of the school as a discourse that conceal mechanisms of power, discipline, and punishment. Foucault's central concern is the way human beings are made "subjects," are subjugated, within the hidden and autonomous workings of power that are the real forces in the world. Other perspectives also enter the picture to criticize the idea that life is about discipline. Neo-humanist thinkers as diverse as Martin Buber and Erazim Kohák stress the intersubjective character of existence and not the need for moral education. The encounter with another is seen as the prism through which to grasp the human relation to the divine.[30] Relations to others constitute the being and dignity of the human person. But the constituting relation escapes a reduction to the self and other to practices of discipline and education. Intra-human goods give way to a transcendent source of value without thereby being subsumed into some supra-human reality of the "community" or "tradition." For Buber, God is the "third" in the relation of I and Thou. The eternal understood to be profoundly personal ingresses into the temporal, as Kohák puts it. By means of encounters with the face of the other, there is disclosed in the concreteness of life the dignity of human existence that commands responsibility. Human life is constituted and not schooled by responsibility.

Humanism and Current Ethics

Various metaphors of freedom enable us to provide an interpretation of the contours of current ethics with respect to the present form of the question of humanism. We have actually unfolded a hermeneutics of freedom; that is, we have grasped the various meanings freedom has taken in and through strands of thought and discourse. Anti-humanistic forms of thought challenge conceptions of the "being of man" that lead to an effacement of other realms of being (an ontological critique) or reduce other forms of life purely to instrumental purposes for human beings (an axiological critique). Anti-humanism can be seen as a response to modern overhumanization. These thinkers look to the fate of Being, machineries of power, or social systems rather than human beings as the object of reflection. Yet it must be asked if the criticism of humanism can sustain itself or if what is needed is a renewed account of the responsibility of human being for life on earth. Does the fate of Being really escape moral evaluation?

In response to these critics, thinkers like Todorov and other neo-humanists argue ontologically that the "I" is an end or goal of action and not its transcendental origin. The "I" that is the goal of action includes the other human being, the finality of the "you." This is what Todorov called lateral transcendence. Yet here too there are questions. In order to avoid overhumanization, must we think beyond lateral transcendence, beyond intra-human ends? Is even that account of transcendence still and finally problematic in its conception of the reach of value? Must we see, as Kohák, Lévinas, and others argue, that our inner-worldly relations are the prisms or traces for a relation to the divine? As one Islamic leader recently put it, "only someone who helps a human being services God."[31] On my understanding, these neo-humanist thinkers are traveling in the direction of "theological humanism." Responsiveness to the other as a form of self-overcoming reveals that which exceeds, transgresses, the kingdom of human power. The claim of the other person is an opening to a realm of value more extensive and intensive than intra-human goods. And yet precisely because it is responsibility for and with others, the human is not submerged into supra-human realities.

The theological humanist departs from fellow travelers in a subtle but important way. As argued throughout this book, the moral space of life is best understood through metaphors of creation. The relation to the divine as the source and scope of value is not limited to, but is inclusive of, the dyadic encounter of self and other. God is not just a trace or ingression within the encounter of self and other. We encounter the other as making a claim upon us because first and foremost self and other exist within a creation that exceeds our encounters. This means that the domain of ethics includes but also goes beyond the relations of justice, care, and love that can and ought to characterize responsiveness to the other.

That insight brings us to the last step in the argument. Why should we embrace theological humanism rather than endorse lateral transcendence and so an inner-worldly humanism, or cling to a seemingly popular antihumanistic outlook? We must engage in a theological account of the various metaphors of freedom we have unfolded as a way to speak about the moral space of life.

On Theological Humanism

This chapter has taken what might appear to be a circuitous route through the question of humanism in ethics. We focused the discussion on freedom and its connection to the reality of human dignity. And we have sketched, albeit too briefly, different conceptions of freedom in the world, expressed in basic metaphors, found among humanistic thinkers. This provided us with a map of current options in ethics. Why take this route of reflection in trying to make a case for theological humanism?

We have followed this pathway of reflection because the question of freedom is part of the greatest challenge facing ethics. Recall that we identified that challenge in terms of how to fashion a form of thought and way of life that respects and enhances the integrity of human existence within but not against other forms of life. The challenge centers on the extension of human power and with it the threat of overhumanization, not only to human beings but also to other forms of life. Insofar as freedom names the distinctive human form of causality, and so our power, what is the nature and extent of our freedom? How does freedom relate to the incompleteness of human life and the struggle for integrity? Does freedom situate us within the wider compass of life on this planet, or is it the very power to create worlds, as Vives and certainly Sartre suggest? In light of the incredible extension of human power in a technological age, what might transform how we value power so that we can limit the seemingly endless expansion of the human kingdom and thereby protect the fragile integrity of life on this little planet?

In order to meet the basic challenge facing ethics one must give a robust, non-reductive, yet naturalistic account of freedom (cf. chapter 2). More pointedly, one has to understand freedom within the deeper claim that the struggle for wholeness, for integrity, is the essence of human life. As the philosopher Mary Midgley has put it,

> human freedom centers on being a creature able, in some degree, to act as a whole in dealing with its conflicting desires ... Though it is only an endeavor – though the wholeness is certainly not given ready-made and can never be fully achieved – yet the integrative struggle to heal conflicts and to reach towards this wholeness is surely the core of what we mean by human freedom.[32]

The human struggle for wholeness, for integrity, situates us in the wider complex of life as well as amid conflicts among our desires. Does this struggle that defines freedom reach beyond intra-human ends and resist submersion into supra-human realities? Can we show why inner-worldly humanism and the legacy of anti-humanism are finally inadequate as visions of the moral vocation of human beings?[33]

Pursuing the question of humanism in ethics, we have seen how various anti-humanist arguments rightly challenged accounts of radical freedom found among some classical humanists. These critics discern in those accounts of freedom the ideology and driving impulse of the overhumanization of the world. The difficulty with the anti-humanist critique is that it has, by and large, been unable to raise itself to offer a positive, constructive vision of how to orient life. Anti-humanism has failed in this respect since, per definition, it must subsume human beings into the working of larger, supra-human agencies devoid of moral purpose – say, the fate of Being (Heidegger), or the coming of the *Übermensch* (Nietzsche), or the mechanisms of power (Foucault). In light of the horror and violence of the twentieth century, inner-worldly humanists, as I called them, rightly challenge the anti-humanist agenda and the eclipse of the individual in supra-human agencies. After gas chambers and killing fields, who honestly believes that objective *Geist* or the fate of Being will save us?

Part of the argument made by inner-worldly humanists has been to refashion traditional accounts of freedom in the direction of responsibility for the you, the other. Lateral transcendence retains the humanistic ideal of the human as the goal of action, but it does so in a way that avoids the loss of the other in the project of self-invention or cultivation. This is a genuine and important advance in ethics. It is a development that must be furthered by theological humanism (cf. chapter 7). And yet there are problems. Insofar as inner-worldly humanism can in principle only account for lateral transcendence, it risks, perhaps unwittingly, joining the project of overhumanization. When the good is defined solely with respect to the "other man," responsibility actually requires the extension and exercise of power to overcome all that thwarts human flourishing. If the *summum bonum* is the "other man," a virtual replacement for the divine, why limit human power aimed at human flourishing? While escaping the solitude of the garden and beliefs about the theatre by placing emphasis on the "you" as the goal of action, the idea of lateral transcendence too easily continues the project of overhumanization that so many anti-humanists have sought to resist. This means that two dominant options in ethics are constantly at struggle and yet neither can meet the challenge facing our present age. Must we really choose between the loss of persons into a supra-human holism, or, conversely, preserve the rights and dignity of individual persons by diverting attention from the interdependence of all forms of life?

It is at this juncture that the symbolic and conceptual resources of a religious tradition function to articulate and respond to the plight that befalls human beings. That is to say, one of the problems that bedevil inner-worldly humanists as well as anti-humanists is a reduction in our moral lexicon due to a banishment of resources from ethics. Inner-worldly humanists must reduce symbols, narratives, and metaphors to concealed expressions of human goods. Anti-humanists, conversely, must isolate hidden workings of power or the destiny of Being or a slave mentality in all religious resources. In this respect, these positions share, ironically, an ardent resistance to the hermeneutical insight that symbolic resources fund and invigorate thought. They seek to decode cultural and religious sources rather than seeing how those very sources have diagnostic and illuminative power to decode the complexity of human action and the moral space of life. Thankfully, a theological ethicist can and may and must critically deploy the full resources of a tradition to constructive ends. Stated otherwise, the religions are treasure troves of symbolic resources for ethical thinking. Buddhist claims about the "defilements," Jewish analyses of temptation, and Hindu arguments about karmic forces could be deployed by thinkers in those traditions in order to isolate the self-refutation of human freedom aimed only at its maximization.

From the perspective of Christian theological humanism, the drive of overhumanization is just what one would expect from beings who struggle relentlessly for wholeness with little awareness of the depth of their plight. Forever fastening on what is believed to redeem us from our brokenness in various "god" images, life is defined by the bad infinity of possession and consumption.[34] Insofar as what is sought is integrity of life, the consumed never satisfies. The heart remains restless. The paradox of freedom is that the extension and exercise of power alone is inadequate to the task of human existence, the struggle for integrity. Freedom must be measured by a good that is not of its making, a good that is received as well as achieved. The good, for a theological humanist, embraces the other, the "you," dwelling amid the wider realms of life. Better stated, the end of freedom, the good, is the integrity of life.

We have now reached the full, dialectical force of this chapter and even the entire book. It hinges on a basic insight. In order to respect and enhance the integrity of life, one can neither limit the good of freedom to intra-human ends nor lose it in supra-human realities. Responsibility with and for the other is a prism for the enactment of what transgresses the reach of human power but is the source and scope of goodness that human freedom can and ought to serve. In this light, the biblical injunction to love thy neighbor rightly articulates an authentic source of a humanistic ethics. The love of neighbor is inescapably bound to the love of what is rightly named "God." And as we have seen throughout this book, the complex double love command situates human responsibility within the whole realm of beings as the further reach of the "neighbor." Despite what many contemporary humanists believe, the love of God does not efface concern for the others, the you. The inner dynamics of responsible love infuses moral relations with sacred worth and conjointly religious longings with moral dynamic. The double love command, and the Golden Rule as well, articulate this insight as a maxim for action. They give religious expression to the imperative of responsibility, just as the symbols of creation signal the complexity of goods that constitute the moral space of life.

Without a *theological* humanism we risk the reduction of value to intra-human purposes, yet without a theological *humanism* political, moral, and religious convictions center on supra-human or trans-human realities unconstrained by the recognition of human dignity. Radical anthropocentrism no less than a totalizing holism of the state or nature, or even ideas about God, are deficient. An adequate interpretation of what it means to be human must situate reflection at the intersection of claims about responsibility, the sacred as the source and scope of value, and the integrity of life.

We have shown why one should consider the project of theological humanism in ethics. One last question remains. How might one engage the various metaphors of freedom in order to present a hermeneutically sensitive and yet realistic account of how we can and should live? To be sure, the idea of responsibility is basic in ethics, as well as a picture of freedom embedded in the complex relations that enable and also limit human action. The central value, the end, of action would be to respect and enhance the integrity of life before God. The human problem, in a nutshell, is our existence as a constant struggle of self-overcoming on the way to integrity. The problem is the orientation of our freedom. A valid answer requires clarity about the form of integrity we can, should, and may seek.

Given the focus on responsibility, freedom, and the integrity of life, a theological humanist is suspicious of deploying any one master metaphor as sufficient to articulate the moral space of life. One provides a pluralistic idea of freedom not reducible to one form of thought or just one metaphor. A religious tradition, as well as every human life, is more complex than one root metaphor, such as narrative, or command, or virtue, or Law and Gospel, or love (cf. chapters 4 and 7). Many metaphors are necessary and actually exist in a moral lexicon, while none alone exhausts the meaning of life and its worth. Theological humanism articulates a multidimensional theory of value in and through the use of a range of metaphors about freedom's place in the world.[35] So we must now trace the interaction between metaphors of freedom in order to grasp the deepest meaning and moral important to the idea of the integrity of life. In doing this, one specifies, theologically speaking, our lives before God.

Like the image of the garden, human life is primordially situated in the realms of life on this planet as this is manifest in terms of basic bodily goods. Yet, with the metaphor of the school, human life and our struggle for the wholeness that is genuine freedom are profoundly social. There are social goods available to us only insofar as we engage in those practices necessary to form character and sustain communities. The insight of the metaphor of the theatre is that human beings are not only participants in the realms of life and profoundly social beings, but are also reflexive creatures whose self-understanding does in some fundamental way shape their existence. Through the metaphors charted, one can see that responsible freedom aims to respect and enhance a complex interaction of natural, social, and reflexive goods in the struggle for integrity.

Other metaphors are needed as well. Especially necessary are complex metaphors of transcendence. With other contemporary neo-humanists, the principal revision theological humanism makes to traditional thought is to understand freedom in terms of responsibility with and for others. So a theological humanist must show that insisting on religious transcendence does not and cannot detract from the pressing inner-worldly challenges people around the world now face. We have already made this case by isolating the deep and profound entanglement of the love of God and the love of neighbor that is disclosed, and yet too often forgotten, in a religious tradition. The daring task of speaking about the divine articulates realms of value beyond human preference and power. It seeks also to evoke a love of life rooted in the reality of the living God.

This theological task can only be accomplished by drawing on the many ways of naming God, as well as images of the whole host of human responses to divine action found in a tradition.[36] Think of the cross and resurrection, or testimonies of the reception of love in the Johannine corpus, or acts of God's own repentance, or the outpouring of the Spirit. The insight of these and other images is that in and through various realms of life (politics, intersubjective relations, historical events, emergent social processes) there is, paradoxically, asserted and yet relativized the drive of human power. Political power, the machinery of punishment and discipline, is asserted and yet its dominance broken in the image of cross and resurrection. The fecundity of the natural world is asserted and yet also exceeded in beliefs about the working of the Spirit. And most radically, the justice of God recasts ideas about the world as just a theatre of human struggle and Jupiter-like power (cf. chapter 1). Further examination of these images cannot be undertaken here, although we have engaged with them elsewhere in this book. A careful examination of the moral meaning of the ways of naming God is part and parcel of a complex vision of human transcendence within and not against the wider realms of life. It is to show that we are beings "in-between" precisely because we live, move, and have our being in God (cf. Acts 17:22–31).

A Stance in Life

In this book we have attempted to articulate the attitude and vision of theological humanism within the compass of contemporary ethics. If one understands the shortcomings of anti-humanism as a moral outlook and also sees the limitations of claims about lateral transcendence, then the requirement to pursue the project of theological humanism in ethics is fully warranted. It is warranted by the deepest insight of humanism, namely, the fragile and fallible struggle of freedom for wholeness. Yet more than an attitude or a vision, theological humanism in the last analysis is a religious and moral stance in life. A theological humanist faces realistically the unhappiness, poverty, pettiness, and violence of human beings, but does not believe that those facts are the truth of life. One confronts honestly the ways in which religious traditions have liberated life and bred human misery and brought destruction to life. One knows existence, human fault, and religious failure and yet loves life. That love can and should ignite efforts to lessen human and non-human misery. It is the call of conscience, a testimony to the moral vocation of people in the time of many worlds. This is also the witness that our own lives reach out through the pathways of responsibility to what one can dare to call the living God.

NOTES

1 This chapter was originally presented in a different form for the European Ethics Network and the Societas Ethica in August 2002 at meetings held in Brussels, Belgium. It was also presented at the annual meeting of the Society of Christian Ethics, January 2003, in Pittsburgh, Pennsylvania.

2 See Immanuel Kant, *Fundamental Principle of the Metaphysics of Morals*, translated by Thomas K. Abbott with introduction by Marvin Fox (New York: Liberal Arts Press, 1949) and *The Westminster Shorter Catechism*, in *The Creeds of Christendom*, edited by Philip Schaff, vol. 3 (Grand Rapids, MI: Baker Book House, 1983). Also see Thomas Aquinas, *Summa Theologiae*, 5 vols. (Westminster: Christian Classics, 1981) and Emmanuel Lévinas, *Entre nous* (Paris: Grasset, 1991). The question of what constitutes human flourishing is of course complex and part of the debate in moral theory about naturalism and non-naturalism. The argument of this book is for a type of ethical naturalism, that is, a theory that holds that what we mean by "good" is linked with, if not limited to, what respects and enhances the integrity of a being's life in relation to others. For a general discussion of the point, see Philippa Foot, *Natural Goodness* (Oxford: Oxford University Press, 2001).

3 For a compelling account of this history, see Jonathan Glover, *Humanity: A Moral History of the Twentieth Century* (New Haven, CT: Yale University Press, 2000).

4 On this see Peter Singer, *Unsanctifying Human Life: Singer on Ethics*, edited by Helga Kuhse (Oxford: Blackwell, 2002).

5 It is important to realize that many of the anti-humanistic arguments – especially Nietzsche and Heidegger – were also attacks on the common person. Heidegger opposed authentic existence to "das Mann" and Nietzsche forever attacked the "herd" and all ideas of democracy from a heroic and elitist perspective. I cannot explore the political implications of anti-humanism in this chapter. For a brief study of these issues, see Kate Soper, *Humanism and Anti-Humanism* (La Salle, IL: Open Court, 1986).

6 While forms of intolerance, fundamentalism, and appeals to "orthodoxy" and traditional structures of power are widespread in the religions, there are nevertheless some in every tradition who adopt something like what I am calling "theological humanism." Think of so-called Critical Buddhism, as well as progressive voices in Judaism, Hinduism, and Islam. Among Christians the critical and yet devote

convictions of Black, Third World, and feminist thinkers have helped to blaze the trail to theological humanism.

7 See Tzvetan Todorov, *Imperfect Garden: The Legacy of Humanism*, translated by Carol Cosman (Princeton, NJ: Princeton University Press, 2002) and Martha C. Nussbaum, *Women and Human Development: The Capabilities Approach* (Cambridge: Cambridge University Press, 2000).

8 Ethical holism is related to but distinct from debates about holism in epistemology. My argument here is simply about those ethical positions that claim the worth of any individual being is completely dependent on the "whole" of which it is a part. While some theologians speak like ethical holists, there are strong impulses within the biblical tradition to resist the utter effacement of the individual for the good of the "whole," however that "whole" might be defined. For the most powerful expression of contemporary theocentrism, see James M. Gustafson, *Ethics from a Theocentric Perspective*, 2 vols. (Chicago, IL: University of Chicago Press, 1981, 1984).

9 Tzvetan Todorov, *Imperfect Garden*, p. 5. Also see R. William Franklin and Joseph M. Shaw, *The Case for Christian Humanism* (Grand Rapids, MI: Eerdmans, 1991); Salvatore Puledda, *On Being Human: Interpretations of Humanism from the Renaissance to the Present*, translated by Andrew Hurley with foreword by Mikhail Gorbachev (San Diego, CA: Latitude Press, 1997); and Timothy G. McCarthy, *Christianity and Humanism: From Their Biblical Foundations into the Third Millennium* (Chicago, IL: Loyola Press, 1996).

10 Laszlo Versényi, *Socratic Humanism* (New Haven, CT: Yale University Press, 1963), p. 131.

11 See Hermann Deuser, *Die Zehn Gebote: Kleine Einführung in die theologische Ethik* (Stuttgart: Philippe Reclaim, 2002). This is also a claim made by Luther in his commentary on the first commandment in the *Large Catechism*. One should also note that this claim is especially found among Protestant thinkers and might well explain the importance of positions like those of Plato and Kant, who make a similar point, for Protestant theology.

12 Todorov, *Imperfect Garden*, p. 30.

13 There are of course many other important metaphors that could be explored, including the idea of life as a contest or, as Erasmus has it in his *Enchiridion Militis Christiani* (1503), spiritual warfare. One could also look at the metaphors of the stadium or athletic training. I am focusing on the images of the garden, theatre, and school insofar as they usefully organize the lines of criticism found among anti-humanistic thinkers. For a discussion of the place of metaphor in humanistic thought, see Ernesto Grassi, *Rhetoric as Philosophy: The Humanist Tradition* (University Park: Pennsylvania University Press, 1980).

14 A cautionary note is in order. Everyone who deploys typologies admits their limitation. One is isolating logical options and not providing a detailed analysis of any one position. Not only does typological thinking seem to rigidify or to freeze each position into a "static" rather than dynamic reality, but it also gives the illusion of clarity in a very complex and messy world. Further, every typology is conceived from some standpoint and so necessarily isolates

logical types with respect to the perspective of the thinker developing the typology. If one is not careful, typological schemes become self-justifying. Granting all of these problems, I still judge the use of typological reflection important for the work of theological ethics. On this issue see Paul Tillich, *Christianity and the Encounter of the World Religions* (New York: Columbia University Press, 1963) and H. Richard Niebuhr, *Christ and Culture* (New York: Harper and Row, 1951).

15 It is the case, of course, that those who use the theatre metaphor for the place of freedom in the world often have very different agendas and also different substantive moral and philosophical outlooks. The same is true of ideas about the garden and the school. Mindful of the differences, I cannot explore them in this chapter.

16 Juan Luis Vive, *A Fable About Man* in *The Renaissance Philosophy of Man*, edited by Ernst Cassier, et. al. (Chicago, IL: Phoenix Books/University of Chicago Press, 1956), p. 388. One should also recall that the idea of person in Western thought had its origins in the theatre in terms of the masks worn by actors.

17 Jean-Paul Sartre, "Existentialism is a Humanism" in *Basic Writings*, edited by Stephen Priest (New York: Routledge, 2001).

18 On this see Heidegger's famous "Letter on Humanism" in *Basic Writings*, edited by David Farrell Krell (New York: Harper and Row, 1977), pp. 189–242. There is considerable debate among scholars about whether or not Heidegger should be seen as an anti-humanist or if he was attacking a specific form of humanism in the name of a new account. This debate cannot be entered in this chapter, and is, furthermore, not essential to my argument.

19 For "Heideggerian-like" arguments among ecological ethicists, see Jim Cheney, "Postmodern Environmental Ethics: Ethics as Bioregional Narrative" in *Environmental Ethics* 11 (summer, 1989): 117–34 and also Mick Smith, *An Ethics of Place: Radical Ecology, Postmodernity, and Social Theory* (Albany: State University of New York Press, 2001).

20 See Gustafson, *Ethics from a Theocentric Perspective* and Sallie McFague, *Life Abundant: Rethinking Theology and Economics for a Planet in Peril* (Minneapolis, MN: Fortress Press, 2001).

21 Voltaire, *Candide and Other Stories*, translated by Roger Pearson (Oxford: Oxford University Press, 1990), pp. 99–100. On this also see Terence J. Martin, *Living Words: Studies in Dialogues Over Religion* (Atlanta, GA: Scholars Press, 1998).

22 Michel de Montaigne, *The Complete Works: Essays, Travel Journal, Letters*, translated by Donald M. Frame (Stanford, CA: Stanford University Press, 1958), III, 10, 766–7.

23 See Emmanuel Lévinas, *Totality and Infinity: An Essay in Exteriority*, translated by Alphonso Lingis (Pittsburgh, PA: Duquesne University Press, 1969).

24 For a helpful discussion of the relation between human beings and other species, see Mary Midgley, *Ethical Primate: Humans, Freedom and Morality* (New York: Routledge, 1994).

25 For discussion of these issues, see Donna J. Haraway, *Simians, Cyborgs, and Women: The Reinvention of Nature* (New York: Routledge, 1991); Mark C. Taylor, *Erring:*

A Postmodern A/Theology (Chicago, IL: University of Chicago Press, 1984); Bill McKibben, *The End of Nature* (New York: Anchor Books, 1990); and Charles E. Winquist, "Person" in *Critical Terms for Religious Studies*, edited by Mark C. Taylor (Chicago, IL: University of Chicago Press, 1998), pp. 225–38.

26 See Todorov, *Imperfect Garden*, pp. 80–93 and Paul Ricoeur, *Soi-même comme un autre* (Paris: éditions du Seuil, 1990). Also see *Paul Ricoeur and Contemporary Moral Thought*, edited by John Wall, William Schweiker, and W. David Hall (New York: Routledge, 2002).

27 Todorov, *Imperfect Garden*, p. 137.

28 See Pierre Hadot, *Philosophy as a Way of Life: Spiritual Exercises from Socrates to Foucault*, edited by Arnold Davidson, translated by Michael Chase (Oxford: Blackwell, 1995). Also see Werner Jaeger, *Humanism and Theology*, The Aquinas Lecture – 7 (Milwaukee, WI: Marquette University Press, 1943). Also see chapter 5 on the meaning of philosophy in the ancient world, even the idea of Christian philosophy.

29 MacIntrye has been the most insistent on the idea of the "school" among virtue theorists. See his *Three Rival Versions of Moral Enquiry: Encyclopedia, Genealogy, Tradition* (Notre Dame, IN: University of Notre Dame Press, 1990). For a Christian version of this position that is also markedly anti-humanistic, see Stanley Hauerwas, *A Community of Character: Toward a Constructive Christian Social Ethic* (Notre Dame, IN: University of Notre Dame Press, 1981).

30 Martin Buber, *I and Thou* (Edinburgh: T. & T. Clark, 1937) and Erazim Kohák, *The Embers and the Stars: An Inquiry into the Moral Sense of Nature* (Chicago, IL: University of Chicago Press, 1984).

31 See the interview by Erich Follath with Karim Aga Khan IV published in *Der Spiegel* Nr. 1/30.12.02, S. 92–3.

32 Mary Midgley, *The Ethical Primate*, p. 168.

33 Of course, given the fallibility and folly of all things human, it is not possible to give an unquestionable "proof" for the necessity of a theological stance in ethics. All I can do is to attempt to show dialectically how this position isolates and answers a range of shared problems more adequately than other ethical outlooks.

34 In chapter 3 we saw how faith in a fallen form has the structure of the bad infinity of greed. On this also see William Schweiker, "Having@toomuch.com: Property, Possession and the Theology of Culture" in *Criterion* 39: 2 (spring/summer 2000): 20–8.

35 This returns us to the claim about naturalism in ethics mentioned in an earlier note, above. My argument here is also an instance of "hermeneutical realism." One explores imaginative forms in order to grasp the realities of our lives and the world. See William Schweiker, *Responsibility and Christian Ethics* (Cambridge: Cambridge University Press, 1995).

36 On this see David Tracy, "Literary Theory and the Return of the Forms of Naming and Thinking God in Theology" in *The Journal of Religion* 74: 3 (1994): 302–19.

Select Bibliography

Adams, Robert Merrihew. *The Virtue of Faith and Other Essays in Philosophical Theology*. New York: Oxford University Press, 1987.

Andersen, Svend. *Einführung in die Ethik*. Translated by Ingrid Oberborbeck. Berlin: Walter de Gruyter, 2000.

Antonaccio, Maria. *Picturing the Human: The Moral Thought of Iris Murdoch*. Oxford: Oxford University Press, 2000.

Antonaccio, Maria, and William Schweiker, eds. *Iris Murdoch and the Search for Human Goodness*. Chicago, IL: University of Chicago Press, 1996.

Apel, Karl-Otto. *Diskurs und Verantwortung: das Problem des übergangs zur Postkonventionellen Moral*. Frankfurt am Main: Suhrkamp, 1990.

Appadurai, Arjun. *Modernity at Large: Cultural Dimensions of Globalization*. Minneapolis: University of Minnesota Press, 1996.

Aquinas, Thomas. *Summa Theologiae*. 5 vols. Westminster: Christian Classics, 1981.

Arendt, Hannah. *The Human Condition*. Chicago, IL: University of Chicago Press, 1969.

Assmann, Jan. *Moses the Egyptian: The Memory of Egypt in Western Monotheism*. Cambridge, MA: Harvard University Press, 1997.

Augustine, Saint, Bishop of Hippo. *The Trinity*. Translated by Edmund Hill. Edited by John E. Rotelle. New York: New City Press, 1991.

—— *On Christian Teaching*. Translated by R. P. H. Green. Oxford: Oxford University Press, 1997.

—— *The City of God against the Pagans*. Translated by R. W. Dyson. Cambridge: Cambridge University Press, 1998.

Barber, Benjamin R. *Jihad Vs. Mcworld*. New York: Times Books, 1995.

Barth, Karl. *Das Wort Gottes und die Theologie: Gesammelte Vorträge*. Munich: Chr. Kaiser, 1924.

—— *The Word of God and the Word of Man*. Translated by Douglas Horton. New York: Harper and Row, 1957.

—— *Church Dogmatics*. Translated by G. W. Bromiley. Edited by G. W. Bromiley and T. F. Torrance. Edinburgh: T. & T. Clark, 1957–70.

Beck, Ulrich, Anthony Giddens, and Scott Lash. *Reflexive Modernization: Politics, Tradition and Aesthetics in the Modern Social Order*. Cambridge: Polity Press, 1994.

Beestermöller, Gerhard, and Hans-Richard Reuter, eds. *Politik der Versöhnung*. Stuttgart: Kohlhammer, 2002.

Benhabib, Seyla. *Situating the Self: Gender, Community, and Postmodernism in Contemporary Ethics*. New York: Routledge, 1992.

Betz, Hans Dieter. *The Sermon on the Mount: A Commentary on the Sermon on the Mount, Including the Sermon on the Plain (Matthew 5:3 – 7:27 and Luke 6:20–49)*. Minneapolis, MN: Fortress Press, 1995.

Boulton, Matthew, Kevin Jung, and Jonathan Rothchild, eds. *Doing Justice to Mercy*. Notre Dame, IN: University of Notre Dame Press, forthcoming.

Browning, Don S. *Religious Thought and the Modern Psychologies: A Critical Conversation in the Theology of Culture*. Philadelphia, PA: Fortress Press, 1987.

——*A Fundamental Practical Theology: Descriptive and Strategic Proposals*. Minneapolis, MN: Fortress Press, 1991.

Buber, Martin. *I and Thou*. Translated by Ronald Gregor Smith. Edinburgh: T. & T. Clark, 1937.

Bultmann, Rudolf Karl. *Jesus and the World*. Translated by Louise Pettibone Smith and Erminie Huntress. New York: Scribner, 1934.

Cahill, Lisa Sowle. *Sex, Gender, and Christian Ethics*. Cambridge: Cambridge University Press, 1997.

Cannon, Katie G. *Black Womanist Ethics*. Atlanta, GA: Scholars Press, 1988.

Childs, Brevard S. *Biblical Theology of the Old and New Testaments: Theological Reflection on the Christian Bible*. Minneapolis, MN: Fortress Press, 1993.

Collins, Adela Yarbro, ed. *Feminist Perspectives on Biblical Scholarship*. Atlanta, GA: Scholars Press, 1985.

Crossan, John Dominic. *Jesus: A Revolutionary Biography*. San Francisco, CA: HarperSanFrancisco, 1994.

Curran, Charles E. *Directions in Fundamental Moral Theology*. Notre Dame, IN: University of Notre Dame Press, 1985.

Davies, Paul. *God and the New Physics*. New York: Simon and Schuster, 1983.

Debray, Régis. *Transmitting Culture*. New York: Columbia University Press, 2000.

Derrida, Jacques. *Dissemination*. Translated by Barbara Johnson. Chicago, IL: University of Chicago Press, 1981.

——*Margins of Philosophy*. Translated by Alan Bass. Chicago, IL: University of Chicago Press, 1982.

Descartes, René. *Meditations on First Philosophy*. Translated by Laurence Julien Lafleur. New York: Macmillan, 1951.

Deuser, Hermann. *Die Zehn Gebote: Kleine Einführung in die Theologische Ethik*. Stuttgart: Reclam, 2002.

Donagan, Alan. *The Theory of Morality*. Chicago, IL: University of Chicago Press, 1977.

Doniger, Wendy. *Other Peoples' Myths: The Cave of Echoes*. Chicago, IL: University of Chicago Press, 1995.

Elshtain, Jean Bethke. *Women and War*. New York: Basic Books, 1987.

——*Real Politics: At the Center of Everyday Life*. Baltimore, MD: Johns Hopkins University Press, 1997.

——*New Wine and Old Bottles: International Politics and Ethical Discourse*. Notre Dame, IN: University of Notre Dame Press, 1998.

Erasmus, Desiderius. *In Praise of Folly*. Translated by Betty Radice. London: Penguin Books, 1971.

Erickson, Victoria Lee, and Michelle Lim Jones, eds. *Surviving Terror: Hope and Justice in a World of Violence*. Grand Rapids, MI: Brazos Press, 2002.

Fasching, Darrell J., and Dell deChant. *Comparative Religious Ethics: A Narrative Approach*. Oxford: Blackwell, 2001.

Finnis, John. *Fundamentals of Ethics*. Washington, DC: Georgetown University Press, 1983.

Fischer, Johannes. *Theological Ethik: Grundwissen und Orientierung*. Stuttgart: W. Kohlhammer, 2002.

Flanagan, Owen J. *Varieties of Moral Personality: Ethics and Psychological Realism*. Cambridge, MA: Harvard University Press, 1991.

Flanagan, Owen J., and Amélie Rorty, eds. *Identity, Character, and Morality: Essays in Moral Psychology*. Cambridge, MA: MIT Press, 1990.

Foot, Philippa. *Natural Goodness*. Oxford: Oxford University Press, 2001.

Fowl, Stephen E., and L. Gregory Jones. *Reading in Communion: Scripture and Ethics in Christian Life*. Grand Rapids, MI: Eerdmans, 1991.

Franklin, R. W., and Joseph M. Shaw. *The Case for Christian Humanism*. Grand Rapids, MI: Eerdmans, 1991.

Freire, Paulo. *Pedagogy of the Oppressed*. New York: Continuum, 1990.

Frymer-Kensky, Tikva Simone, et al., eds. *Christianity in Jewish Terms*. Boulder, CO: Westview Press, 2000.

Gadamer, Hans-Georg. *Der Anfang der Philosophie*. Stuttgart: Philipp Reclam, 1996.

——*Truth and Method*, 2nd revd. edn. Translated by Joel Weinsheimer and Donald G. Marshall. New York: Continuum, 1998.

Gamwell, Franklin I. *The Divine Good: Modern Moral Theory and the Necessity of God*. San Francisco, CA: HarperSanFrancisco, 1990.

——*The Meaning of Religious Freedom: Modern Politics and the Democratic Resolution*. Albany: State University of New York Press, 1995.

Geertz, Clifford. *Local Knowledge: Further Essays in Interpretive Anthropology*. New York: Basic Books, 1983.

Gewirth, Alan. *Reason and Morality*. Chicago, IL: University of Chicago Press, 1978.

Giddens, Anthony. *Modernity and Self-Identity: Self and Society in the Late Modern Age*. Stanford, CA: Stanford University Press, 1991.

Gill, Robin. *Churchgoing and Christian Ethics*. Cambridge: Cambridge University Press, 1999.

Girard, René. *Violence and the Sacred*. Translated by Patrick Gregary. Baltimore, MD: Johns Hopkins University Press, 1977.

——*The Scapegoat*. Baltimore, MD: Johns Hopkins University Press, 1986.

Grassi, Ernesto. *Rhetoric as Philosophy: The Humanist Tradition*. University Park: Pennsylvania State University Press, 1980.

Gustafson, James M. *Christ and the Moral Life*. New York: Harper and Row, 1968.

—— *Varieties of Moral Discourse: Prophetic, Narrative, Ethical, and Policy*. Grand Rapids, MI: Calvin College and Seminary, 1988.

—— *Ethics from a Theocentric Perspective*, 2 vols. Chicago, IL: University of Chicago Press, 1992.

—— *A Sense of the Divine: The Natural Environment from a Theocentric Perspective*. Cleveland, OH: Pilgrim Press, 1994.

Habermas, Jürgen. *Moral Consciousness and Communicative Action*. Translated by Christian Lenhardt and Shierry Weber Nicholsen. Cambridge, MA: MIT Press, 1990.

—— *Postmetaphysical Thinking: Philosophical Essays*. Translated by W. M. Hohengarten. Cambridge, MA: MIT Press, 1992.

Hadot, Pierre. *Philosophy as a Way of Life: Spiritual Exercises from Socrates to Foucault*. Translated by Michael Chase. Edited by Arnold I. Davidson. Oxford: Blackwell, 1995.

Haraway, Donna Jeanne. *Simians, Cyborgs, and Women: The Reinvention of Nature*. New York: Routledge, 1991.

Harrison, Beverly Wildung. *Making the Connections: Essays in Feminist Social Ethics*. Edited by Carol S. Robb. Boston, MA: Beacon Press, 1985.

Harvey, David. *The Condition of Postmodernity: An Enquiry into the Origins of Cultural Change*. Oxford: Blackwell, 1989.

Hauerwas, Stanley. *A Community of Character: Toward a Constructive Christian Social Ethic*. Notre Dame, IN: University of Notre Dame Press, 1981.

—— *Christian Existence Today: Essays on Church, World, and Living in Between*. Durham, NC: Labyrinth Press, 1988.

Hauerwas, Stanley, and William H. Willimon. *Resident Aliens: Life in the Christian Colony*. Nashville, TN: Abingdon Press, 1989.

Hays, Richard B. *The Moral Vision of the New Testament: Community, Cross, New Creation: A Contemporary Introduction to New Testament Ethics*. San Francisco, CA: HarperSanFrancisco, 1996.

Heidegger, Martin. *Being and Time*. Translated by John Macquarrie and Edward Robinson. New York: Harper and Row, 1962.

Hirsch, E. D. *Validity in Interpretation*. New Haven, CT: Yale University Press, 1967.

Huber, Wolfgang. *Konflikt und Konsens: Studien zur Ethik der Verantwortung*. Munich: Chr. Kaiser, 1990.

Hume, David. *An Enquiry Concerning the Principles of Morals*. La Salle, IL: Open Court, 1966.

Jaeger, Werner Wilhelm. *Humanism and Theology, The Aquinas Lecture, 7*. Milwaukee, WI: Marquette University Press, 1943.

—— *Early Christianity and Greek Paideia*. Oxford: Oxford University Press, 1961.

Janowski, Bernd, and Michael Welker, eds. *Opfer: Theologische und Kulturelle Kontexte*. Frankfurt am Main: Suhrkamp, 2000.

John Paul II. *On the Hundredth Anniversary of Rerum Novarum = Centesimus Annus*. Washington, DC: Office for Publishing and Promotion Services, United States Catholic Conference, 1991.

Johnson, Elizabeth A. *She Who Is: The Mystery of God in Feminist Theological Discourse*. New York: Crossroad, 1992.

Johnson, Mark. *Moral Imagination: Implications of Cognitive Science for Ethics*. Chicago, IL: University of Chicago Press, 1993.

Jonas, Hans. *The Imperative of Responsibility: In Search of an Ethics for the Technological Age*. Translated by Hans Jonas and David Herr. Chicago, IL: University of Chicago Press, 1984.

——*Mortality and Morality : A Search for the Good after Auschwitz*. Edited by Lawrence Vogel. Evanston, IL: Northwestern University Press, 1996.

Kant, Immanuel. *Fundamental Principles of the Metaphysics of Morals*. Translated by Thomas K. Abbott. New York: Macmillan, 1989.

——*Critique of Pure Reason*. Translated by Paul Guyer and Allen W. Wood. Edited by Paul Guyer and Allen W. Wood. Cambridge: Cambridge University Press, 1998.

Kelsay, John, and Sumner B. Twiss. *Religion and Human Rights*. New York: Project on Religion and Human Rights, 1994.

Kirk, Kenneth E. *Conscience and Its Problems: An Introduction to Casuistry*, Library of Theological Ethics. Louisville, KY: Westminster/John Knox Press, 1999.

Klemm, David E., and William Schweiker, eds. *Meanings in Texts and Actions: Questioning Paul Ricoeur*. Charlottesville: University Press of Virginia, 1993.

Kohák, Erazim V. *The Embers and the Stars: A Philosophical Inquiry into the Moral Sense of Nature*. Chicago, IL: University of Chicago Press, 1984.

Krueger, David A. *The Business Corporation and Productive Justice*. Nashville, TN: Abingdon Press, 1997.

Küng, Hans. *Global Responsibility: In Search of a New World Ethic*. Translated by John Bowden. New York: Continuum, 1993.

Küng, Hans, and Karl-Josef Kuschel, eds. *A Global Ethic: The Declaration of the Parliament of the World's Religions*. Special edn. New York: Continuum, 1995.

Lange, Dietz. *Ethik in Evangelischer Perspektive: Grundfragen Christlicher Lebenspraxis*. Göttingen: Vandenhoeck and Ruprecht, 1992.

Lévinas, Emmanuel. *Totality and Infinity: An Essay on Exteriority*. Translated by Alphonso Lingis. Pittsburgh, PA: Duquesne University Press, 1969.

——*Otherwise Than Being: Or, Beyond Essence*. Translated by Alphonso Lingis. Boston, MA: Martinus Nijhoff, 1981.

——*Alterity and Transcendence*. Translated by Michael B. Smith. New York: Columbia University Press, 1999.

Lindbeck, George A. *The Nature of Doctrine: Religion and Theology in a Postliberal Age*. Philadelphia, PA: Westminster Press, 1984.

Lippman, Walter. *A Preface to Morals*. New York: Time, 1964.

Lovin, Robin W. *Reinhold Niebuhr and Christian Realism*. Cambridge: Cambridge University Press, 1995.

Lovin, Robin W., and Frank Reynolds, eds. *Cosmogony and Ethical Order: New Studies in Comparative Ethics*. Chicago, IL: University of Chicago Press, 1985.

Luhmann, Niklas. *Theories of Distinction: Redescribing the Descriptions of Modernity*. Translated by Joseph O'Neil et al. Edited by William Rasch. Stanford, CA: Stanford University Press, 2002.

McCarthy, Timothy. *Christianity and Humanism: From Their Biblical Foundations into the Third Millennium*. Chicago, IL: Loyola Press, 1996.

McClendon, James William. *Ethics: Systematic Theology*, vol. 1. Nashville, TN: Abingdon Press, 1986.

McFague, Sallie. *Models of God: Theology for an Ecological, Nuclear Age*. Philadelphia, PA: Fortress Press, 1987.

——*Life Abundant: Rethinking Theology and Economy for a Planet in Peril*. Minneapolis, MN: Fortress Press, 2001.

McGinn, Bernard. *The Presence of God: A History of Western Christian Mysticism*, 5 vols. New York: Crossroad, 1991.

MacIntyre, Alasdair C. *After Virtue: A Study in Moral Theory*. Notre Dame, IN: University of Notre Dame Press, 1981.

——*Three Rival Versions of Moral Enquiry: Encyclopaedia, Genealogy, and Tradition: Being Gifford Lectures Delivered in the University of Edinburgh in 1988*. Notre Dame, IN: University of Notre Dame Press, 1990.

——*Dependent Rational Animals: Why Human Beings Need the Virtues*. Chicago, IL: Open Court, 1999.

Mack, Burton L. *Who Wrote the New Testament?: The Making of the Christian Myth*. San Francisco, CA: HarperSanFrancisco, 1995.

Maguire, Daniel C. *The Moral Core of Judaism and Christianity: Reclaiming the Revolution*. Minneapolis, MN: Fortress Press, 1993.

Martens, Ekkehard. *Zwischen Gut und Böse: Elementare Fragen Angewandter Philosophie*. Stuttgart: Philipp Reclam, 1997.

Martin, Terence J. *Living Words: Studies in Dialogues over Religion*. Atlanta, GA: Scholars Press, 1998.

Mathewes, Charles T. *Evil and the Augustinian Tradition*. Cambridge, MA: Cambridge University Press, 2001.

Meeks, Wayne A. *The Moral World of the First Christians*. Philadelphia, PA: Westminster Press, 1986.

Menzel, Peter. *Material World: A Global Family Portrait*. San Francisco, CA: Sierra Club Books, 1994.

Metz, Johannes Baptist. *Faith in History and Society: Toward a Practical Fundamental Theology*. Translated by David Smith. New York: Seabury Press, 1980.

Midgley, Mary. *Beast and Man: The Roots of Human Nature*. Brighton: Harvester Press, 1979.

——*Can't We Make Moral Judgements?* New York: St. Martin's Press, 1991.

——*The Ethical Primate: Humans, Freedom, and Morality*. New York: Routledge, 1994.

Milbank, John. *Theology and Social Theory: Beyond Secular Reason*. Cambridge, MA: Blackwell, 1991.

Mill, John Stuart. *On Liberty*. Edited by John Gray. Oxford: Oxford University Press, 1991.

Miller, Richard B. *Interpretations of Conflict: Ethics, Pacifism, and the Just-War Tradition*. Chicago, IL: University of Chicago Press, 1991.

Moltmann, Jürgen. *The Crucified God: The Cross of Christ as the Foundation and Criticism of Christian Theology*. Translated by R. A. Wilson and John Bowden. New York: Harper and Row, 1974.

——*The Coming of God: Christian Eschatology*. Translated by Margaret Kohl. Minneapolis, MN: Fortress Press, 1996.

Montaigne, Michel de. *Complete Works: Essays, Travel Journal, Letters*. Translated by Donald M. Frame. Stanford, CA: Stanford University Press, 1957.

Mouw, Richard J. *The God Who Commands*. Notre Dame, IN: University of Notre Dame Press, 1990.

Murdoch, Iris. *The Sovereignty of Good*. London: Routledge and Kegan Paul, 1970.

——*Metaphysics as a Guide to Morals*. New York: Penguin Press/Allen Lane, 1992.

Murphy, Jeffrie G., and Jean Hampton, eds. *Forgiveness and Mercy*, Cambridge Studies in Philosophy and Law. Cambridge: Cambridge University Press, 1988.

Murray, Patrick, ed. *Reflections on Commercial Life: An Anthology of Classic Texts from Plato to the Present*. New York: Routledge, 1997.

National Conference of Catholic Bishops. *The Challenge of Peace: God's Promise and Our Response: A Pastoral Letter on War and Peace: May 3, 1983*. Washington, DC: Office of Publication Services, United States Catholic Conference, 1983.

——*Economic Justice for All: Pastoral Letter on Catholic Social Teaching and the US Economy*. Washington, DC: Office of Publication Services, United States Catholic Conference, 1986.

Newhauser, Richard. *The Early History of Greed: The Sin of Avarice in Early Medieval Thought and Literature*. Cambridge: Cambridge University Press, 2000.

Niebuhr, H. Richard. *The Meaning of Revelation*. New York: Macmillan, 1941.

——*Christ and Culture*. New York: Harper and Row, 1951.

——*The Responsible Self: An Essay in Christian Moral Philosophy*, Library of Theological Ethics. Louisville, KY: Westminster/John Knox Press, 1999.

Nietzsche, Friedrich Wilhelm. *The Birth of Tragedy and the Genealogy of Morals*. Translated by Francis Gilffing. Garden City, NY: Doubleday Anchor, 1956.

——*Thus Spake Zarathustra*. Translated by R. J. Hollingdale. New York: Penguin Books, 1961.

Nussbaum, Martha Craven. *Love's Knowledge: Essays on Philosophy and Literature*. New York: Oxford University Press, 1990.

——*Women and Human Development: The Capabilities Approach*. Cambridge: Cambridge University Press, 2000.

Otto, Rudolf. *The Idea of the Holy: An Inquiry into the Non-Rational Factor in the Idea of the Divine and Its Relation to the Rational*. Translated by John H. Harvey. New York: Oxford University Press, 1958.

Patrick, Anne E. *Liberating Conscience: Feminist Explorations in Catholic Moral Theology*. New York: Continuum, 1997.

Perry, Michael J. *The Idea of Human Rights: Four Inquiries*. Oxford: Oxford University Press, 1998.

Picht, Georg. *Wahrheit, Vernunft, Verantwortung: Philosophische Studien*. Stuttgart: Ernst Klett, 1969.

Pinckaers, Servais. *The Sources of Christian Ethics*. Translated by Sr. Mary Thomas Noble. Washington, DC: Catholic University of America Press, 1995.

Plato. *Symposium*. Translated by Benjamin Jowett. Indianapolis, IN: Bobbs-Merrill Educational Publishing, 1980.

——*Philebus*. Translated by Dorothea Frede. Indianapolis, IN: Hackett Publishing, 1993.

——*Phaedrus*. Translated, with introduction and notes, by Alexander Nehamas and Paul Woodruff. Indianapolis, IN: Hackett Publishing, 1995.

Polkinghorne, J. C. *The Faith of a Physicist: Reflections of a Botton-up Thinker : The Gifford Lectures for 1993–4*. Minneapolis, MN: Fortress Press, 1996.

Polkinghorne, J. C., and Michael Welker, eds. *The End of the World and the Ends of God: Science and Theology on Eschatology*. Harrisburg, PA: Trinity Press International, 2000.

Rabelais, François. *Gargantua and Pantagruel*. Translated by J. M. Cohen. New York: Penguin Books, 1955.

Radhakrishnan, S. *The Hindu View of Life*. London: Mandala, 1960.

Radin, Margaret Jane. *Reinterpreting Property*. Chicago, IL: University of Chicago Press, 1993.

Ramsey, Paul. *The Just War: Force and Political Responsibility*. New York: Charles Scribner's Sons, 1968.

——*Fabricated Man: The Ethics of Genetic Control*. New Haven, CT: Yale University Press, 1970.

——*The Essential Paul Ramsey: A Collection*. Edited by William Werpehowski and Stephen D. Crocco. New Haven, CT: Yale University Press, 1994.

Randall, John Herman, Jr. *The Making of the Modern Mind: A Survey of the Intellectual Background of the Present Age*, 50th anniversary edn. New York: Columbia University Press, 1976.

Rawls, John. *Political Liberalism*. New York: Columbia University Press, 1993.

Ricoeur, Paul. *The Symbolism of Evil*. Translated by Emerson Buchanan. New York: Harper and Row, 1967.

——*Interpretation Theory: Discourse and the Surplus of Meaning*. Fort Worth: Texas Christian University Press, 1976.

——*Essays on Biblical Interpretation*. Edited by Lewis Seymour Mudge. Philadelphia, PA: Fortress Press, 1980.

——*Hermeneutics and the Human Sciences: Essays on Language, Action, and Interpretation*. Translated by John B. Thompson. Cambridge: Cambridge University Press, 1981.

——*Time and Narrative*, 3 vols. Translated by Kathleen Blamey and David Pellauer. Chicago, IL: University of Chicago Press, 1984.

——*Oneself as Another*. Translated by Kathleen Blamey. Chicago, IL: University of Chicago Press, 1992.

——*Figuring the Sacred: Religion, Narrative, and Imagination*. Translated by David Pellauer. Edited by Mark I. Wallace. Minneapolis, MN: Fortress Press, 1995.

Rigby, Cynthia L., ed. *Power, Powerlessness, and the Divine: New Inquiries in Bible and Theology*. Atlanta, GA: Scholars Press, 1997.

Ritzer, G. *The Macdonaldization of Society: An Investigation into the Changing Character of Contemporary Social Life*. Thousand Oaks, CA: Pine Forge Press, 1993.

Robbins, Lionel. *A History of Economic Thought: The LSE Lectures*. Edited by Steven G. Medema and Warren J. Samuels. Princeton, NJ: Princeton University Press, 1998.

Robertson, Roland. *Globalization: Social Theory and Global Culture*. London: Sage, 1992.

Rorty, Richard. *Contingency, Irony, and Solidarity*. Cambridge: Cambridge University Press, 1989.

Ruether, Rosemary Radford. *Sexism and God-Talk: Toward a Feminist Theology*. Boston, MA: Beacon Press, 1983.

Saddhatissa, Hammalawa. *Buddhist Ethics*. Boston, MA: Wisdom Publications, 1997.

Sassen, Saskia. *Globalization and Its Discontents: Essays on the New Mobility of People and Money*. New York: New Press, 1998.

Scharlemann, Robert P. *The Reason of Following: Christology and the Ecstatic I*. Chicago, IL: University of Chicago Press, 1991.

Schleiermacher, Friedrich. *Hermeneutics: The Handwritten Manuscripts*. Translated by James Duke and Jack Forstman. Edited by Heinz Kimmerle. Missoula, MT: Scholars Press for the American Academy of Religion, 1977.

Schüssler Fiorenza, Elisabeth. *Bread Not Stone: The Challenge of Feminist Biblical Interpretation*. Boston, MA: Beacon Press, 1984.

——*But She Said: Feminist Practices of Biblical Interpretation*. Boston, MA: Beacon Press, 1992.

Schweiker, William. *Mimetic Reflections: A Study in Hermeneutics, Theology, and Ethics*. New York: Fordham University Press, 1990.

——*Responsibility and Christian Ethics*. Cambridge: Cambridge University Press, 1995.

——*Power, Value, and Conviction: Theological Ethics in the Postmodern Age*. Cleveland, OH: Pilgrim Press, 1998.

Schweitzer, Albert. *The Philosophy of Civilization*. Buffalo, NY: Prometheus Books, 1987.

——*The Quest of the Historical Jesus*. Edited by John Bowden. Minneapolis, MN: Fortress Press, 2001.

Schwöbel, Christoph, and Dorothee von Tippelskirch, eds. *Die Religiösen Wurzeln der Toleranz*. Freiburg im Breisgau: Herder, 2002.

Screech, M. A. *Laughter at the Foot of the Cross*. Boulder, CO: Westview Press, 1999.

Shklar, Judith N. *Ordinary Vices*. Cambridge, MA: Belknap Press of Harvard University Press, 1984.

Shriver, Donald W., Jr. *An Ethic for Enemies: Forgiveness in Politics*. New York: Oxford University Press, 1995.

Singer, Irving. *Meaning in Life: The Creation of Value*. New York: Free Press, 1992.

Singer, Peter. *Unsanctifying Human Life: Essays on Ethics*. Oxford: Blackwell, 2002.

Sittler, Joseph. *The Structure of Christian Ethics*. Louisville, KY: Westminster/John Knox Press, 1998.

Smart, Ninian. *World Philosophies*. London: Routledge, 1999.

Smith, Jonathan Z. *Imagining Religion: From Babylon to Jonestown*. Chicago, IL: University of Chicago Press, 1982.

Smith, Wilfred Cantwell. *The Meaning and End of Religion: A New Approach to the Religious Traditions of Mankind*. New York: Macmillan, 1963.

Spohn, William C. *What Are They Saying About Scripture and Ethics?* revd. edn. New York: Paulist Press, 1995.

Stackhouse, Max L. *Public Theology and Political Economy: Christian Stewardship in Modern Society*. Grand Rapids, MI: Eerdmans, 1987.

Stackhouse, Max L., Peter J. Paris, Don S. Browning, and Diane Burdette Obenchain, eds. *God and Globalization*, 4 vols. Harrisburg, PA: Trinity Press International, 2000–2.

Stead, Christopher. *Philosophy in Christian Antiquity*. Cambridge: Cambridge University Press, 1994.

Sugirtharajah, R. S., ed. *Voices from the Margin: Interpreting the Bible in the Third World*. Maryknoll, NY: Orbis Books, 1991.

Summerell, Orrin F., ed. *The Otherness of God*. Charlottesville: University Press of Virginia, 1998.

Sundermeier, Theo. *Was Ist Religion?: Religionswissenschaft Im Theologischen Kontext : ein Studienbuch*. Gütersloh: Kaiser Gütersloher Verlagshaus, 1999.

Swift, Jonathan. *Gulliver's Travels, and Other Writings*. Edited by Ricardo Quintana. New York: Modern Library, 1958.

Tanner, Kathryn. *Theories of Culture: A New Agenda for Theology*. Minneapolis, MN: Fortress Press, 1997.

Taylor, Charles. *Philosophy and the Human Sciences*, vol. 2. Cambridge: Cambridge University Press, 1985.

—— *Sources of the Self: The Making of the Modern Identity*. Cambridge, MA: Harvard University Press, 1989.

Taylor, Mark C. *Erring: A Postmodern A/Theology*. Chicago, IL: University of Chicago Press, 1984.

Thomas, Günter. *Medien – Ritual – Religion: Zur Religiösen Funktion des Fernsehens*. Frankfurt am Main: Suhrkamp, 1998.

Tillich, Paul. *The Courage to Be*. New Haven, CT: Yale University Press, 1952.

—— *Christianity and the Encounter of the World Religions*. New York: Columbia University Press, 1963.

—— *Morality and Beyond*. Louisville, KY: Westminster/John Knox Press, 1995.

Todorov, Tzvetan. *Imperfect Garden: The Legacy of Humanism*. Princeton, NJ: Princeton University Press, 2002.

Tödt, Heinz Eduard. *Perspektiven Theologischer Ethik*. Munich: Chr. Kaiser, 1988.

Tomlinson, John. *Globalization and Culture*. Chicago, IL: University of Chicago Press, 1999.

Toulmin, Stephen. *Cosmopolis: The Hidden Agenda of Modernity*. New York: Free Press, 1990.

Tracy, David. *Plurality and Ambiguity: Hermeneutics, Religion, Hope*. San Francisco, CA: Harper and Row, 1987.

Traina, Cristina L. H. *Feminist Ethics and Natural Law: The End of the Anathemas*. Washington, DC: Georgetown University Press, 1999.

Versényi, Laszlo. *Socratic Humanism*. New Haven, CT: Yale University Press, 1963.

Vlastos, Gregory. *Socrates: Ironist and Moral Philosopher*. Ithaca, NY: Cornell University Press, 1991.

Voltaire. *Candide and Other Stories*. Translated by Roger Pearson. Oxford: Oxford University Press, 1990

von Rad, Gerhard. *Genesis: A Commentary*. Translated by John H. Marks. London: SCM Press, 1961.

Wall, John, William Schweiker, and W. David Hall, eds. *Paul Ricoeur and Contemporary Moral Thought*. New York: Routledge, 2002.

Wallace, Mark I., and Theophus Harold Smith, eds. *Curing Violence*. Sonoma, CA: Polebridge Press, 1994.

Wallwork, Ernest. *Psychoanalysis and Ethics*. New Haven, CT: Yale University Press, 1991.

Walzer, Michael. *On Toleration*. New Haven, CT: Yale University Press, 1997.

Welker, Michael. *God the Spirit*. Translated by John F. Hoffmeyer. Minneapolis, MN: Fortress Press, 1994.

Wesley, John. *Sermons on Several Occasions*. London: Epworth Press, 1975.

Whitehead, Alfred North. *Science and the Modern World*. New York: Macmillan, 1948.

——*Process and Reality: An Essay in Cosmology*. Edited by David Ray Griffin and Donald W. Sherburne. New York: Free Press, 1978.

Yoder, John Howard. *The Priestly Kingdom: Social Ethics as Gospel*. Notre Dame, IN: University of Notre Dame Press, 1984.

Index of Names

Index of Scripture

Index of Subjects